Horse Behavior Explained

Margit H. Zeitler-Feicht

Horse Behavior Explained

Origins, Treatment, and Prevention of Problems

Margit H. Zeitler-Feicht
Technical University of Munich, Germany

English translation by
Katharina Lohmann
University of Georgia
Athens, Georgia

Consultant
Katherine A. Houpt, VMD, PhD
Cornell University
Ithaca, New York

Trafalgar Square Publishing
NORTH POMFRET, VERMONT

First published in the United States of America in 2004 by
Trafalgar Square Publishing
Howe Hill Road, North Pomfret, Vermont 05053

Printed in China

ISBN 1–57076–262–7

Library of Congress Control Number 2003107943

Disclaimer
The Author and Publisher shall have neither liability nor responsibility to any person or entity with respect to any loss or damage caused or alleged to be caused directly or indirectly by the information contained in this book. While the book is as accurate as the Author can make it, there may be errors, omissions, and inaccuracies.

English edition © 2004 Manson Publishing Ltd
73 Corringham Road, London NW11 7DL, UK

Original German edition © 2001 Eugen Ulmer GmbH & Co,
Wollgrasweg 41, 70599 Stuttgart (Hohenheim), Germany

Project manager: Paul Bennett
Copy-editor: Joanna Brocklesby
Designer: Cactus

Picture credits
Numbers refer to figure numbers:

Feicht, Dr. Ernst: 51, 52, 56, 86, 98, 99, 104.

Guni, Klaus-Jürgen: front cover.

Huber, Markus: 23, 100, 103, 119, 127, 131, 145.

Lehmann, Britta: 31, 53.

Research Institute and Natural History Museum Senkenberg, Dept. of Messel Research SMF: 1.

Sambraus, Prof. Hans Heinrich: title page verso, 4, 6, 7, 8, 9, 10, 15, 16, 17, 18, 22, 24, 25, 26, 27, 28, 29, 30, 32, 33, 37, 46, 47, 54, 58, 105, 116, 118, 121, 124, 136, 139.

Stuewer, Sabine: half title page, title page.

Werkbild (Schöttstall): 38.

Wittmann, Ulrike: Figure 72.

All other pictures are by the author.

Drawings were made according to sketches by the author:

Flutbacher, Helmut: 35, 36, 48, 61, 95.

Lokau, Siegfried: 2, 3, 5, 19, 39, 40, 55, 80, 81, 83, 89, 95, 97, 138, 142, 143, 146, 147, 148.

Contents

Preface

Aside from the dog, the horse is a human's best friend. Sayings such as "the world's happiness rests on a horse's back" signal this close relationship and are evidence of our appreciation of the horse. Can the horse, however, always perceive the way it is treated by human beings in our society as fortunate?

Formerly, the horse had to work hard in front of a plough or carriage, was used in wars, or was needed for the fast delivery of messages to remote locations. In many cases, horses were worn out far too early. In the past few decades, this has changed. In our current society, the horse serves mostly sports and leisure purposes. Even this type of use, however, can carry great risks for these animals. It is not uncommon for a horse to be asked to perform tasks that are overwhelming from both a physical and psychological standpoint; or the horse may be treated as a partner and friend, but the required expertise is lacking.

If a horse is not treated according to its nature, however, this may result not only in the development of diseases but also of behavioral abnormalities. These do not come out of nowhere: a causative trigger is always present. Most often, mistakes made in management and handling are responsible and virtually force the horse into the abnormal behavior. While this behavior is often dismissed as a "flaw", it is not infrequently significant from an animal cruelty standpoint.

Nobody should assume that problem behavior arises from a horse's moodiness. The common description as a "vice" suggests this way of thinking; however, it is wrong and alarming.

This book takes a remarkable approach to working against this assessment. It convincingly clarifies why and how problem behavior develops. Only by understanding this context, can one prevent abnormalities from occurring or, if they have already arisen, treat them with appropriate measures and a lot of patience. Taking problem behavior seriously means to actively prevent cruelty against animals. For this reason, I hope that this comprehensive and thorough work will become widely distributed. Here's to the well-being of the horse!

Prof. Dr. Hans Heinrich Sambraus

Foreword

The foreword to this book should, for good reason, be prefaced with a quotation of the famous horse expert Hans Heinrich Isenbart: "Whenever people did not regard it below their dignity to use all their mental capacity to deal with the horse's psyche, the art of riding experienced flowering times."

In the past 40 years or so, the horse and the occupation with it have boomed in a way that no-one could imagine during the 1950s and 60s. A species that was almost condemned to becoming extinct prior to the beginning of the 1960s has nearly tripled in number and developed into a nationwide population (Germany) of about 800,000 animals. This development was exclusively caused by the discovery of horses as partners for sports and leisure activities. Even today, it can be foreseen that the equine sport, with currently about 750,000 riders, drivers and vaulters belonging to horse clubs, and certainly at least the same number of non-affiliated horse lovers, will continue to grow in the future.

As encouraging as this development may be, it has to be stated that this "coin of growth" also has its flipside. Never before have as many people with as little or no experience in dealing with horses occupied themselves with these animals. Many problems arising in the relation-ship between human and horse are, therefore, attributable to the person's ignorance regarding correct handling of horses. The German Rider's Association has attempted to address this situation for many years with a number of different measures and projects.

This book distinguishes itself particularly by the fact that it not only offers a thorough description of the causes and possible therapies of problem behavior in horses, but also describes ways to prevent its occurrence in the first place. Anyone who does not understand the natural requirements of horses, or who even humanizes them, will always make a bad friend for a horse. As painful as this realization may be, problem behavior in horses primarily results from mistakes made by the people dealing with them. In her discussion, the author does not limit herself to the often-encountered generalizations of problem solving. She rather demonstrates the necessity to investigate thoroughly the horse's needs in detail in order to arrive at individual-ized solutions. The essence of this book could, therefore, be reduced to this one sentence:

Knowledge is animal protection.

Dieter Graf Landsberg-Velen
President of the German Riders'
Association (FN)

Part A: The horse's adaptability to the environment

Adaptation denotes a process that alters animals and plants in the course of their dealing with the environment, in order to allow them to maintain themselves and their species. Horses have had to adapt to a changing environment over millions of years. Only those well adapted to the particular circumstances at any one time survived ("survival of the fittest"). Long-term adaptation was made possible by a broad genetic variety. Genotypes that most successfully dealt with the environmental circumstances had a selection advantage. They also reproduced most successfully, so that over time their genetic make-up dominated their population.

According to modern theories of evolution, the development of new types of equids occurred, aside from mutation, primarily by natural selection. Later on, during domestication, further selection took place, which is referred to as artificial selection, because man instead of nature determined the selection criteria.

The most important selection criterion at the beginning of domestication was undoubtedly the ability of the wild horse to adjust to a life in captivity. To a certain extent, today's domesticated horse has adjusted to this life; however, it remains much closer to its original wild form than many other domestic animals. For this reason, current animal husbandry practices still demand constant adjustment (adaptation) by the horse. During ontogeny, i.e. the development of the individual, adaptation of the individual horse occurs by means of certain behaviors. Its success depends on many factors. The development of behavioral abnormalities indicates that the limits of adaptation capacity have been exceeded. In order to be able to recognize when one is in danger of expecting too much from the adaptation capacity, a look at the phylogenic development of behavior has practical significance, aside from being of scientific interest.

Evolution

Development of equids

The horse's prehistoric development can be followed exceptionally well because its genealogical development is very well documented by many fossil findings. As a result, the horse's evolution can be traced back almost completely into the Eocene, approximately 60 million years ago.

In this epoch, *Eohippus* (also called *Hyracotherium*) populated North America, Europe, and presumably Asia. It is the oldest known representative of the horse-like animals (Equidae) and is therefore regarded as the earliest ancestor of today's horse. Its appearance, however, had little in common with today's equids, as it resembled a polled duiker antelope. It was approximately fox-sized with a height of 25–45 cm (10–18 in) at the withers, and had an arched back. The front feet of this eocenian ancestor had four toes, and the hind feet, three toes, with hoof-like, blunt nails. The teeth formed a closed row with only few small gaps. The crowns of the teeth were low and had a bumpy chewing surface, so that only crushing, chewing movements were possible.

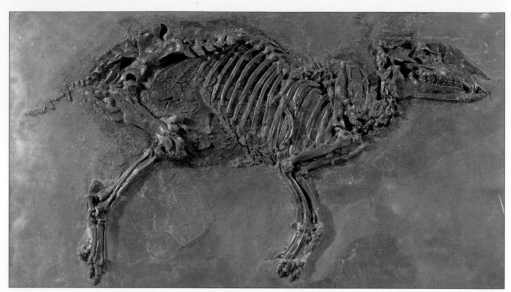

I Skeleton of the Messeler primeval horse (*Propalaeotherioum parvulum*) found in the Messel oil slate pit near the Odenwald, Germany. The *Eohippus* (*Hyracotherium*) is thought to be the earliest, horse-like form of a hoofed animal.

These morphological attributes suggest that the eohippus primarily consumed leaves and berries and lived in the woods. This assumption was proven to be correct several years ago, when a 50-million-year-old primeval horse was found in the Messel pit near Darmstadt, Germany (1). Its fossilized stomach contents consisted of leaves. The number of excavation findings in North America and Europe further indicates that *Eohippus* was a common inhabitant of the primeval forest, and primarily lived *alone* or in small groups.

Further development of the Equidae (2) took place in North America, while all European sidelines became extinct in the course of evolution. In the Miocene, approximately 25 million years ago, a new type of equid appeared, the genus *Merychippus*. This ancestor, with a height of 90–100 cm (36–40 in) at the withers, was the first to show attributes definitively indicating an adaptation to life in the plains. Its feet, although still having three toes, showed a very strongly developed center toe such that the other toes no longer touched the ground. In addition, the teeth had greatly elongated crowns with enlarged chewing surfaces, and had acquired cement as an additional substance besides dentin and enamel. These substances formed an effective grinding surface that could be used to grind coarser plant parts such as grasses. These morphologic changes allow the conclusion that *Merychippus* had left the protective environment of the forest and was populating open or semi-open areas.

With *Merychippus*, therefore, the transition from the leaf-eating inhabitant of the forest to the grass-eating inhabitant of the plains was completed. This transition was accompanied not only by the described anatomical alterations of the teeth and extremities, but also by extensive physiological and behavioral adaptation. Among other changes, this included the formation of complex social structures, because in the open plains, life in larger groups increases the chance of survival of the individual.

Pliohippus, an approximately donkey-sized grass-eater, which lived in North America some 7 million years ago, achieved an even higher developmental state. This is especially true for the development of its extremities. It was the first genus to exhibit true monodactyly (possession of only one hoof) by reduction of the side toes to the splint bones. At the end of the Pliocene, about 2 million years ago, the advanced developmental stages of *Pliohippus* were already very similar to today's domestic horse.

Via the land bridges which existed at that time, the descendants of the American *Pliohippus* reached Asia, and subsequently Europe and Africa at the beginning of the ice age, the Pleistocene, approximately 1–2 million

Eohippus (height 35 cm (13.8 in)) four toes: the front foot had four toes and a ball.

Miohippus (height 60 cm (23.6 in) or more) three toes: the lateral toes are still clearly developed.

Merychippus (height 90 cm (35.4 in)) three toes: most of the weight is borne on the center toe.

Pliohippus (height 122 cm (48 in)) one toe: one (the center) toe supports the entire body weight.

2 The most important developmental stages of equids during evolution.

years ago. While the migrated equid populations were able to adapt to the environmental circumstances on the Eurasian continent, the descendants of *Pliohippus* in North and South America became extinct for unknown reasons approximately 12,000 years ago. The further development of the horse from the Pleistocene to today's phenotypes, therefore, took place in Europe and Asia.

Until the mid-Pleistocene, the ancestors of the "true" horse showed predominantly zebra-like (zebrine), donkey-like (asinine) or half-donkey-like (hemionine) characteristics. This long history of development of horses alongside donkeys, half-donkeys and zebras is the basis for their close relationship. They all belong to the same genus, horse (*Equus*), within the family of horse-like animals (Equidae) (Table 1).

There is little concrete evidence for the further development of the Equidae. This fact is most likely responsible for a sometimes inconsistent nomenclature used in the literature concerning horse types that lived during the ice age. According to current scientific knowledge, however, all domestic horses are likely to have derived from just one species of wild horse with variable genetic make-up (theory of mono-

phyletic descent). The work of Nobis (1997) in particular, presents extensive evidence for this theory (**3**). According to his research, only one wild horse species with great genetic variability populated Europe and Asia during the ice age. In the course of the ice age, it developed from *Allohippus* (a transitional stage between *Pliohippus* and *Equus*) to various forms of *Equus*. In the late Pleistocene, a long-lasting separation of the different populations probably occurred, which led to the development of subspecies. They differed in body size and outer appearance depending on the landscape and the climatic conditions of the particular area they lived in. As an example, the Eastern and Western subspecies was relatively small while the variant found in Southern and Central Russia was taller. The different populations are, however, thought never to have lost their sexual affinity, which confirms that they belong to the same species. The only representative of the original subspecies still existing today is the Przewalski horse, while all others have become extinct. The domestic horse (*Equus przewalskii f. caballus*) is thought to have developed from a different subspecies of the original wild horse, although this has not been proven.

Table I Phylogeny of the domestic horse (Grzimek 1987)

Order group:	Ungulates (hoofed animals)	Ungulata	Species and chromosome number (2N):
Order:	Ungulates with unpaired ("odd") hooves	Perissodactyla	• Mountain zebra (*Equus zebra*) with 2 subspecies — 32 • Plains zebra (*Equus quagga*) with 6 subspecies — 44 • Grevy zebra (*Equus grevyi*) — 46
Family:	Horse-like animals	Equidae	• Onager (*Equus hemionus*) with 5 subspecies — 56
Genus:	Horses	*Equus*	• Wild donkey (*Equus africanus*) with 2 subspecies — 62 • Wild horse (*Equus przewalskii**) — 66

Equus przewalskii f. caballus = Domestic horse (64)
(f=forma=form: denotes a domestic animal)

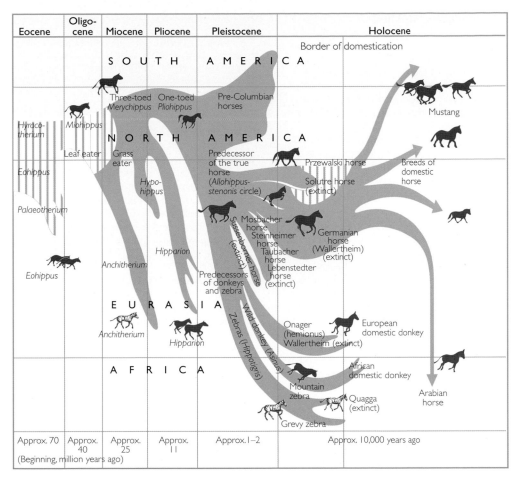

Eocene	Oligo-cene	Miocene	Pliocene	Pleistocene	Holocene

3 Graphical representation of the spatial and geological development of the equine tribe (Museum of Natural History Mainz, Germany, according to Nobis 1997).

Theory of monophyletic descent:
- One original species according to Grzimek (1987): *Equus przewalskii* (Przewalski horse) with three subspecies: *Equus przewalskii silvaticus* (forest tarpan, extinct), *Equus przewalskii gmelini* (plains tarpan, extinct) and *Equus przewalskii przewalskii* (wild horse of the plains).
- One original species according to Nobis (1997): *Equus ferus* with three subspecies: *Equus ferus solutreensis* (Western and Central Europe, Solutré horse, extinct), *Equus ferus gmelini* (South and Central Russia, tarpan, extinct) and *Equus ferus przewalskii* (Northern China and Mongolia, Przewalski horse).

The theory of polyphyletic descent, which is still found in many publications today, is based on the state of knowledge dating back 50 years and more. It claims that our domestic horses can be traced back to three or four different species of wild horses, whose genetic make-up is mixed to differing extents in the currently existing breeds. This theory refers to the species definition applied to fossil findings, which is limited to morphological criteria (=morphological species definition).

Theory of polyphyletic descent:

- Three original species according to Hilzheimer: tarpans, celtic ponies, and draft horses (cited according to Nobis 1997).
- Three original species according to Antonius: *Equus orientalis* (South Russian tarpan), *Equus ferus* (Przewalski horse) and *Equus robustus* (Western European horse) (cited according to Nobis 1997).
- Four original species according to Speed and Ebhardt (Ebhardt 1958): Northern pony (type I), tundra pony (Type II, Przewalski horse), Roman-nosed horse (type III) and original Thoroughbred (type IV).

According to the definition of present species (biological species definition) the theory of polyphyletic descent has proven untenable. This definition implies that only those groups that are able to produce fertile offspring with each other can be denoted a species. This is without doubt the case for all "true" horses. Although the Przewalski horse with 2N=66 has 2 more chromosomes than the domestic horse with 2N=64, the two can be bred to produce fertile offspring. In contrast, all other species of equids can be bred to each other but almost always will produce infertile offspring.

> The outer appearance, conformation, physiology, and species-specific behavior of horses are the result of development over approximately 60 million years.

Species-specific behavior

Evolution is responsible for the species-specific behavior of all animal species. Basic equine behavior, therefore, results from an adaptation process engraved in the genetic make-up of horses for millions of years. Three keywords can be used to describe their typical behavior: horses are animals of the plains, herd animals, and flight animals.

ANIMALS OF THE PLAINS

It can be deduced from the evolutionary process that horses have lived as grass-eating inhabitants of the plains (or steppe) for over 25 million years. Because this feed is low in energy and high in fiber, daily requirements had to be satisfied by long feeding times. It is therefore not "greed" but instead an inborn behavior, when our domestic horses experience the need

4 Under near-natural conditions, horses move around for up to 16 hours a day within their social group to consume feed.

to consume feed for approximately 15 hours a day. Exercise behavior is closely associated with feeding behavior, because grazing is coupled with a steady forward movement. For the purpose of feed intake, therefore, our horses' wild ancestors spent approximately two-thirds of the day at a slow walk. Equine conformation, physiology and behavior have also been adjusted to this continuous movement over millions of years. For this reason, our present horses still require several hours of movement at a slow pace every day (**4**).

Plains-like landscapes have one characteristic in common: a high nightly emission of heat. Consequently, large temperature differences exist between day and night. For millions of years, horses have been adapted to these extreme climatic conditions and are provided with excellent thermoregulation. Our modern horses still deal with heat, cold, and temperature changes better than all other domestic animals. However, not only are temperatures extreme in plains-like landscapes, sun exposure is as well. Horses have been adapted to this for millions of years. As a consequence, they tolerate light very well and even have a preference for exposure to a lot of natural light.

HERD ANIMALS

Horses have most likely lived in close social union with other members of their species for at least 25 million years, because for flight animals and defenseless herbivores living in open landscapes, the advantages of a group outweigh its disadvantages. For example, many pairs of eyes and ears see and hear more than those of an individual animal. Only in a group was it possible for the individual animal to satisfy its varying needs sufficiently without always having to be "on the lookout". As a consequence, our domestic horses still only feel safe when in close contact with members of their own species. The need for social contact and life in a community is inborn.

FLIGHT ANIMALS

For millions of years, flight has been the horse's best defense against enemies. This was evidenced by an ongoing specialization of the tips of their toes until they became the hoof. It is not only the legs and body functions (heart and circulatory system, respiratory apparatus, and so on) that are designed for flight, but also the sensory organs, as chances of survival are increased the sooner the horse can recognize the enemy and flee.

The flight reaction occurs according to an "inborn elicited mechanism" and is genetically fixed. Experiences can positively or negatively influence a horse's reaction to a frightening situation. The behavior is then determined by an "acquired and inborn elicited mechanism". Through adaptation and positive reinforcement, many situations that elicit fear in a horse can be defused and, as a result, the escape reaction can be controlled or even prevented.

Escape is still the horse's first reaction to fear, fright, and threats. As a horse owner, therefore, one should always be aware that a fleeing horse is afraid. Punishment is the wrong response because it only increases the horse's fear. It would also be wrong to regard the horse as cowardly due to its flight reaction. Horses are not predators, as, for example, are cats, who stop because a noise is of interest to them. It is normal behavior when a horse reacts to danger by running away, and stops to assess the situation only when a certain distance is reached. Only when the option to escape no longer exists, will a horse turn toward danger and defend itself by kicking or biting.

Domestication

Morphological and ethological changes

Domestication denotes the process of change from a wild to a domestic animal. The first domestication of wild animals took place prior to the year 12,000 BC. The dog was the first animal to become domesticated, followed by the sheep, pig, goat, and cow; the horse came much later (5). It can be assumed that humans in those times already had sufficient experience with the process when they began to domesticate the horse.

The horse's domestication probably began in several locations throughout its wide area of distribution during the 5th millennium BC. The oldest fossil findings of domestic animals can be traced back to approximately 4,000 years BC. They stem from the Southeastern European region, with the Ukraine most likely being the area where domestication took place for the first time. Throughout the 3rd millennium BC, horse husbandry spread through large parts of Southwest Asia. Around 3,000 BC, horses also first appeared in Central Europe. They had a slender body and a height at the withers of 120–135 cm (47–53 in). Their appearance resembled that of the local tarpans more closely than that of the Eastern European domestic horses. It is therefore assumed that domestication in Central and Eastern Europe occurred independently.

Year BC	Fertile crescent	Northern Greece	Central Europe	Ukraine	North America
12,000			🐕		
11,500					
11,000					
10,500					
10,000	🐕				
9,500					
9,000	🐑				
8,500					🐕
8,000				🐖	
7,500	🐄 🐐		🐕		
7,000	🐖				
6,500		🐄 🐕			
6,000	🐄 🐐	🐄 🐖			
4,000				🐎	

5 Earliest evidence for the existence of domestic animals in different regions of the world (Sambraus 1994). Open symbols = evidence in dispute.

Domestication required the horse's adaptation to new living conditions. One can imagine the following sequence of events:

At first, small groups of horses were caught and penned up in an escape-proof enclosure. Man provided feed for the animals, tended to their health, provided protection from their natural enemies, and often also reduced their tendency to fight among each other. Interbreeding of animals in captivity with their wild original form was diligently avoided. Only those horses were kept that were not too dangerous, that tolerated human approach, and that could be tamed with time. As a consequence, only horses that were able to adapt to living conditions dictated by man were domesticated. This required a long process extending over many generations. As a result, alterations in phenotype and modifications of behavior were genetically fixed. No behavior that had developed in the course of evolution was completely lost due to domestication, however.

How extensive are these changes, and how much do today's horses differ from their wild ancestors? This question is difficult to answer, because free-roaming "truly wild" horses no longer exist. The only ones to consider are the Przewalski horses. They, however, have become accustomed to life in the care of humans as well, and the animals living in semi-natural reserves and wilderness stations cannot easily be used as comparisons. Although, according to recently published information by BBC Wildlife, there might be a small group of free-roaming Przewalski horses in the border region between China and Mongolia, further information about these horses is not yet available. Similarly, so-called "wild horses" in the USA and Australia cannot be considered useful subjects for comparison, because they merely represent escaped domestic horses and not truly wild ancestors.

One can, therefore, answer the above question only by referring to known general differences between domestic animals and their wild ancestors, as have been described by Herre and Röhrs (1990), and applying them to the horse. Accordingly, today's domestic horse is likely to differ from its wild ancestors as follows:

• **The domestic horse is tamer than its original wild form. This tameness is inborn.**
This statement refers to the fact that domestic animals are less timid than their wild ancestors, not only as individuals, but also as a group.

• **The domestic horse is less aggressive than its wild ancestors.**
It is assumed that when domestication began,

humans preferred quiet, controllable animals. Only those were used for breeding, and a less aggressive behavior became genetically fixed over time. This difference can still be noted when comparing domestic horses and Przewalski horses today. Even though the latter have been kept in zoological gardens for generations, the number of conflicts within groups is still higher than it is for domestic horses.

• **Sensory performance is decreased in comparison to the original forms.**
Due to domestication, the brains of domestic animals have undergone profound changes within a relatively short period of time. These include a large quantitative decline of the "higher" nervous systems (or cortical system), the limbic system and the optic centers. Changes in brain size have not been proven in horses, but this information has been extrapolated from what is known in other species. These changes in brain structure due to domestication must not, however, be interpreted as degenerative in a negative sense. They rather represent a hereditary, useful adaptation to a change in the environmental circumstances. For example, a loss of vigilance in our domestic horses, which of course requires sensory performance, is associated with a decreased tendency to flee. This facilitates handling and human use of the horse for riding, carrying loads, and pulling carts. On the other hand, it is also of advantage for the horse itself in the sense of decreasing stress, because the horse no longer continuously needs to be "on the lookout".

• **Domestic horses show a much greater variability with regard to their size, color patterns, performance, and behavior than their original forms.**
All horses adapted to a particular region by natural selection showed a high degree of similarity in their color, size, and performance ability. Man set different standards than nature and, over the last 5,000 years, created different breeds by selective breeding according to his wishes. Selection criteria included color, markings, size, pulling strength, speed, and jumping ability.

Breed-specific behavior

In equine literature, it is quite common to describe the presumed different horse species (theory of polyphyletic descent) as "types" instead of species in order to avoid a direct contradiction of the genealogical history. In popular as well as scientific literature, the type doctrine according to Speed and Ebhardt (Ebhardt 1958) gained particular recognition.

The fossil remains, on which this hypothesis is based, however, are rarely present in one location in large enough numbers and to a sufficient degree of similarity, to be able to derive statistically significant evidence. Through radiographic evaluation and comparison of skeletons and teeth, the two researchers concluded that the bone structure of different fossil horse types was similar to that of the modern horse to a large extent. Based on their findings, they differentiated four equine "primeval types" that differed in their phenotype and behavior depending on their region of origin. This statement is based on experiments to breed back original horses, which showed that certain skeletal features are associated with certain morphological and ethological characteristics. According to Speed and Ebhardt (Ebhardt 1958), these four primeval types are the origin of our modern domestic horse breeds and still influence their essential traits.

When Speed and Ebhardt interpreted their results, the science of genetics was still in its infancy. It was thought that hereditary traits that determined a "breed" were fixed once and for all, and it had not yet been realized how quickly features can change in a population that experiences a high selection pressure. The English thoroughbred serves as a good example of how rapidly horses have developed into certain breeds, as it evolved due to strict selection in only 200 years. A breed or subspecies can disappear just as quickly. At the time of Speed and Ebhardt, people did not yet realize how important gene fluctuation is in living populations. Its significance, however, has become more and more evident through research done since the 1960s.

It is, therefore, more plausible that the phenotype and behavior of our domestic horses today is influenced less by the different wild horse types that lived during the ice age, but instead was shaped by the breeding practices of humans during the past centuries. It is undisputed, however, that the basis of all breeding is represented by the originally existing breeds or, according to Nobis (1997), the three subspecies of *Equus ferus*. These geographical breeds were characterized by a high genetic variability and were optimally adapted to the conditions of their country of origin. Based on these basic breeds, targeted selection with criteria determined by economical needs and individual human preference resulted in the different cultural breeds. These can be differentiated by certain features such as exterior, performance characteristics, and behavior. Some of these breeds can be categorized in groups showing similar morphological and ethological features, which are expressed in the usual denominations as pony, draft horse, warmblood, and thoroughbred. These correspond to a certain extent to the "primeval types" described by Speed and Ebhardt, namely the pony type, draft horse type, plains horse type, and Arabian type. Independent of the doubtful theory of evolution of the primeval types, the named groups agree with the observations of Speed and Ebhardt regarding modern breeds.

PONIES

Typical features of "true" ponies are a rounded shape, a wider croup in relation to the withers height, plentiful mane and tail hair, a straight nose, wide forehead, short ears and a tendency toward shortness (6). Most ponies, such as the Icelandic, Shetland, and Exmoor ponies, are characterized by a very social behavior and an agreeable nature even in larger groups. They are generally well suited for keeping in groups or for management in indoor/outdoor paddocks. They are very tolerant to cold as they develop a thick winter coat. The coarse superficial layer of hair allows running off of rain water and protects against moisture to a certain extent. Many ponies are "easy keepers" and tend to become fat when kept on highly nutritious pastures. Ponies are usually alert, lively, very capable of learning, and have strong nerves; furthermore, their endurance deserves special mention. With their compact, rounded stature, their muscular, high-set neck, and their short extremities, they present themselves as strong, small riding horses. A potential problem, however, is their tendency towards low withers leading to instability in saddle positioning. In addition, the often strongly developed lower neck, coupled with a narrow throatlatch, poses problems with a dressage-type posture. Another disadvantage can be their strong herd-boundness in that ponies tend to "stick together". Their response to harsh correction can often include aggressiveness.

DRAFT HORSES

The exterior of the draft horse mirrors their original use as a strong pack animal and carriage horse (7). Characteristic of the draft horse are its heavy stature, "split" croup, heavy plump head, small eyes, narrow forehead, and Roman nose. The classical type with its low-set neck and narrow throatlatch is less suitable for the sport of

6 Typical ponies are undemanding, tireless and very capable of learning (Exmoor pony).

7 Aside from its stocky physique, characteristics of the draft horse include gentleness and a rather limited need for exercise (Southern German Draught Horse).

riding; however, draft horses are extremely sure-footed in difficult terrain. Draft horses are generally known for their calmness and gentleness. Their exercise requirements are rather low and they are generally predictable and tend to be phlegmatic and headstrong. They are slow learners but retain a lesson once they understand it. Problems with draft horses are often the result of a lack of relationship to and respect for humans, paired with stubbornness and reluctance to move. They are well suited for group management; however, groups should be stable and of limited size as draft horses have a tendency toward fierce fighting.

WARMBLOODS AND THOROUGHBREDS

Warmbloods and thoroughbreds are taller than ponies and of lighter build than draft horses (**8**). Their coat is short and fine in the summer and they develop a limited winter coat. Given a feed sufficiently high in energy and shelter against heavy rain, however, they can still be kept outside during the winter months. The goal of breeding warmbloods and thoroughbreds has always been suitability for riding and performance (speed, endurance, and jumping ability). Refined warmbloods and thoroughbreds in particular, therefore, have high exercise requirements. For this reason, they need several hours of free exercise in addition to their daily work. These "hot-blooded" horses increasingly tend to be over-excitable and are therefore predisposed to behavioral abnormalities. When kept in traditional barns with individual stalls, they show an above average number of aggressive or attention-seeking behaviors such as kicking the stall wall, and biting metal bars. Some warmbloods and thoroughbreds also require a strikingly high individual distance and exhibit comparatively high intraspecies aggressiveness. This may be explained by the fact that an agreeable nature has never been a selection criterion in the breeding of riding and racing horses. In addition, for generations the predominant manner of keeping these horses has been individual confinement, where conditioning of social behaviors is of lesser importance.

A special type is the pure-blooded Arabian (**9**). It is distinguished by a particularly dainty stature with a narrow croup, a refined short head with a concave profile, as well as short ears and large eyes and nostrils. Another typical feature is the high carriage of its head and neck. Arabians have the highest need for exercise of all horses paired with very fast reactions. Their extreme sensitivity and excitability are characteristic, and lead to a flight reflex that can be easily elicited. They therefore tend towards panic-like reactions when confronted with frightening situations. They do, however, build strong relationships with human beings. For this reason, correct management based on trust-building measures can redirect their hyperexcitability toward a calm and reliable behavior. Arabians are characterized by an agreeable nature. They are sociable and very affable, so that they are well suited for group management. With management problems, they show an increased tendency toward stereotypical movements such as weaving and stall pacing.

8 Thoroughbreds and refined warmbloods can tend towards overexcitement if management and handling are less than optimal (German warmblood).

9 The Arabian is characterized by a high sensitivity and great need for exercise (pure-blooded Arabian).

Ontogeny

Ontogeny, or individual development, is defined as the development of any living being from the fertilized oocyte (egg) until its death. It is the short-term adjustment of an animal to its given environment in the course of its life. Aside from morphological development and maturation, learning processes are of particular significance for this process. They allow the animal to adapt transiently to its particular living conditions.

The term maturation is used to denote the development or slow refinement of behavioral patterns during ontogeny, which occur in the absence of experience. Hereditary behaviors are based on maturation. In contrast, experience is necessary for behaviors based on learning processes. The animal learns through habituation, conditioning, imitation, and insight. Most behaviors result from a combination of maturation and learning processes.

The period of greatest behavioral change is during juvenile development. In this period, learning ability is maximal for all individuals. It is easy to recognize the biological significance of this phenomenon. The young animal comes into particularly close contact with other members of its species (parents and other immediate family members) and can, therefore, more easily acquire skills and experiences for later life than it can after dissolution of the family bond. Being receptive to this type of impression early in life is an advantage for the individual's adaptation to its enviroment.

Starting immediately after birth, horses are relatively independent and very capable of learning (Table 2). For this reason, the newborn foal is known as the prototype of the truly precocious animal. Imprinting on the dam, a special learning process, begins at birth and is often successfully completed within a few hours. Furthermore, a foal, independent of breed, learns to rise and lie down in a coordinated manner shortly after birth (**10**), and to find the udder more or less accurately. From day one, healthy foals are able to follow their dam and the group for relatively long distances and at all gaits.

In our modern management systems, a horse's ontogeny is strongly influenced by humans. The conditions and influences of management and training in particular have a formative influence on its future behavior. Positive as well as negative experiences occur from the first hour of life onwards and become irrevocably fixed within the horse's memory. Human influence of the individual's development, therefore, begins at birth and is of greatest importance during further upbringing. An example is the separation of the foal from its mother. If an approach is taken that is similar to the original way of equine life, the foal's necessary separation process from its dam can take place without traumatizing the foal. Great psychological strain, however, can be exerted if the foal is abruptly separated from its dam and has no further contact with other familiar companions. This negative experience can be profound and may represent the foundation of a future behavioral abnormality.

In general, negative experiences during early development are particularly far-reaching. For this reason, behavioral problems originating from this period are very difficult or impossible to treat and reverse. As a general rule, difficult horses or horses showing behavioral abnormalities are not born as such, but are made to be this way either by management, training, or both.

> Collectively, equine behavior is based on:
> - Species-specific behavior.
> - Breed-specific behavior.
> - Individual behavior.
>
> Individual behavior results from the experiences made during ontogeny.

10 Viable foals attempt to stand within minutes of birth.

Table 2 Inborn and learned behavioral patterns after birth
(Dillenburger 1982; Waring 1983; Schäfer 1993)

Immediately	Commencement of breathing and thermoregulation, tearing of the umbilical cord
	Freeing from the fetal membranes
	Beginning of imprinting on the dam and its own species
After several minutes	Attempts to stand
After approx. 10–60 minutes	First standing
After approx. 40 minutes	Visual and auditory orientation
After approx. 30–120 minutes	Seeking the udder Inborn: • Seeking dark corners. • Pushing and bumping movements towards the food source. • Suckling posture, suckling reflex, swallowing reflex. Learned: • Finding the udder.
After approx. 30–120 (420) minutes	First suckling
After approx. 30 minutes	Exploring behavior and curiosity (licking of and sniffing at objects, flehmen, pawing) Comfort behavior (grooming, rolling) Agonistic behavior, subordination posture
After approx. 60 (−180) minutes	Defecation
After approx. 100 minutes	Playing behavior (solitary play)
After approx. 120 minutes	Urination
Within the first day of life	Moving at all gaits

Limitations of behavioral adaptability

The conclusion drawn from the previous discussion is that the horse has had to continuously adapt to changing living conditions for millions of years. Again and again this adaptation was successful; at times, however, the limitations of adaptability were exceeded. As a result, during evolution, when natural selection dictated survival, entire sidelines became extinct due to a lack of adaptability. This is not the case for horses under human care today, except when one considers possible breeding failures. Does this mean that behavioral problems are to be taken less seriously? According to the concept of need satisfaction and damage avoidance of Tschanz (1993), living creatures are capable of establishing and maintaining themselves, and can therefore actively and passively avoid damage. Their success or failure can be assessed by evaluating whether body and body organs as well as behavior are within the normal range of a group of individuals having the same characteristics and belonging to the same breeding community. Behavioral abnormalities can impair self-establishment and self-maintenance or even make it impossible. Therefore, behavioral abnormalities attributable to inadequacies in management and handling are signs that must be taken seriously. They are a signal that under the circumstances in question, the limitations of a horse's adaptability have been exceeded. They are further an indication of living conditions that would make survival more difficult or even impossible for the horse.

How are limitations of a horse's adaptability exceeded? It has to be mentioned that in free-roaming animals, a balance between a behavior-eliciting situation and an inner impetus normally exists. If digressions from this state occur, the animal will try to restore the balance by means of an appropriate behavior. An example can be used to illustrate this: if a free-roaming horse feels hunger, it can seek food and satisfy its eating need. Given average grazing conditions, this activity occupies approximately 13 hours of every day. Now, on day X, an aberration from the normal state occurs. Grass growth is very poor and the feeding need is not satisfied after the usual feeding time. The free-living horse adapts to these conditions by means of behavioral adaptation. It prolongs its grazing time and, additionally, covers greater distances. Conse-

quently, the horse is able to restore the balanced state by means of appropriate behavior. The horse's motivation determines which need is prioritized at any one time.

Under our management conditions, the horse still attempts to adapt by means of certain behaviors. For example, horses that are fed small amounts of roughage and large amounts of energy dense feed to meet their requirements and are stalled on shavings, inevitably only spend a few hours per day on feed intake. Their eating need, however, would only be satisfied after a much longer time. The horse now attempts to adapt to this situation in order to restore the balanced state. Some horses simply spend the extra time resting or dozing, others however try to satisfy their eating need and start to chew on the wooden partitions (11). In both cases, the horse attempts to adapt to the given conditions. While the first variant is viewed favorably, the second variant is considered to represent aberrant behavior.

This example shows that under inadequate management conditions, some horses still show normal behavior, while others already show aberrant behavior. When are the limitations of the adaptation capacity reached? Generally speaking, an aberration only occurs if the horse, depending on its individual disposition, is unable to control a situation by behavioral adaptation. When adaptation and avoidance are no longer possible, an escape into aberrant behavior can result. The limitations of the adaptation capacity may be reached if:

- The horse's environment does not satisfy its behavioral needs.
- Handling of the horse during training and use exceeds the horse's adaptation capacity.

Under these conditions, conflicts, deprivation, and frustration can arise. These will, if they occur repeatedly and for a long time, lead to an emotional build-up. This build-up will ultimately be the origin of problem behavior. Because conflict, deprivation, and frustration are in the end responsible for such a situation, these terms will be explained in more detail.

CONFLICT
In a conflict situation, two mutually exclusive behavioral patterns are stimulated concurrently and to about the same extent. The resulting behavior

11 Rationed feeding on sawdust bedding does not satisfy the eating need of horses. Possible consequences are replacement activities such as rubbing the teeth against and gnawing of the stall walls (see the marks on the inside of the stall door).

is termed conflict behavior. Mutually exclusive behavioral patterns are, for example, "avoidance–approach" (flight and attack), "avoidance–avoidance" and "approach–approach".

The following is an example of the conflict "avoidance–avoidance" under human influence: a jumper is afraid of the jump and wants to refuse it. He is, however, afraid of punishment by the rider if he does not jump. This horse finds itself in an insoluble conflict situation: fear of jumping and, at the same time, fear of not jumping. Free-roaming horses are also exposed to conflict situations. In contrast to those arising under human influence, however, these can almost always be solved. Another example is as follows: a stallion willing to breed approaches a mare in early heat. Two behavioral patterns are activated concurrently: libido, which demands approach, and inborn social behavior, which causes avoidance because the stallion knows from experience that the mare may kick if he breaks her individual distance barrier. This stallion's conflict can be solved, even if the mare is not ready to be bred. He abandons his initial plan and turns to an activity rated the second most important, for example eating.

One can use the animals' behavior to detect that they are in a conflict situation. They will show either ambivalent behavior, redirected activities, or substitute activities. With ambivalent behavior, two different behaviors are exhibited in rapid alternation, for example feeding and flight. Redirected activities occur when a behavior is elicited by a certain object but cannot be exhibited toward it. This can, for

example, be observed in a group management situation when desired resources are limited. A horse may want to approach the feeding trough that is already occupied by a higher ranked animal. The lower ranked animal does not dare to attack this horse, but instead lets its aggression out on an uninvolved horse standing close by. This is also called redirected aggression. As a substitute reaction, one denotes a behavioral pattern that is inappropriate for the current situation (**12**). Known substitute reactions in horses are hasty eating, pawing, and headshaking.

12 Yawning can represent displacement behavior if it is exhibited in the absence of a relaxed, stretched-out head position.

DEPRIVATION

Deprivation, lack, or want exists when the horse is denied the possibility to satisfy its behavioral needs by means of target activities in a species-specific manner. An extreme example is the raising of a foal in complete isolation. Due to a lack of contact with members of its own species, deprivation with regard to social behavior occurs. This results in misdirected social development to the extent that the foal may become afraid of its own species. Such an extreme situation does not usually occur in practice. It is, however, enough to significantly limit a foal's social contact during its up-bringing, as occurs, for example, when dam and foal are kept isolated from other horses. Only within a herd can foals acquire all aspects of social behavior. As a general rule, mammals must practice social behavior in their youth, because associated behavioral patterns cannot otherwise be fully developed. It also appears that from a certain age on, animals cannot make up for an existing deficit. Deficient social behavior, therefore, can hardly be corrected later on. Deprivation of social behavior in horses leads to inappropriate behavioral expressions and a lack of ability to communicate with members of the same species, which results in significant problems in group management situations and breeding behavior.

> A deprivation, or want, exists when the horse is prevented from actively satisfying behavioral needs in a species-specific fashion. The result of deprivation is fear or aggression.

FRUSTRATION

Frustration arises when emotional tension is evoked because an expected action, that would satisfy a specific need, cannot be carried out. In this case the object, towards which the action is usually directed, is present. The need is there-fore evoked, but external influences prevent the completion of the appropriate behavioral pattern. In horse management, these situations arise especially frequently in association with feeding. How many horses are kept on shavings and are fed rations because they are too fat or, because of a hay dust allergy, they can only eat complete feeds and no hay? Their neighboring horses do not have these problems. They have sufficient hay and straw and, subsequently, they spend an appropriately long time eating. The former horse is exposed to a classically frustrating situation. The object, namely the feed, which could serve to satisfy the eating need, is present. It is, however, in the neighboring stall and the separating bars prevent the action that would satisfy the need, i.e. the feed intake, from occurring. Aggressive biting and grinding of the bars may be the result. Other horses, however, react to this type of situation with striking apathy.

> Frustration arises when emotional tension is created because an expected, need-satisfying action does not occur. Aggression can occur as a result of recurring frustration. Chronic frustration can lead to resignation.

Part B: Inborn behavioral patterns – implications for management and handling

Knowledge of natural equine behavior is a prerequisite for management that meets behavioral needs and for appropriate horse handling. Problem behavior is almost exclusively attributable to inadequacies in management, upbringing, training, and current use. For this reason, knowledge of the behavioral needs of horses is the basis for successful prevention and therapy of problem behavior.

The following ethogram, or behavioral inventory, provides insight into the essential behavioral patterns of the horse. Only if these are satisfied, can the horse live in psychological harmony with its "artificial" environment and its "social partner" human being. According to the ethological convention, the ethogram is presented as a division into individual functional areas. These are differentiated according to their different biological functions such as social behavior, feeding behavior, dam-foal behavior, and so on. Behavioral patterns can intersect at times, however, because not all behaviors are limited to one functional area.

The division of behavioral patterns into functional areas has didactic advantages and facilitates recognition of mistakes made in management and handling. Needs can only be satisfied within their functional area. Consequently, excellent design of one functional area cannot compensate for inadequacies in another. It is, for example, not possible to make up for deficiencies in resting behavior by an optimal and nutritionally sound feeding practice.

Because behavioral abnormalities attributable to management and handling always occur when the adaptation capacity of horses has been exceeded, knowledge of their behavioral needs in each operational area is very helpful when investigating the source of a problem. It is, therefore, the goal of this section to analyze natural equine behavior in more detail and derive inferences for management handling. For each functional area, predisposing factors for problem behavior are demonstrated, and solutions for its correction are presented.

Because free-roaming horses no longer exist, the following discussion of natural equine behavior stems from observations made in related equid species, in domestic horses living in the wild (such as Mustangs) or the semi-wild (such as Koniks, Camargue horses, New Forest ponies), or in horses living under near-natural conditions. Suitable related species for comparison are first and foremost the plains zebra and the mountain zebra, because they exhibit a similar social organization to the Przewalski horse and the domestic horse. Relevant findings are based on observations made by Klingel (1972).

Daily routine of free-roaming horses

Natural behavioral patterns

Under natural conditions, horses spend the greater part of their day eating: 50–70% of a 24-hour day. Following feed intake, standing in an awake (5–20%) or dozing state (10–20%) and locomotion independent of that during feeding (5–15%) take up most of their time. Comparatively little time is spent on behaviors such as lying down, drinking, comfort behavior, and so on. Many activities such as eating and resting are exhibited simultaneously by the members of a group. The reason for this synchronization of behaviors is the tendency to remain close to companions. The trigger for synchronous behavior is social facilitation.

Similar to physiologic processes, most behavioral patterns are subject to a daily rhythm that is determined by endogenous ("inner clock") and exogenous factors (light, temperature). Independent of this circadian rhythm, however, other factors such as the weather, insects, and predators influence the daily routine. As a result, free-roaming horses do not have a strict daily routine, as is sometimes claimed, but are rather flexible.

Seasonal influences also have an effect on the behavior of free-roaming horses. A well known example is the seasonal migration of some equid populations, which is caused by extensive climatic changes and the resulting shortage of feed or water. The circannual rhythm is thought to be responsible for some behavioral changes of horses that occur during certain seasons. Among these are an increased unrest and a greater need for exercise during the spring and fall as well as increased feed intake at the beginning of winter.

Implications for management and handling

ADAPTATION TO THE NATURAL TIME BUDGET

In captivity, depending on the type of management system and their use, the daily routine of horses differs to a greater or lesser extent from the natural activity rhythm. Figure 13 shows the time budget of horses living under near-natural conditions on the one hand and in captivity on the other. The comparison shows that under natural conditions, horses spend approximately 60% of their time eating. When kept in a stall with hay and straw being offered *ad libitum*, this time portion is already reduced by one third to 47%. An extreme shortening of eating time occurs with rationed feeding and strawless management. The time spent on feeding under those conditions is reduced to 16%. Divergences from the natural time budget such as these are not infrequently found in practice. They should, however, be strictly avoided because the emotional build-up resulting from an insufficient satisfaction of needs is the primary cause of management- and handling-induced behavioral aberrations.

REGULAR OR IRREGULAR ORGANIZATION OF THE DAY?

With stalled horses it is customary to have a regular daily routine and, specifically, to maintain precise feeding times. The inner clock of horses is frequently given as a reason for this measure because horses react to delay in a very sensitive manner. They kick against the stall walls or rub their teeth against the bars or in general show an increased level of unrest and aggression. As a result, one tries very hard to maintain the correct time again at the next feeding. Is this exact timing necessary? As can be seen from the preceding explanations, horses tend to exhibit certain activities at certain times, but they are flexible and not at all fixed. The described behavior is caused, therefore, more by a learning process than by an inborn behavior. With stall management, it is therefore sensible not to let horses get too used to a fixed schedule. Horses show a more balanced behavior if they, as under natural conditions, have unlimited access to feed, or if they are fed several times during a 24-hour period without paying attention to a minute-by-minute time schedule. Many problem behaviors can be avoided in this manner. A divergence from schedule of several hours or more should, however, be avoided for ethologic and physiologic (digestion) reasons.

- An extreme divergence of individual activities from the natural daily routine leads to an insufficient satisfaction of needs and is the primary cause of behavioral disturbances.
- Letting horses get used to precise times, for example with regard to feeding and riding, can lead to problem behavior due to excessive anticipation and excitement.

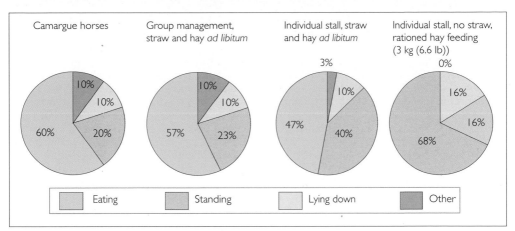

13 Time budget of horses under different management conditions (according to Duncan 1980, Kiley-Worthington 1989).

Social behavior

Natural behavioral patterns

SOCIAL ORGANIZATION AND GROUP SIZE

Horses are social animals. Due to disease or exclusion from the group, they can temporarily become loners, but in most cases, social isolation ends in re-association with a different group or in the animal's speedy death. Naturally, horses live in harem groups (or bands) or in stallion or bachelor groups that can temporarily form herds of 100 animals or more. The individual groups are, however, independent of each other. While bachelor groups are structured more loosely, harem groups often stay together for years or even for life. The group's core usually consists of the leading stallion and his older mares. Bands with two or more cooperating stallions also exist, while one stallion always maintains the absolute alpha position.

Horse bands are relatively small and at most comprise 20 members. From observations of wild equids and mustangs that have run wild, it is known that a harem group usually consists of only one to six mares, their foals up to an age of 2 or 3 years and an adult stallion. The leadership of such a band is primarily incumbent on the dominant mare. The stallion also participates in this task. He is, however, primarily responsible for keeping the band together and for defense against attacks from other individuals, such as other stallions and predators.

Even though horse bands have offspring every year, group size only varies within certain limits. This is primarily due to voluntary or forced wandering off of the offspring. The former often depends on the number of siblings, social pressure, and playmates. Young stallions are always driven away by their sire when they exhibit a strong interest in the older mares. If their advances are limited to the younger mares, the dominant stallion often is remarkably tolerant. In general, the relationship between the sire and his sons can be regarded as friendly, as long as the latter are not very dominant and do not claim an older mare. Young stallions that have wandered off form bachelor groups of most often two or three but up to 20 members. At an age of 5–6 years, when they have reached physical and psychological maturity, young free-roaming stallions can finally found their own band. In doing so, the keeping together of a group of mares appears to be more challenging than their acquisition. Only the strongest successfully "extract" mares from another stallion's band through fighting or take over a harem in its entirety. Most often young stallions take over roaming, superfluous female offspring to found a band. Many young stallions never found their own band and remain in a bachelor group for life.

Similar to the stallions, young mares voluntarily leave their bands or are forcibly taken, which means they are kidnapped. Kidnapping occurs when other stallions are prompted to take over mares during their first pronounced and long-lasting heat. The dominant stallion tries to prevent kidnapping, but his interest in his daughters is less than that in his older mares, as has been observed in Camargue horses by Goldschmidt-Rothschild and Tschanz (1978). This behavior helps to keep the incest rate low. In rare instances in nature, however, the harem stallion does mate with his own daughters.

It is not at all unusual for adult mares to switch bands. Observations by Berger (1986) and Stevens (1990) in semi-wild horses in the great basin and North Carolina showed that up to 50% of mares 4 years and older switched to a different family within 3 years. Researchers presume that the availability of feed, which differs according to the living area, is a possible reason for this behavior. It was observed that with unfavorable resources, mares increasingly tended to wander. Age, rank, and pregnancy, on the other hand, do not seem to influence the frequency of wandering off. It was, however, observed that mares which were frequently threatened, left the band union more often than others.

RANK ORDER

All horse groups operate under a relatively solid rank order. It ensures that competence problems do not always result in fights, and therefore contributes to smooth cohabitation. As soon as a hierarchy is established, it remains relatively stable. A condition for this stability is that all animals in a group have to be individually acquainted. The horse uses visual, auditory, and, especially, olfactory features to orient itself within the group.

In the wild, the stallion is frequently the animal holding the highest rank. He is followed in rank by the dominant mare, usually an older and experienced animal, which is also very strong. She is then followed in rank by the remaining mares in a mostly linear fashion. Not infrequently, however, more complicated rank structures such as triangle relationships occur (A is dominant to B, B is dominant to C, but C is dominant to A). The reason for this lies in the multitude of rank-determining factors. These multifaceted relationships primarily occur in larger groups; in smaller groups the hierarchy is mostly linear.

What determines the rank of an animal? What makes it the most dominant one? While physical factors such as age, sex, weight, and size may contribute, they do not necessarily determine the rank of an animal. For example, the age-dependent level of experience is of major importance. While stallions are usually dominant over geldings and those, in turn, over mares, experienced animals that are still strong and fit often dominate over younger ones.

Furthermore, small or female animals can be of higher rank than larger ones or males. This is due to the fact that next to physical features, psychological factors such as willingness to fight, temperament, reaction speed, and self-confidence are important in determining rank. These behavioral features can vary with breed. According to Schäfer (1993) and personal experiences, ponies and small cold-blooded breeds (Haflinger, Norwegian Fjord horses) often occupy positions higher in rank than large breed horses within mixed breed groups, which is presumably due to their strong psychological expressiveness. Foals and young horses initially occupy a position low in rank. They have to achieve the bodily and social maturity required for a higher ranked position over time. Only a suckling foal occupies the social rank of its dam without its own doing, as long as it stays close to her. When comparing different species, horses dominate over mules, donkeys, and cattle.

When trying to assess a rank order, we do it subjectively and therefore often come to different conclusions. Certainly, horses that fight the most, the so-called tyrants, are typically not the highest in rank. The frequency of aggression or aggressive behavior does, therefore, not indicate the rank position of individual animals. An objective assessment of a rank order is possible when using the rank index calculation according to Sambraus (1975) (see Table 3).

Dominant animals have certain privileges compared with the subordinate members of the group. For example, they always have first pick and, therefore, the choice of the best feeding place, the most convenient sleeping and resting place and so forth. In return, they provide safety and security for the lower ranked animals, which in the end is of great importance for their well-being. An interesting question is whether under natural conditions, foals of highly ranked mares become highly ranked animals themselves. In this context it is observed that when mares come into heat simultaneously, highly ranked mares can prevent lower ranked mares from being bred by the stallion. By this means, the former achieve an earlier birth of their own foals, which gives them a lead with regard to growth, age, and size and, therefore, a rank advantage. Additionally, dominant mares and their foals frequently exhibit a better body condition as the dams claim the better grazing areas for

Protocol						Interpretation		
Horse	1	2	3	4	5	Calculation (see formula)	Rank index	Rank order
1		‖‖ ‖‖ ‖‖ / ‖	/ / ‖‖‖	‖‖ ‖	‖‖ ‖‖	1/4	0.25	4
2	‖ / ‖‖ ‖‖ ‖‖		‖ / /	‖‖ ‖‖ ‖‖	‖‖ ‖‖	1/3	0.33	3
3	‖‖ / /	/ / ‖		‖‖ / ‖‖	‖‖ / ‖	0/3	0	5
4	‖‖ ‖‖ /	‖‖ ‖‖ ‖‖ /	‖‖ / ‖‖		‖‖ ‖‖	4/4	1.00	1
5	‖‖ ‖‖ / ‖‖	‖‖ ‖‖ / ‖‖	‖‖ / ‖ ‖‖	‖‖ ‖‖		3/4	0.75	2

Table 3 Protocol and interpretation of a rank index calculation (Sambraus 1975).

Rank index calculation (Sambraus 1975)

To calculate the rank index, one starts by recording the conflicts and their outcome for each horse over an extended period of time (Table 3). For each interaction, the dominant as well as the subordinate horse receives a mark above or below a horizontal line. This means that the horse denoted at the top of the table is dominant or subordinate to the one denoted in the left column with regard to its social rank. To calculate the rank index, the number of animals that an individual has proven to dominate is divided by the number of group members to which an established rank relationship exists. By definition, a rank relationship is considered established if one animal shows at least twice as many dominant activities than the other.

$$\text{Rank index} = \frac{\text{number of subordinate animals}}{\text{number of established rank relationships}}$$

According to this formula, the rank index is always between 0.0 and 1.0. The higher an animal is in rank, the closer the rank index becomes to 1.0.

themselves. Therefore, foals of higher ranked mares may have certain privileges. Some authors further suggest that inborn behavior and behavior learned from the dam plays a certain role. In the end, however, individual ranking factors decide the rank of an animal. The rank is not static and can change throughout life dependent on the animal's physical and psychological condition.

As an additional comment, it should be noted that aside from ranking factors, the momentary motivation of animals can decide the outcome of a conflict. For example, a lower ranked animal with a high motivation such as hunger can transiently stand up against a higher ranked animal. Such a one-time event does not, however, permanently alter the established relationship in rank between the two animals.

CONFLICTS

In general, horses only exhibit as much aggressive behavior as is required by the momentary situation. This has economic reasons because a fight implies the risk of injury for both, even the winner, and therefore could ultimately jeopardize survival. Many confrontations are therefore ritualized; at times, however, serious damaging fights can take place. Which type of confrontation is chosen depends on many factors such as rank, sexual libido, age, sex, and the individual willingness to fight. For this purpose, horses possess a fine-tuned repertoire of threatening and submissive gestures. These are inborn, like all types of social expression.

To threaten, the horse uses a specific facial expression, characterized by laid-back ears, and narrowed nostrils, with the corners of the mouth pulled back and downwards. The degree of intensity of the threat is differentiated according to the risk of injury. Confrontations without bodily contact such as threatening swinging of the head, rear leg threats, and bite threats are regarded as less dangerous. Biting and kicking with bodily contact, on the other hand, are more likely to cause injury. Aggressive forms of threat such as head swinging, charging, and biting are used primarily by highly ranked individuals against those of lower rank. Defensive behaviors such as rear leg threats and rear leg kicks are independent of rank. They are, however, typical for mares, while aggressive forms of threats are predominant in stallions.

If in the course of a confrontation, one horse signals its subordination, it generally prevents further aggression by the dominant animal; this is referred to as social inhibition. In this manner, serious confrontations can mostly be avoided. The recognition of another horse as being higher in rank is demonstrated by avoidance, leaving or rapid flight. A tail tucked between the hind legs explicitly demonstrates subordination and fear. In an established hierarchy and with sufficient available space, subordination is demonstrated by avoidance. This form of subordination is difficult to detect for the observer because the animals maintain their rank-dependent social distance without being threatened. Young horses exhibit a specific gesture of subordination, which is referred to as snapping or tooth clapping (**14**). For this purpose, the suckling posture is taken and with a rigid facial expression and semi-opened jaws, the mandible (lower jaw) is moved back and forth. Presumably, this gesture inhibits aggression or has a calming effect as it is only exhibited towards older, or very dominant, or threatening animals. It is, however, not always successful. The behavior is also interpreted as a displacement behavior. This gesture of subordination is generally only exhibited by young animals up to an age of approximately 4 years, but can in rare cases be maintained for life.

If the hierarchy is established and a stable herd structure exists, slight laying back of the ears and curling of the nostrils and lips is generally sufficient to put the opponent in its place. However, even well organized groups show certain shifts in their hierarchy. For example, younger animals try to stand their ground against older animals, those that are becoming weaker, or those that are sick. Over time, these will give up their position without a fight.

FIGHTS

Horses are not territorial. Serious fights between stallions, therefore, do not occur with the goal of defending territory.

Therefore, a meeting between stallions of different bands outside the mating season usually takes place rather peacefully. They usually limit themselves to ritualized behaviors such as foreleg kicking, squealing, circling, rearing, and marking by defecation, with which they try to impress and threaten their rival. After such a ritualized fight, the stallions separate and return to their mares, which are then usually herded closer together. Herding is decidedly an aggressive but ritualized behavioral pattern of stallions. It does not result in injury as long as the mares know how to interpret the behavior correctly, which is usually the case in free-roaming herds. During herding, which can be

14 Snapping, or tooth clapping, is a subordination gesture of young horses. Occasionally, it is also exhibited by adult animals.

15 Under natural conditions, serious damaging fights between stallions only occur during the breeding season.

performed at any speed and gait, the stallion exhibits a threatening expression. The head is lowered towards the ground and the head and the extended neck are swung vertically or, less frequently, horizontally. Herding is first shown after the 3rd year (34–38 months) of age and is exhibited fully at approximately 5 years (50–58 months) of age.

Under natural conditions, escalating fights between stallions only occur during the mating season (**15**). Then, however, they are real, hardly ritualized, damaging fights in which the opponents frequently inflict many bite wounds and bruises. These fights are exhibited particularly frequently and vehemently between younger and older stallions, because with increasing maturity, the adolescent animals increasingly refuse to accept the rank claim of the leading stallion. In the wild, however, grave injuries or death of the subordinate animal are the exception. Approximately 3% of adult stallions die as a consequence of fighting injuries such as infected wounds, jaw injuries, and lameness, because they are weakened and become easy prey for predators.

The manner of fighting during a stallion fight is always similar: minor differences in opinion are settled standing by means of neck- and bite-fights. With crossed necks, the stallion attempts to push the opponent to the ground and to place bites on his fore legs. This is usually followed by "circling" nose-to-tail (also called an anti-parallel position), during which the animals try to hurt each other's hindlegs.

The harsher form of a stallion fight is the rearing-kicking-fight. For this, the stallion rises on his hindlegs and tries to hurt the opponent with foreleg kicks and bites to the neck, throat, and ears. These rearing fights are frequently interrupted by running fights. During these, the pursuer tries to bite the front horse in the flank and the rear until he turns around and faces him again. Kicking and the rapid flight of the subordinate animal end this fight, although the winner will pursue the escapee for some additional time.

Mares fight in a different manner than stallions. For them, a typical feature is the hindleg kick. Most often, mares will back into each other and squeal loudly before starting to kick. When defending themselves against stallions, mares also generally kick with their hindlegs. Only in extreme situations do they strike and bite, charge, or chase their opponent. Massive conflicts with hindleg kicking among mares primarily serve to establish rank order.

BONDING AND RELATIONSHIPS

Formation of relationships, i.e. the need for social contact and the readiness to follow others, determines the behavior of socially living animals. It is no coincidence that all animals that are easy to work with live in communities and have a natural understanding of "friendship" and establishment of contact. Horses as social animals have the ability and the need to form friendships. While the presence of a stallion serves to strengthen the stability of a band union, the friendly connection between group members is the decisive factor. Band unions are maintained even in the absence of a stallion. The group connection is strengthened, among other factors, through certain social activities such as being together and mutual grooming (16). The reasons for friendships are diverse, but certain common motivations are recognizable. For example, a strong connection exists between a dam and her foal, often also between her and her older offspring. Playmates of early days also sometimes remain friends for life, as long as they are not separated. Color is of certain relevance: animals of the same color are preferred as friends. It is not known for certain, whether imprinting on the dam's color, which frequently is the same as the foal's, or the horse's own color is of importance for this behavior. A common fate, such as simultaneous introduction into a strange group together, can also lead to formation of ties between animals. Rank is not of importance for friendship formation. Not infrequently, one of the animals in a friendship is braver and of higher rank than the other. This friend then protects the subordinate animal as long as it remains in his vicinity. Stallions have their favorite mares with which, even outside the breeding season, they spend time and exhibit grooming activity. Despite friendship, however, agonistic behavior can be observed between partners and may even occur relatively commonly due to their closer relationship.

Absolute dislike between horses can be observed in the wild but is rare. Some stallions reject certain mares completely without an obvious reason from the observer's standpoint. These stallions will attack the rejected mares so violently that the attacked animal does not dare to come close to the community again. These rejected animals, however, connect with another band.

16 Aside from hygienic purposes, mutual grooming serves to stabilize social relationships.

INDIVIDUAL DISTANCE

Individual distance is defined as the distance that is usually maintained between individuals of a certain species or between members of a community. It is not uniform in size but in fact is dependent on the rank relationship between animals. As a general rule, the greater the difference in rank between two animals, the greater the distance they keep from each other. Foals and youngsters have the smallest individual distance between each other; it increases with increasing age. There also appear to be breed-dependent and individual differences. Highly bred warmbloods and thoroughbreds in general require a greater distance to their neighbors than ponies, draft horses, and Arabians. Finally, the individual distance differs depending on the situation and activity. For example, the distance during grazing is significantly greater than that during rest periods (17).

Sambraus (1978) points out that the term individual distance is confusing because it implicates a fixed distance between one animal and each member of its group. This is not the case. The distance is determined by the rank relationships. For example, the individual distance between horse A and horse B may be 1 m (39 ins), but 3 m (117 ins) between horse A and horse C. According to Sambraus, the term avoidance distance is better suited to describe these relationships. Because the term individual

17 During resting periods, the individual distance is generally reduced while rank order relationships are maintained.

distance has become established in recent years, however, it will be used for the remainder of this text. It does seem appropriate though to point out the possibility of an incorrect interpretation of the term, as the literature frequently evokes the impression that the individual distance is of uniform size for a certain horse.

- Horses are social animals and live in communities of at least two and maximally 20 members. The union formed with members of the same species provides security.
- Their inborn social behavior forces horses to establish a rank order. Once it is established, further serious conflicts do not arise. The union does, therefore, remain mostly stable.
- Rank factors are physical and psychological features, the latter of which are decisive in mixed breed groups.
- The connection within communities is mostly a matter of social ties. Voluntary and forced switching of groups occurs in all age groups.
- Maintenance of individual distance is a requirement for smooth cohabitation. The outer appearance, conformation, physiology, and species-specific behavior of horses are the result of a development over approximately 60 million years.

If one animal crosses another's individual distance, this represents an aggressive act, which in return evokes submission or attack. To cross the individual distance peacefully, therefore, friendly intentions have to be signaled. This is, for example, achieved during social grooming by showing the "grooming face". For breeding purposes, the stallion also has to cross the mare's individual distance. An experienced stallion will therefore indicate his peaceful intentions by courting and a slow approach during foreplay.

Implications for management and handling

Note: all measurements and recommendations for horse housing given are according to German regulations. There are no specified Federal regulations concerning housing of privately owned horses in the US. However, recommendations for barn design, measurements, building materials, and so on, are available from State Extension Services and different equine organizations. Regulations exist for research horses. Useful publications include the *"Guide for the Care and Use of Laboratory Animals"* (Institute of Laboratory Animal Resources, Commission on Life Sciences, National Research Council, National Academy Press, 1996) and the *"Guide for the Care and Use of Agricultural Animals in Agricultural Research and Teaching"* (Federation of Animal Science Societies, 1999).

Life in a group represents the natural behavior of horses. According to the guidelines of the German Federal Ministry for Nutrition, Agriculture and Forestry (*Bundesministerium für Ernährung, Landwirtschaft und Forsten, BMELF, 1995*), therefore, horses should, whenever possible, be kept in groups of two or more horses. As these groups are formed according to the wishes of human beings and with restrictions in regard to space, instead of being formed freely as they would under natural conditions, special attention has to be paid to measurements and spatial design. In the end, however, the success of any group management always depends on the knowledge and "horse sense" of the manager. His or her qualification for the task is of utmost importance.

SOCIAL BEHAVIOR – A LEARNING PROCESS
All social behavior is inborn, but mutual understanding of the forms of expression has to be acquired. It is, therefore, of utmost importance for foals and young animals to grow

up in groups. The best environment is a herd with companions of similar age as well as adult horses. At the very least, they should grow up in a herd of brood mares and, after weaning, be transferred to a foal-raising operation. Even here, however, contact with older animals is advantageous. Geldings are very suitable as they will interfere in an educational manner but still also be playful. Under these conditions, the social behavior of the younger animals can unfold in its entirety. Horses raised in this manner understand the "language" of their peers and are capable of resolving rank relationships in an appropriate manner. Unfortunately, it is not rare, and may even become more and more common, for mistakes to be made when raising horses. Horse owners wish for a foal out of their mare and this foal is then born and raised at a boarding stable or at their home. Other foals are not present. The owner also fails to transfer the weanling to an appropriate foal-raising operation because he or she does not want to be separated from the little one, or the owner makes a point for the training advantages of an intensive horse-human-relationship early on. The young horse, therefore, remains in the same place with only the dam as a social partner. Raising a horse in this manner predisposes it to a misdirected social development. Horses that lack sufficient social experience during the first years of their life remain problematic throughout life, whenever they come into close contact with other horses. It also appears that the missing experience can only be compensated for insufficiently or not at all. Horses raised in this manner are afraid of other horses because they are not able to appropriately judge their expressions and behavior. Because of this fear, they often overreact or react inappropriately in a given situation, i.e. they kick or bite when given the slightest opportunity. Other horses show the opposite behavior; they stand aside from the rest and are always "on guard" and are wary of the other group members. These horses are usually not suited for management in a group because they become stressed and the risk of injury for themselves or the other group members is disproportionately high.

CONCEPTION OF GROUP MANAGEMENT – HOW CAN AGONISTIC BEHAVIOR BE REDUCED?

Group management is often regarded skeptically in practice, in part because of the increased risk of injury. This concern is valid in a situation where horses are brought together without any preparations or special measures. Group management, which is possible in a barn with loose housing, a run-out shed, or in a pasture with a shed, only works smoothly if the manager knows enough about equine behavior, is familiar with the type of management in question, and has planned the operation correctly. A general rule for all types of group management is that animals of inferior rank must have the opportunity to withdraw at all times (**18**). Circular runs are useful because they allow rapid withdrawal and thereby help to resolve conflicts as smoothly as possible. In contrast, dead ends and acute angles are dangerous. They can only be entered and exited via one opening. Once a horse has been driven inside, there is no escape. More than one horse has been seriously hurt or even killed in this manner. To avoid situations like these, run-out sheds must have two entryways or a permanently open front. A box stall that has been turned into a group management situation can also contain dangerous dead ends if one only opens the doors and lets the animals roam freely. A risky situation always occurs when two or more horses enter a stall simultaneously, because they invariably cross each other's individual distance. Agonistic behavior is, therefore, bound to occur.

Of particular importance for group management is the availability of sufficient space. Only then can horses practice their natural avoidance behavior and keep their rank-dependent individual distances without conflict. For this purpose, minimum measurements exist that are calculated by formulas based on the withers height (wh). With these formulas, space requirements for horses of all sizes can be calculated exactly. The minimum space per horse in a barn with loose housing is $(2 \times wh)^2$. For a horse with a wh of 1.65 m (65 in), this translates into approximately 11 m² $[(2 \times 1.65)^2 = (3.3)^2 = 3.3 \times 3.3 = 10.9$ m²$]$ (117 sq ft). To calculate the space requirements for all horses together, the formula is multiplied by the total number of horses (n $\times$ $(2 \times wh)^2$; so, for 10 horses, the area required is 109 m² (1,173 sq ft)), where the wh of the tallest horse is used as a reference point. For a run-out shed, a run of $2 \times (2 \times wh)^2$ per horse has to be added to the resting area of $(2 \times wh)^2$. According to personal experience, these measurements represent the absolute minimum and every responsible horse owner will plan with greater dimensions. For a run-out shed, for example, the outside space available for smaller groups of less than 10 horses should, as a guideline, provide an area of at least 300 m² (3,229 sq ft). If adequate room is not available and the opportunity to avoid others is not given,

18 Agonistic behavior is to be expected if feeding or watering devices are placed in corners without any opportunity for a horse to escape, as is the case with this incorrectly positioned water source.

lower ranked animals have no way to escape and constantly live in a stressful environment.

However, sufficient room is not enough. Run-out sheds lend themselves to a breakdown into different functional areas such as eating, drinking, resting, and exploring, and thereby avoid concentration of too many animals in certain places. The most attractive area in any barn is the eating area. It has to be placed and designed with great care, as otherwise massive conflicts arise even in well integrated groups. One prerequisite is a ratio of animals to feeding places of at least 1:1, i.e. each horse must have its own feeding place (trough, hay rack, and so on) where it can eat while maintaining its individual distance. A hay rack for five horses in a barn with six or more animals is not suitable because horses want to eat together. It is part of their natural behavior. In practice, feeding stalls have proven to be suitable with regard to this issue. Feed-related aggression occurs with increased frequency during the expectancy period prior to feeding or near computer-regulated feeding systems, where only asynchronous feed intake is possible. Redirected aggression (p.124) can then be observed more frequently.

CORRECT GROUP STRUCTURE

In naturally formed equine bands, the maximal group size is 20 animals. Within this order of magnitude, the animals are guaranteed to know each other well, which is the primary requirement for smooth cohabitation. In group managements, especially in boarding facilities, this group size should, therefore, not be exceeded. It has been proven that the number of agonistic behaviors increases with increasing group size. Furthermore, the risk of discrimination against certain animals in the resting and dozing area, or when they are seeking shelter from insects or extreme weather, is increased. A different situation occurs when many horses are kept on large pastures, which represents a herd situation and allows formation of smaller groups that can keep an appropriate distance from each other. With breeding herds, larger groups are also unproblematic because the groups remain stable for several years and the animals are very familiar with each other.

In captivity, horses cannot choose their group affiliation themselves as they can in the wild. When putting together a group, it is therefore of utmost importance to pay attention to the agreeability of horses with each other. Ponies, draft horses, and Arabians, for example, are well suited for group management. Some highly bred warmbloods and thoroughbreds, on the other hand, are sometimes difficult to integrate into a group. If certain horses continue to be disruptive and cause problems after having been given sufficient time to get used to the situation, they should be removed from the group. In a different group with more equal companions, they may then be much easier to manage. The original group will most often settle down peacefully after the troublemaker has been removed.

The age of horses should not be overlooked when putting a group together. Younger horses, for example, are subject to threats by older ones.

A single young animal will, therefore, not be comfortable in a group of older horses and its psychological development may be impaired. If two young animals are present in the group, however, living with adult animals can be of significant advantage. Very old horses should also have a partner in order to be better able to deal with the age-related loss in rank status. In general, it can be observed that poorly integrated animals are attacked more frequently and more aggressively. As a general rule, an animal low in rank has to be tolerated by at least one animal in a dominant position. Otherwise, discrimination of this animal with regard to feeding, drinking, cover, and so on, will be excessive.

Because of ties and "friendships" between horses, smaller groups of less than 10 animals should have an even number of horses. It is otherwise possible that one horse will be excluded and left by itself. Such loners are increasingly involved in fights because they lack a friendly relationship. Color also plays an important role. A white horse within a group of dark-colored horses will have difficulty being accepted or will not be accepted at all. It is better to integrate two white horses or pintos. These will become attached in most cases. Size and breed are frequently less important than color in the choice of a partner. It is with good reason that some breeding operations form their herds according to color.

Geldings and mares often form close friendships. Some geldings will even develop stallion-like behavior, which can increase the danger of serious conflicts in a mixed-gender group. It is often recommended that horses are separated according to gender and form groups with exclusively mares or geldings. According to experiences by Kolter (1987), groups with an excess of mares are more agreeable than those with an even gender distribution.

APPROPRIATE MANAGEMENT OF STALLIONS

Adult stallions, especially breeding stallions, are often kept strictly isolated and without the possibility of going out to pasture with companions of the same species. They do, therefore, show a remarkable number of behavioral abnormalities. These horses can, however, be integrated into groups, especially outside the breeding season. Special measures need to be taken to do this. For example, it is important to keep groups of stallions, or of geldings and stallions, outside the range of mares. If not, there is a reason for rivalry and fighting. Furthermore, sufficient opportunity to avoid

one another and as much space as possible has to be available. If this is not the case, there is a great risk of massive conflicts that can even be fatal. If stallions are kept separated from others, an outside stall with paddock and pasture access is recommended. With extremely disagreeable stallions, it may be useful to keep the immediately adjacent paddock empty (**19**).

Stallions not intended for breeding should be castrated if they exhibit sexually motivated or aggressive behavior. Although this operation is associated with a noticeable effect on the behavioral inventory, it appears to be justified from an animal welfare standpoint. In most cases, castration is the prerequisite for appropriate management of male horses.

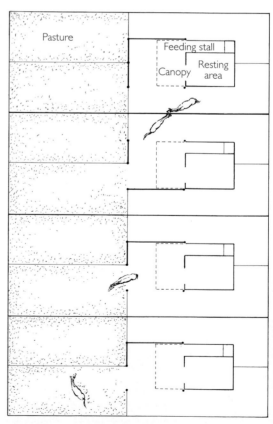

Pasture

Feeding stall

Canopy   Resting area

19 Layout of a run-out system for stallions.

CAUTION WHEN INTRODUCING NEWCOMERS

The most important criterion for integrating a horse into a group is probably that it should have sufficient social experience. As described earlier, horses with deprivation (insufficient experience) in this functional area are afraid of their own species and tend towards misdirected social behavior. These horses will be much more comfortable when kept separated from others, for example in a stall with an attached paddock.

As a general rule, each new addition to a group represents a change in the existing rank order. Consequently, frequent fluctuations in a group result in constant disruptions. Only operations in which just minor changes of the group constellation can be expected over the years are, therefore, suitable for group management.

The newcomer that is added to a horse group has to establish its rank in relation to every single one of the herd members. This can be done relatively peacefully by means of threatening and avoidance behavior, but it can also lead to more aggressive confrontations that can sometimes last for several days. These confrontations will be the fiercer the more highly ranked the new animal was in its previous group. For this reason, it makes sense not to let the horse simply "take a leap into the dark" but instead to take some precautions.

Brief removal of a horse from its group for hours or even a few days does not usually lead to significant rank order conflicts upon its return. If, on the other hand, a horse is removed from the group for a longer period of time, it may be advisable to treat the re-integration as one would a new addition. According to experience, the group members remember highly ranked animals for longer periods of time than lower ranked ones.

ARE INDIVIDUAL STALLS APPROPRIATE?

Management in individual stalls is, strictly speaking, opposed to the inborn social behavior of horses. In a comparative study by Houpt and Houpt (1989) it was shown that separated management of horses in stalls with paddocks can be a viable alternative to group management, as long as the opportunity for visual, olfactory, and auditory contact is given at all times.

Considering that only a few horse operations are suitable for group management with regard to the required small fluctuation in the horse population, and that to date some of our horses exhibit damage due to social deprivation, and further that only few operation managers have

Practical tips for the integration of newcomers

Decrease home advantage
The new horse should be given the opportunity to explore the barn by itself or together with other familiar horses for several hours prior to introduction into the group. This has the advantage that it can orient itself better once the other horses are added. Furthermore, it will adopt some of the barn odor and loose some of its foreign smell.

The settling-in stall – the secure retreat
A "must" for every group management is an appropriately sized (approximately 16–20 m^2 (172–215 sq ft)) settling-in stall, which allows a first meeting via nasonasal contact over a chest-high separation but provides a secure retreat at all times. This stall can also be used as a sick stall as needed.

Everything's easier with a "friend"
It has proven useful to introduce the newcomer to only one especially agreeable group member at first. With an already familiar partner, the integration is handled much better psychologically. One can also introduce the horse successively, i.e. one first introduces the animal of lowest rank, then after a certain time (for example one day) the next highest one and so on until it knows the entire group.

Provide relaxation
The integration of new horses is least problematic if the other horses are sufficiently "busy" so that "the new guy" does not represent the "event of the day". The optimal time is the pasture season when horses are mostly busy with grazing.

Lots of space – the A and O
The more space there is available and the better the opportunity to avoid others during the integration period, the smaller the risk of injury will be for all members of the group.

the necessary qualifications, "horse friendly" individual stall management is definitely acceptable. It is very positive that in practice the trend has increasingly gone towards an open stall design with improved visual contact with others via half-open doors or separation walls.

Nowadays, stalls without paddocks are virtually impossible to rent out in some areas. Of the individual stall management options, this variant and the type with a half-open door most appropriately meet the horse's need for social contact because they allow physical contact with the neighbor above the partition (**20**). It is imperative that only horses that get along well with each other are stalled next to each other. This measure is in fact recommended for any type of stall management, otherwise aggressive behaviors such as kicking the walls and biting the bars are preprogrammed. In addition, the incompatible animals suffer from constant stress. For the attacked animal, this stress is caused by an insoluble and fear-producing conflict situation, and for the aggressor by frustration as his attacks remain without success. Modern stall designs are not at all comparable to the isolation created by traditional stalls that are completely closed off by bars or, even worse, high partition walls. It is a proven fact that horses that are kept separately in this manner, and are therefore deprived of contact with others and the environment, are more prone to developing behavioral abnormalities (**21**).

The best way to satisfy social behavior in a management situation with individual stalls is to allow daily exercise or pasture access of horses together or in small groups. It has to be considered, however, that horses separated in closed off stalls can estimate their rank position towards each other, but do not know their exact rank position. In order to resolve rank conflicts, horses need to have physical contact. To avoid injury, therefore, appropriate preventive measures should be taken when stalled horses are brought together for the first time, similarly to introducing a newcomer to a group. Only when the hierarchy is established, can they be herded together and put out to pasture together as a group. Because horses in individual stalls with a common turnout are repeatedly separated for several hours, a higher number of agonistic behaviors has to be expected in comparison to that seen in horses continuously managed in groups.

20 Outside stalls can be designed to allow closer social contact.

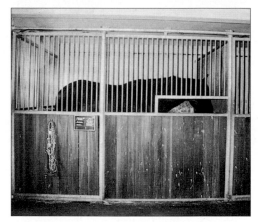

21 In traditional box stalls, social contact is severely limited.

MANAGEMENT OF HORSES WITHOUT EQUINE COMPANIONS

Keeping a horse without companions of the same species has to be judged entirely differently than management in individual stalls. It is not appropriate from a behavioral standpoint; in Germany it is a violation of the Animal Welfare Act, although this is not the case for the US. The German Animal Welfare Act (§2) requires that an animal must be fed, cared for, and kept according to its species and its needs. It is a popular counter-argument that the isolated management of horses is not so bad because they can also form strong bonds with members of other species such as goats and dogs. The horse will indeed act towards this "replacement" partner as if it were another horse. Such relationships stem from times in which it was common to keep horses without companions of the same species. They are, therefore, only an indication of a previous or existing unsuitable management! In general, therefore, keeping a horse with animals of a different species must only be considered as a temporary solution (**22**).

22 Keeping a single horse without equine companions is not appropriate from a behavioral standpoint. Using other species for company is only acceptable as a temporary solution.

THE HUMAN BEING AS A SOCIAL PARTNER

While dogs regard their human companions as members of the pack and behave towards them mostly as they would towards other dogs, the relationship between human being and horse is less obvious. This is primarily attributable to differences in the socialization processes. The relatively long critical period of the dog allows a secondary imprinting onto humans to a certain extent. This is not possible in horses. The risk of imprinting a foal onto a human being will be discussed in more detail later (p. 56).

In addition, the daily contact between human beings and horses is typically very short and is often limited to 1 hour. Full members of a horse group, on the other hand, spend day and night united with their band.

Despite these restrictions, horses appear to include the human being in their social behavior and regard him as a "social partner". Consequently, a horse will attribute a social rank to every person dealing with it. According to the person's behavior, this rank may be higher, equal to, or lower than that of the horse. Inferiority in rank makes handling and training difficult. An equal rank is not desirable either because it results

in constant power struggles. Problem behavior, such as the horse being difficult to catch, kicking, and biting, results, among other reasons, from the horse not recognizing the person as being higher in rank. It is, therefore, not sensible to raise a horse in an anti-authoritarian manner because it will be forced by its inborn social behavior to establish who is on top and who is on the bottom of the hierarchy.

How does one achieve the dominant position? One definitely does not do this by force, because it creates neither dominance nor trust but fear and pain instead. The resulting insoluble conflict situation sooner or later makes the horse become resigned or aggressive; a keen and willing cooperation will, however, never be achieved. To achieve the dominant rank, one has first to consider that the horse will measure us by our rank factors. As our physical features are comparatively insignificant, one has to rely more on psychological rank factors such as charisma, experience, and self-confidence in order to dominate the horse. One should therefore always be aware that one signals inferiority or superiority as soon as one approaches a horse. The dominant position will be developed further in the course of daily handling and training, which begins with ground work (**23**). Each exercise has to be completed consistently and with absolute determination and has to be – and this is very important – planned carefully in order to result in success. Therefore, it has to be thought through beforehand, and has to be structured such that it ends with praise and positive reinforcement. In this manner, trust in the human being can develop. This trust, paired with the person's dominance, will create a feeling of safety that is necessary for the horse's comfort and that will allow a positive communication between human and horse. Daily handling in the form of feeding, grooming, and so on, further reinforces the gain in trust.

When working with several horses simultaneously, one has to know and consider their hierarchy with one another. If the human being takes on the alpha position, he can use his authority to forbid contact between certain horses as long as he is present. It would, however, be wrong to punish a higher ranked animal for aggression shown toward a lower ranked one. The aggressor regards its behavior as normal because it does not understand the human interpretation of "do not hurt the weaker one". In this case, punishing the dominant horse would only enhance its agonistic behavior towards the other horse.

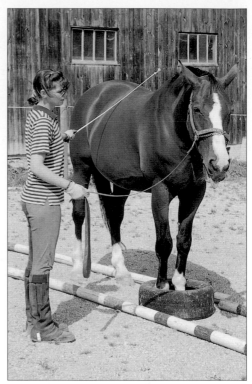

23 Ground work is the best way to achieve dominance over the horse.

Deficits in the social field often play a part in problem behavior

- Raising a horse without sufficient contact with companions of the same species can result in a misdirected social development (deprivation damage).
- Life in isolation or with greatly reduced contact with companions predisposes to behavioral abnormalities such as weaving and auto-mutilation.
- Grouping together of horses that do not get along, or frequent changes in the group constellation, lead to conflicts, discrimination, and stress.
- Many undesirable behaviors such as unwillingness to be caught, biting, and kicking frequently result from hierarchy problems between humans and horses.

Reproduction behavior

Natural behavioral patterns

SEXUAL MATURITY

Sexual precocity can be observed in many colts (**24**). They playfully mount their dams and playmates. Sometimes the penis will even be extended completely. When young stallions play, mounting is not an unusual occurrence either. It serves as practice for the breeding procedure later on. A prerequisite for the ability to breed, on the other hand, is the achievement of sexual maturity. It will be reached at an age of 12–20 months depending on the breed and the plane of nutrition. As soon as sperm is produced, stallions are theoretically capable of breeding. In the wild, however, a certain psychological maturity is required for breeding aside from the mere physical ability. It is reached at an age of approximately 5 years, coinciding with the time a harem band is founded. Only then do free-roaming stallions breed more frequently. The highpoint of sexual potency for thoroughbred and warmblood stallions lies between 7 and 17 years of age. The senium (old age), when stallions may become impotent, begins at 20–25 years of age.

In mares, the first heat occurs between 12 and 20 months of age, depending on the breed and the plane of nutrition. The first estrus is frequently very strongly developed so that under natural conditions, mares are bred by the end of their first year of life. Conception on the other hand rarely takes place before the end of the second year so free-roaming mares usually give birth for the first time when they are 3 years old.

The mares' readiness to breed is seasonal. Horses are long-day breeders. With increasing length of daylight, i.e. in the spring and early summer, mares show the signs of estrus more and more strongly. This seasonality of the heat cycle is caused by the light-dependent production of sex hormones. Stallions are fertile year-round, but their sexual drive is also significantly increased in the springtime.

READINESS TO MATE

Most mares come into heat every 3 weeks for 5 days, and ovulation occurs on the second to last day of estrus. The externally recognizable heat most often begins 2–3 days prior to ovulation and can last for another 1 or 2 days afterwards. The physiological range of 2–16 days is, however, quite large. The mare is ready to mate only at the time of ovulation, during the so-called peak of the heat cycle; at other times she will refuse the stallion.

Within the undisturbed band with one stallion and only a few familiar older mares, sexual behavior is exhibited relatively calmly.

24 Early sexuality is normal behavior.

Through daily inspection of feces and urine, the stallion detects mares in heat via olfactory signals (pheromones) (**25**). He is, however, not capable of detecting whether the mare is at the peak of the heat cycle, at the beginning, or already at the end. To test this, he starts with mating foreplay. He grazes close to the mare, makes frequent nasonasal contact, courts her with a collected gait and a bent neck, engages in frequent grooming with her, and sniffs and nibbles at her flanks, rear legs, and the anogenital region (**26**). He will often extend his penis and sometimes he will try to mount her. Early in the heat cycle copulation generally does not take place because the mare will try to avoid the stallion (**27**) by passively moving forward or by actively kicking at him, the latter of which is frequently accompanied by squealing and urine squirting. In this case, the experienced stallion will retreat so that, under natural conditions, injuries are the exception.

Prerequisites for successful mating of sexually mature horses in the wild are:

- Familiarity of the mare with the stallion.
- Peak of the mare's heat cycle.
- Readiness to mate on the part of the stallion.
- No intervention of other animals.

Consequently, mares within a harem band are only willing to mate with the dominant stallion. They will flee from strange or young stallions or will ward them off with their rear hooves. Although "rapes" can be observed under natural conditions, they are the exception. Even with the dominant stallion, the feeling of familiarity has to be strengthened prior to mating. This is, among other things, achieved by foreplay. It contains the so-called tenderness behavior consisting of establishment of nasonasal contact, licking, and nibbling. This results in an increase and synchronization of readiness to mate. Young mares need to be stimulated in this manner longer than older mares. With the latter, foreplay can be reduced to a short nasonasal contact. During foreplay, a stallion with breeding experience will always stay to the side of the mare to avoid the danger of being kicked. Once the peak of the heat cycle, which lasts 1–2 days, is reached, the mare indicates her readiness to mate by distinct "presenting". She takes on a characteristic position that functions as a signal for the stallion. Horses do not show a "heat face", such as the yawning described for donkeys and zebras, but careful observation reveals that many mares in heat will turn their ears back and exhibit a "loosening" of the lips and a subtle opening and closing of the jaws (Houpt 1998).

> ### Characteristic features of a mare's readiness to mate
>
> - Standing with spread legs (sawhorse stance).
> - Lifting and sideways turning of the tail.
> - Frequent elimination of mucoid urine.
> - Winking (rhythmic opening and closing of the vulva) (**28**).
> - Increased willingness to make contact with group members.

A healthy stallion will usually be ready to mate whenever one of his mares comes into heat. A preference for certain mares can, however, be observed. This will be for his older mares. He is usually less interested in the younger mares that are often his daughters. Furthermore, a preference for certain colors is known to occur. Wild-living stallions with only bay or chestnut colored mares in their herd have been described. Processes similar to imprinting are likely to be responsible for this behavior.

In general, the other members of the family will hardly pay attention to the mating process and there is no interruption. In larger herds where several mares come into heat at the same time it can happen that an older mare causes the stallion to withdraw from another mare in heat. In isolated cases, it has even been observed that mares not in heat tried to prevent mating of the stallion with a lower ranked mare.

Other stallions do not disturb the mating process in natural societies. The leading stallion will further try to keep his mares in heat out of the immediate reach of other males. These will usually observe the mating process from a distance and will sometimes masturbate. Even though the dominant stallion has the copulation privilege, he can abstain from it. He will, however, only leave his mare in heat to those 2- to 3-year-old young stallions that he tolerates within his group because of their obvious subordination.

MATING

If the above-mentioned prerequisites for mating are met, the harem stallion will usually mount the mare with a completely erect penis, while his sternum rests on her croup and his forelegs tightly clutch the flank region in front of her hips. During mating, most stallions rest their head in the region of the withers or the shoulders of the mare; some hold onto her mane by their teeth. Downright biting, however, is not part of the mutual communication

Testing of the readiness for breeding under semi-natural conditions

25 Flehmen after olfactory investigation of eliminations.

26 Careful approach and sniffing at the mare.

27 Refusal of the stallion by the mare, which is not ready to be bred.

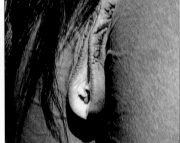

28 Among other signs, the mare signals her readiness to mate to the stallion by rhythmic opening and closing of the vulva and exposing the clitoris (winking).

during the natural mating act. Some stallions do not become erect until after they have exhibited searching motions or have mounted repeatedly. After penetration, on average 10 (4–15) friction movements occur and then ejaculation takes place. In some cases, vocalization such as moaning of the mare and grunting of the stallion can be heard. In large breed horses, a strong muscle contraction in the region of the tailbase and a rhythmic nodding of the tail (five to ten times) are characteristic signs that ejaculation is occurring. With pony stallions, the tail nodding is frequently absent or only weakly observed. The duration between penetration and ejaculation followed by dismounting of the stallion is very short and amounts to only 5–60 seconds in adult animals. Young, inexperienced stallions usually require more time.

During the peak of the heat cycle, mares are bred several times such that under natural conditions, stallions will mate between 8 and 15 times daily. The frequency with which a stallion breeds is dependent not only on his individual disposition and breed (testicle size), but also to a great extent on his health and nutritional status. Additional factors are his age, his capacity, and the time point during the breeding season. A strong stallion can copulate again only minutes after the previous breeding act.

Mares that are ready to mate will seek out the stallion deliberately. This behavior can also be observed in domesticated mares, which at times even attempt to stimulate any other horse. While older mares can push back during the mating act, younger inexperienced mares, or mares not familiar with the breeding stallion, try to escape copulation by walking forward or by fleeing.

Prerequisites for successful breeding

- Growing up in a herd in order to condition expressions and social behavior during the mating process.
- Physical and psychological maturity of the stallion (5–6 years of age).
- Heat of the mare (spring and early summer).
- Familiarity of the mare with the stallion.
- Space and time for exchange of signals during foreplay and the mating process.

Implications for management and handling

SERVICE IN-HAND

While in the wild the conception rate of horses is above 90%, that of national breeding operations is often at or below 60%. One of the major reasons is the horses' health status. However, medical prevention and control including culturing of mares, ultrasound, examination, and so on, has already reached a very high standard. Could ethological factors also be of importance? For example, many breeders are of the opinion that, in addition to the gynecological examination, sufficient stimulation of the mare by the stallion is an important prerequisite for successful breeding.

Servicing mares in-hand is common practice. The sequence of events is as follows. Man determines the optimal time point for breeding according to the signs of heat shown by the mare. The mare is then presented to the breeding stallion or a teasing stallion (**29**). If she shows the appropriate behavior, she is then bred. Both mare and stallion are restrained by handlers. The mare may further be restrained by hobbles or ropes in order to prevent her from kicking the stallion. The entire procedure takes place within a few minutes. Afterwards, mare and stallion are again separated.

This type of breeding procedure contradicts the natural, very complex breeding behavior of horses in almost every detail. First of all, intimacy between the mare and the stallion is lacking, which is a major requirement for completion of the breeding process in the wild. Another frequently overlooked issue is the need for sufficient time and space to allow exchange of signals between mare and stallion. Foreplay plays an important role in mood synchronization but is reduced to a minimum when horses are placed in stocks for the purpose of teasing. Furthermore, the mare is frequently teased with the "wrong" stallion, i.e. a teasing stallion. And last but not least, the horses are restrained with ropes or reins, resulting in a negative experience of fear and pain associated with the breeding process (**30**). Another consideration is that many of the mares bred in this fashion do not have any direct contact with stallions for the remainder of the year. Without proximity to a male horse hormonal imbalances can develop that will complicate conception right from the start. In addition, transport and change of environment associated with bringing the mare to a stallion translate into stress for the mare, especially if she is not used to it or has a foal by her side. The time of year can also affect the expression of the signs of heat and should be considered. Although the cycle of domestic horses is less dependent on daylight length than that of free-living horses, mares generally show their readiness to be bred much more overtly in the spring and early summer than during the other months. The conception rate during these seasons is also clearly the highest.

Can service in-hand be designed more appropriately from a behavioral standpoint? Are alternatives such as "back to nature" or artificial insemination preferable? The latter is, as long as fear of the veterinarian is limited, certainly the better solution for most female animals, because it "only" represents a medical procedure and, if contact with a stallion is possible at home, makes transport unnecessary. One has to be aware, however, that the important operational area of reproduction behavior is even further limited during artificial insemination than is the case with service in-hand. As an ultimate consequence, this represents "negative selection" with regard to fertility. Service in-hand can be made more appropriate from a behavioral standpoint only to a limited extent. Options to improve the procedure primarily include management issues such as improvement of the above-mentioned deficits and increased regard for the animals' individual needs and characteristics. The fact that mare and stallion are not familiar with each other remains. This can also be a problem when allowing horses to breed freely in a herd. If unfamiliar horses are brought together without any preparation or precaution, confrontations invariably result. It is wrong to assume that "feelings" during the breeding season will suppress the normal course of rank order behavior. Due to constraints of space and time, therefore, the notion of "back to nature" is currently unrealistic for most horses used for breeding.

29 Testing of a mare's readiness to mate with the help of a teaser stallion behind a testing wall.

30 Mares which are prevented from kicking by hobbles, can retain a negative association with the mating process.

FREE MATING IN A HERD

Even with domestic horses, it is possible to manage a stallion together with mares in a sort of harem band; a practice that many private breeders of pony and specialty breeds have adopted for some time now (**31**). In these situations, breeding occurs in a relatively calm manner similar to the observations made in the wild. This management does not preclude additional use of the horses for breeding outside the herd, as stallions can learn to accept the fact that they themselves or one of their mares is removed from the herd. For operations with several stallions living with their bands, it is recommended to separate the herds by at least one empty pasture. A peaceful co-existence of several bands is possible only if sufficient space is available and an appropriate distance between herds can be maintained.

If one wants to breed horses freely in a herd, it is a primary prerequisite that the breeding animals must have been raised in a herd. Only then do they master the adequate behavioral patterns required for safe and successful mating. Of particular importance is sufficient experience in behavioral expressions and signal exchange. Without this knowledge, mating in a herd may turn into a dangerous event for both mare and stallion from the start. One has to further con-sider that animals in captivity do not have the opportunity to choose their group affiliation. True aggression of stallions against mares is rare, but absolute incompatibilities are possible. If they occur, horses should definitely be separated because, with limited space to avoid each other, the risk of injury is too great.

Breeding herds, into which the stallion is only introduced for several months during the breeding season, exhibit a different group dynamic than under natural conditions. The mares, which live without a stallion for most of the year, form relatively stable units, which are each led by a dominant mare. When the stallion is introduced at the beginning of the breeding season, he is treated as a newcomer and mares often behave quite aggressively towards him. This can become problematic, especially for young stallions because they will be tolerated only for breeding purposes, if at all, and will occupy a low rank in the hierarchy due to their youth and lack of psychological maturity. Under these conditions, mating may even become dangerous for the stallion. Further, it cannot be excluded that living with unfamiliar mares belonging to their own established groups only for the breeding season represents a severe psychological burden for the "outsider" stallion.

31 As long as upbringing and management by humans is adequate, a stallion can be kept together with mares and foals in a band without problems.

BREEDING STALLIONS

Problems with regard to sexual behavior are not uncommon among intensively used breeding stallions. Aside from genetic aspects – gentleness towards other horses is not a selection criterion for stallions of the warmblood and thoroughbred breeds – they can mostly be attributed to management and psychological causes. Being stalled without access to a run or pasture and without contact with other horses is just as predisposing a factor for problem behavior as is insufficient or total lack of experience in natural breeding behavior. These stallions will often overreact or even become violent when they come into contact with mares. Insufficient erection, reluctance to breed, excessive nervousness, and premature ejaculation can also be associated with this problem. According to Schäfer (1993), use of stallions for breeding at an age of 2.5–3 years, which is too young when compared to natural behavior, can also be responsible for development of a reluctance to breed later. Refusal to breed mares of a specific color, on the other hand, has to be attributed to imprinting-like events. Occasionally, one can also observe that stallions refuse to breed lactating mares that have a milk odor about them. This is likely to be caused by a lack of experience and unfamiliarity with the situation as most breeding stallions are kept separated from mares. Under natural conditions, on the other hand, the stallion is exposed to the odor of lactating mares throughout the year and is, therefore, used to it.

If one wants to establish a harem band, it is advisable to use a young stallion and to introduce mares one by one. Caution must be exercised when using older stallions that have exclusively been mated at hand, because they are often conditioned unnaturally. For some of them, even a horse without a rider can represent a mare ready to be bred, and they have never learned to approach a mare slowly and test her willingness to mate. These stallions will frequently attempt to mate immediately or they become downright aggressive, which is not without danger for themselves and the mare.

- Consideration of ethological aspects is not at all irrelevant for the success of breeding.
- Many problems with sexual behavior of stallions and mares result from incorrect upbringing and management and from a lack of consideration for essential behavioral patterns during the breeding process.

Dam–foal behavior

Natural behavioral patterns

The average length of gestation (pregnancy) in domestic horses is 340 days. However, due to placental characteristics, a wide range of 320–360 days is observed. Breed- and gender-specific differences also occur: ponies and smaller horses typically carry their foals for a shorter time, draft horses tend to carry them longer, and colts are usually born 1 or 2 days later than fillies.

BEHAVIOR AT BIRTH (PARTURITION)

In the wild, births take place throughout the day and night with many occurring during the early morning hours. As with all flight animals, equids need a sense of absolute security in order to give birth. For this reason, some mares will separate from the group to give birth and not return to their band until a few days afterwards. Others will give birth directly within the group or in its immediate vicinity. The birthing process is not interrupted by the other group members, but does evoke great interest in some of them. Outer features of an impending birth (parturition) are:

- "Bagging up" (udder enlargement).
- "Waxing" (pre-colostrum drops on the teat ends).
- An edematous vulva and secretion of cervical mucus.

All these features indicate the end of pregnancy. In a number of mares, however, parturition occurs without any of these signs. The birthing process can be divided into three stages: the opening stage (stage I), the delivery stage (stage II), and the afterbirth stage (stage III). During stage I the foal is brought into the correct birth position by uterine contractions, and the amniotic fluid bubble is pushed towards the cervix in order to widen the birth canal. This process is already painful. The mare will show unrest and colic-like signs. Periods with these signs, however, can be interrupted by intervals of complete rest. During these times, mares will show normal behavior and some will eat, although they may do so hastily. There are always mares, however, that will commence parturition without any of the described signs.

> ## Ethological and physiological features of stage I of parturition
>
> - Walking in circles, looking back and kicking at the abdomen, pawing.
> - Lying down repeatedly for short periods of time, rolling (mostly without shaking off bedding afterwards).
> - Frequent elimination of small amounts of feces and urine.
> - Heavy sweating (neck and shoulders).
> - Letting down of milk, dripping, and sometimes streaming of milk.

Stage I can be very short and last only 50 minutes, but can also last 12 hours or more. This is due to psychogenic influence on uterine activity. It will either strengthen contractions or interrupt them entirely. In some cases, the impending birth can be delayed for several days. As soon as the waters break, however, parturition occurs without any further possibility for delay.

Most horses will lie down in lateral recumbency to give birth; only about 1.5% of mares foal standing. Severe pain from contractions can occur. It can be severe enough to make mares throw themselves to the ground as they would with colic.

As long as the position and posture of the foal within the uterus is normal, stage II only lasts for about 10–20 minutes, and rarely more than 30 minutes. Mares giving birth for the first time usually require a little more time than those that have given birth several times before. With a normally positioned foal, the forelegs with the head resting on top will appear first, then the rump, and finally the hindlegs extending backwards.

The newborn foal's movements often will rupture the fetal membranes during the delivery period, which ensures that breathing can take place. A viable foal also will attempt to free itself from the fetal membranes by tossing its head and exhibiting running motions as soon as it is born. The dam seems to help by more or less systematically licking the foal. This process not only serves to remove the fetal membranes and to stimulate circulation, but also allows an intense olfactory bond to develop between the mare and her foal.

The afterbirth detaches relatively rapidly from the mare's uterus. It is usually passed within 15 minutes, and no later than 120 minutes, after parturition. In contrast to many other mammals, horses do not usually eat the afterbirth. Exceptions, however, have been noted in Icelandic and Przewalski horses.

BEHAVIOR OF THE NEWBORN FOAL

After several unsuccessful attempts, the foal will stand for the first time after about 45 minutes (10–120 minutes). Gender and breed differences can be observed. Fillies are often able to stand sooner than colts, and foals of stocky, smaller horse breeds will usually stand about 10 minutes earlier than highly bred warmbloods and thoroughbreds.

Once the foal is able to stand and keep its balance, it immediately begins to search for the udder. This search is directed by an inborn elicited mechanism (IEM). This mechanism is relatively inaccurate and mistakes are normal at first. The IEM directs searching movements only in a vertical direction, preferentially towards angles. The search for the udder is supported by the inborn suckling position with an almost horizontally extended head and neck. This position, which is adapted to the height of the udder is only of use if the size of the foal matches that of the mare. Conversely, a correct suckling position is of little use if the foal is born too large in relation to the mare, which is not uncommon when humans determine the breeding criteria.

Experienced dams will aid their foal's search for the udder by lifting one hindleg. Olfactory inspection of the anal region probably also contributes to the foal finding the udder, as it makes the foal face in the right direction (an anti-parallel position)(32). Most newborn foals will find the udder within 30–120 minutes of being able to stand. At this point, the suckling reflex has already been present for some time. It usually sets in about 20 minutes after birth and is recognizable by the "suckling tongue". Only when foals show their tongue folded into

32 Young foals prefer the reverse-parallel suckling posture.

a groove do they appear to be ready to suckle. Following the first milk ingestion, the udder is found more accurately and rapidly each time, until this learning process is completed after several hours or at most 2 days.

Frequency and duration of suckling vary between individuals. They are primarily dependent on the foal's vitality and age as well as milk flow and the amount of milk given by the dam. Suckling, however, does not merely serve the purpose of nutrition, but has an additional important function: it has a calming effect. This can be recognized by the fact that foals that are startled or are separated from their dams will immediately begin to suckle once they are back in their dam's care. According to Wolff and Hausberger (1994), this behavior can indicate the future usefulness of the horse for riding. In their experiments, foals that more frequently sought protection by their dams and suckled, showed an increased jumpiness later on in training. This behavior and the correlated suckling frequency appear to have a genetic basis.

During the first week of life, a foal will suckle on average approximately four times in an hour, and from the 6th month onwards, only once every hour. At the time of natural weaning, at 8–10 months of age, foals only ingest small amounts of milk once every 2 hours. Under natural conditions, a dam that remains open (unbred) continues to nurse her foal up to an age of about 1.5 years.

DAM–FOAL RELATIONSHIP

Essential prerequisites for an undisturbed relationship between a dam and her foal are the imprinting of the foal onto its dam as well as bonding of the mare and the newborn. For the purpose of imprinting, the foal has a tendency towards bond formation from birth. The instinct to follow is also inborn. The foal, however, does not know whom it is supposed to follow and what its dams looks like; it only appears to have the notion of a large object. It therefore has to learn who its dam is and, accordingly, to which species it belongs. This learning process, which is known as imprinting, is of limited duration and can only take place during the sensitive, or critical, period. This period is very short in precocious animals such as horses, while it is longer in altricial animals such as dogs and cats. The result of imprinting, once completed, is irreversible.

This learning process can be compromised by interruptions, which may result in misdirected imprinting onto other living creatures or even inanimate objects. To avoid this, foals and their dams need an atmosphere of undisturbed solitude following birth. Under natural conditions, the mare will shield her foal from other horses and animals of other species as much as she can. Her motivation to do this is so strong that even a lower ranked mare will successfully keep other horses away from her foal by putting herself in between them and the foal and threatening them. This behavior is equivalent to a temporary elevation in rank and is described as such by some authors. The degree of dominance achieved by the dam during the imprinting period varies on an individual basis. There also appear to be breed differences. Haflinger mares, for example, will dominate even the leading stallion in this situation.

Imprinting of the foal and bond formation between the dam and her foal occur based on olfactory, auditory, and visual characteristics. Olfactory bonding is the first to be completed for both of them (**33**). Its importance for the mare, despite the availability of additional visual and auditory information, is demonstrated by the fact that even after several months, nursing is preceded by an olfactory inspection of the anogenital region. This prevents any error from occurring.

Bonding between a dam and her foal occurs very rapidly. She frequently is able to clearly identify her foal during the first half hour. Imprinting of the foal onto its dam takes a little longer. It is completed at no less than half an hour but can take up to 2 days. The completion of imprinting is recognizable by the foal actively following its dam. Once imprinting is completed, alternative partners are rejected as dams or foals.

DURATION OF THE DAM–FOAL BOND
The foal spends most of its first weeks of life in close proximity to its dam. With increasing age, the close bond between the dam and her foal will loosen. During the first week of life, the foal spends 90% of its time close to its dam, but it is that close only about 50% of the time at 5 months of age, and 20% of the time at 8 months of age. Parallel to this development, the foal increasingly will establish contact with other members of the group, mostly to age-matched companions, yearlings, and siblings.

A few days after birth, the mare will already tolerate contact between her foal and other family members. She can, however, react very aggressively to other horses or animals of other species and may even actively attack them by making use of her front hooves and teeth. Strange foals that approach her will also be driven away by threats and will be chased off violently if they attempt to nurse.

The time point of weaning differs between different populations of free-roaming horses. Most often, foals are between 8 and 10 months of age at weaning. Koniks, Camargue horses, and mustangs are often weaned at 8 months of age, while New Forest and Dülmen pony foals are allowed to nurse up until several days prior to the birth of the next foal. Following birth of the new foal, the dam will be somewhat more tolerant towards her own older foal as opposed to others; she will, however, keep it strictly away from her newborn and the milk source. The weaned foal will then associate with other horses with which it has already established a close bond during its first months of life. Within 2–4 weeks, the activity rhythm of the weanling will be indistinguishable from that of other yearlings and 2-year-olds. Even after weaning the bond between dam and foal still exists. Here, contact is initiated mostly by the offspring. Only when it leaves the band at an age of 2 or 3 years, is the relationship between dam and foal terminated for good.

33 Nasonasal contact immediately after birth establishes the olfactory connection between dam and foal.

Implications for management and handling

FOALING AREA

Under management conditions, most births take place in a stall. It is advantageous for each mare to remain in her stall and, therefore, in her familiar surroundings. The stall does, however, have to be sufficiently large. The minimum measurement for foaling stalls is $(2.3 \times wh)^2$. This translates into a stall floor space for large breed horses of about 16 m² (172 sq ft). The typical stall size of 3×3 m (10×10 ft) found in many places is not sufficient for horses of this size. A general recommendation is to pad the stall walls with straw bales. This allows for more room to be made if the mare becomes recumbent in a corner of the stall and the foal is in danger of being pushed against the wall during birth. If this precaution is taken, the mare does not have to be forced to stand up again, but instead the straw bales behind her simply have to be removed.

When births occur within a group of horses, an unintentional separation of dam and foal can take place, which increases the risk of disturbance of the dam–foal relationship. Especially in mixed-breed groups, lower-ranked mares cannot always keep other horses away from their foals, even though they exhibit increased aggressiveness during the critical period. It is therefore advisable to separate a mare that is expected to give birth from the other horses in good time, especially if they are kept in a barn with loose housing or a run-out shed. The best way to separate a mare is to place her in a sufficiently large stall that allows her to retreat from the others but still provides adequate contact with the group members. An undisturbed imprinting process and establishment of the dam–foal bond is then possible and, in addition, medical attention is provided more easily.

HANDLING OF THE MARE

With breeding horses, the mares' great need for security results in most births taking place during the night. Approximately 90% of stalled horses therefore foal in the evening, during the night, or in the early morning hours. To give birth, the dam requires a secure and shielded environment. Many mares delay their births until no human beings are around. Only people with whom they are very familiar are allowed to be present without being regarded as a disturbing factor. Even though most foalings take place without complications, they should be monitored. Proven monitoring aids are technical devices such as video cameras and birth monitors with moisture or heat sensors. Repeated walk-by checks, on the other hand, tend to disturb a mare. One should definitely not behave in a fashion different from the usual routine, because whispering and walking on tiptoes can have an irritating effect and give the impression of an approaching enemy. Hectic behavior and nervousness on the part of personnel can also negatively influence the foaling process or even interrupt it entirely.

Disruptions during the period immediately following birth can seriously impair the dam–foal relationship. A disturbance by people, horses, or other animals can stress the mare and result in a misdirected defense reaction, i.e. one that is directed against the foal. In this case, the newborn foal can be seriously hurt.

With young primiparous mares, i.e. mares giving birth for the first time, as well as with brood mares that have previously served as riding horses for many years, aggressive behavior directed against the first foal can sometimes be observed. Some will kick at the newborn while it is still recumbent, others will try to prevent it from nursing by means of kicking and biting. This behavior is usually caused by a lack of experience and further motivated by pain or fear. In these cases, helpful intervention is indicated and, rather than punishing the mare for her behavior, one has to teach her with praise to associate the foal with a positive experience (p.160). Most of the time it is sufficient to restrain the mare temporarily until the foal has nursed for the first time. As long as no disease processes are present, the first nursing represents a positive experience for the mare as well, because it relieves the painful pressure caused by a full udder. In addition, several hormones such as endorphins are released and create a pleasant sensation. Most often, the problem is solved after a few repetitions and the mare accepts her foal.

Sometimes, albeit rarely, aggressive behavior occurs unrelated to the foal's attempts at nursing. Among other causes, a genetic component for this behavior has been suggested. Mares of Arabian descent, and among them particularly those of certain blood lines, appear to have a tendency towards aggression against their own foals more frequently than other horse breeds (Houpt 1995). These horses should not be used for breeding.

An increased aggressiveness of mares against animals of other species and people during the critical period has to be regarded as normal behavior. If, however, aggressive behavior against humans persists after the imprinting period is completed, one has to take appropriate measures to demonstrate one's superiority in rank. Otherwise, a permanent shift in the hierarchy can result and significantly impair further handling of the mare.

HANDLING OF THE FOAL

A healthy foal does not require human help. It does not need to be lifted to its feet, nor does it need to be held up against the udder. To ensure an optimal supply with immunoglobulins via the colostrum, one should only help the foal if it continues to search in the wrong place 2 hours after birth. Similarly, medical attention should be given only if really indicated. As soon as the dam–foal relationship has been successfully established, however, nothing stands in the way of development of a closer relationship between a human being and the foal.

Disturbances during the critical period can result in misdirected imprinting. This will lead affected horses later on to have difficulties in understanding horse-specific behavioral patterns. Furthermore, especially with colts, aggression and sexual behavior directed against human beings have to be expected. The risk for a misdirected social development in this manner is especially high in orphaned animals. To avoid misdirected imprinting, one should find surrogate mares for these foals as soon as possible, if necessary by using the services of an appropriate agency, and in the meantime put them with another particularly gentle horse. As a general rule, mares will not allow foals other than their own to nurse. Exceptions are rare. For this reason, certain precautions have to be taken when bringing a foal together with its surrogate mother. Proven practices are to cover up the foal's original scent (rub bodily substances of the mare or its deceased foal onto it such as manure or used bedding) and to restrain the mare during the first nursings. If the mare does not accept the foal at all, raising it by hand is the only alternative. Aside from the consideration of medical problems and an appropriate feeding frequency, one has to be careful that the foal does not build too strong a relationship to people. Bottle-feeding can cause the bond with the human to become too strong. Buckets equipped with feeding nipples or automatic feeders such as those used in calf raising operations are, therefore, more suitable. This procedure will satisfy the foal's suckling needs sufficiently and will prevent it from becoming too closely attached to the human being. If contact with equine companions, especially other youngsters, is available at the same time, these foals will build normal relationships to other horses as well as to humans later on.

The imprint training method according to Miller (1995) is not entirely without risk. Its goal is to utilize the great learning ability during the critical period and to imprint the foal onto human beings in parallel with its imprinting on its own species. This "imprint training", which uses imprinting effects but is, in addition, based on a systematic conditioning program, is intended to make the foal recognize the human being as a member of its own species in order to facilitate future handling and training. The problem with this procedure is that the critical period of horses is very short compared to that of the dog. It can be as short as 30 minutes but sometimes lasts for several hours. If the contact between the human being and the foal is too intense during this period of time, a misdirected imprinting is preprogrammed. While, according to Waring (1983), temporary misdirected imprinting can be corrected, this can only be done as long as the imprinting process has not been completed. For this reason, it is risky to use the method of sensory overload (p.130) in newborn foals because it must be performed consistently until tolerance without fear is achieved. If it is interrupted prematurely because one fears a misdirection of imprinting, long-term learning effects in a negative sense can result. According to Miller's method (1995), the foal is touched and confronted with all sorts of noises as early as 1–2 hours after birth. To get it used to having its ears touched, for example, the outside and inside of its ears are touched repeatedly until the foal ceases to show any avoidance reaction. To do this, it is restrained on the ground in order to hinder it from getting up and attempting to escape. Learning therefore primarily takes place under fear according to the method of "sensory overload". Miller incorrectly describes his method as desensitization.

STRESS-FREE WEANING

The experiences of a foal during and after weaning have a profound effect on its further development. The internationally common practice of weaning at 6 months is still very early. If weaning occurs abruptly, or contact with equine companions does not exist, or the foal is removed from its familiar environment, the separation from the dam is compounded by an unnatural social isolation, which represents a tremendous psychological burden for the young animal. Several behavioral abnormalities have their origin in psychological trauma occurring during this time. The weaning process should, therefore, be adapted as much as possible to the natural detachment process of a foal from its dam under free-roaming conditions. Weaning in this manner has the added advantage that the digestive tract can slowly adapt to an entirely solid diet, and additional feeding stress, which would occur after the separation, can mostly be avoided. For psychological as well as physiological reasons, therefore, weaning must not occur prior to 6 months of age.

Mistakes in the management of brood mares and during birth and upbringing are frequently causes of problem behavior

- A lack of experience of maternal behavior can result in aggressive behavior of the mare towards her foal.
- Disturbance of the mare immediately following birth can impair bonding with the foal and result in aggressive behavior.
- Disruptions of the imprinting process during the critical period can be responsible for a foal's misdirected social development.
- Abrupt weaning without contact with familiar companions and a change of location result in a severe psychological strain and predispose for future behavioral abnormalities of the foal such as cribbing and weaving.

Tips for stress-free weaning of foals

Raising in a herd
Stress-free weaning is ensured if the foal can grow up in a herd or brood mare band with many other youngsters. Under these conditions it will already have formed close relationships with other horses prior to weaning. In the company of familiar group members the foal will much better be able to tolerate temporary absence of its dam as well as the final separation.

Practicing separation
If the foal has already learned to be separated from its dam prior to weaning, the final "cutting of the cord" will occur without trauma. To begin the exercise, the foal should be approximately 2–3 months of age. In the first part of the exercise, the mare is removed for short periods of time while the foal is allowed to remain with its playmates. Her absence is then successively lengthened while adapting the absolute time span to the foal's individual behavior. It would be wrong to leave the foal in a stall by itself where it will potentially "climb the walls". As soon as the foal has learned to be led, it is removed from the group itself. This has to be done very carefully and without force and, in the beginning, a few meters are enough. The distance is then increased slowly until the first longer walks with the foal by itself can be undertaken.

Weaning together with friends
A stress-free final weaning is achieved when the foal can remain with its companions and the dam is removed. At least one playmate or well acquainted "aunts" and "uncles" should remain with the foal.

Remaining in the familiar environment
After weaning, the foal remains in its familiar surroundings and with familiar horses and playmates. The dam is situated in a different barn. It is wrong to take the foal immediately to a different location and integrate it into a new group of horses. To do this would represent a significant psychological burden for the weanling.

Eating behavior

Natural behavioral patterns

FEED SPECTRUM AND FEED SELECTION

Like all equids, horses are herbivores and live primarily on grasses and herbs. Depending on the habitat's vegetation and the season, free-roaming horses also consume leaves, bark, twigs, young shoots, swamp and reed grasses, moss, and so on (**34**). In doing so, they differentiate carefully between the different plants; some are preferred, others rejected. This behavior is not inborn, the foal has to learn it by imitation of its dam. Feedstuffs that have been available to it in its youth leave an especially strong impression. This is also denoted as feed imprinting. In conjunction with an adaptation to certain feedstuffs, it is decisive for future feed preference. Aside from these factors, horses choose their feeds according to taste, structure, and availability rather than nutritional value. If the feed supply is rich, they are very picky. If feed is scarce, they are hungry, or have increased nutritional requirements (e.g. during pregnancy), the quantity of ingested feed becomes more important than its quality and time-consuming selective grazing is abandoned.

The senses of smell and taste play an important role in choosing feed; optical impressions, on the other hand, are not particularly important. Feed that has an unpleasant odor will not be ingested at all. Horses also have a very strong sense of taste. Bitter tasting plants are rarely consumed and sweet ones are preferred. As far as is known, horses are not able to distinguish poisonous plants from non-poisonous. As most toxic plants have a strong odor or bitter contents, however, they have a repellent effect on horses and are usually avoided.

Because of selective grazing, horses do not use pastures and greens evenly. In some places grass will be gnawed down to the root (**35**) while in others it may stand up to 1 m (3 ft) high. These so-called roughs develop because domestic horses refuse to graze plants that grow on their manure. The reason for this behavior likely lies in the odor that sticks to the ground. This behavior has not been observed in horses in the wild or in Przewalski horses. The latter even prefer to eat the lush grass growing close to their manure piles.

Foals will occasionally ingest small amounts of fresh manure, specifically that of their dam, during the first weeks of life. This behavior can also be observed in perissodactyla ("odd-hoofed ani-

mals") in the wild. It is assumed that this behavior results in an improved intestinal flora and vitamin B supply. In adult horses, coprophagia (manure eating) is the exception. If it occurs with increased frequency, it represents a behavioral abnormality. Most often, mistakes in feeding are the cause (p.145). Gnawing of wood and bark, on the other hand, is part of the natural eating behavior of horses. It can be observed in horses in the wild as well as adequately nourished and sufficiently exercised horses under human care. Horses obviously like the taste and the texture of wood. Excessive wood chewing, however, also represents a behavioral deviation and in general indicates inappropriate management (p.143).

34 Ingestion of leaves and nibbling of bark represent normal eating behavior of horses.

35 Horses eat selectively and can bite off tasty grasses and herbs to the root.

36 Rhythm of feed intake in pasture horses (according to Krull 1984).

Month of observation	Sunrise ↓	Sunset ↓	Grazing time (hours)
May			15.5
July			12.1
September			13.8

4^{00} 6^{00} 8^{00} 10^{00} 12^{00} 14^{00} 16^{00} 18^{00} 20^{00} 22^{00} 24^{00} 2^{00} 4^{00}

DURATION AND REGULATION OF FEED INTAKE

As horses eat selectively and chew carefully and as their natural feed is low in energy and high in fiber, they require very long eating times to satisfy their nutritional requirements. Feral horses in the natural state as well as pasture horses spend about 12–18 hours of a 24-hour day on feed intake. Eating time is dependent on nutrient supply. However, the duration of feed intake has an upper as well as a lower limit. Even if they are unable to satisfy their nutritional needs, horses rarely eat for more than 18 hours a day. Other activities such as resting and social activities take preference. The lower limit is at about 12 hours: even with a very good feed supply, horses will eat for that period per day. This behavior has an inborn determining component.

Feeding trials of Sweeting *et al.* (1985) in ponies and of Meyer (1995) showed that stalled horses with *ad libitum* access to feed showed a similar rhythm of feed intake as pastured horses (**36**) even when they were fed concentrated feed. If mixed feed was offered free choice, animals divided the entire amount into approximately 10 daily portions. The feed intake per meal was never above 0.25 kg/100 kg body weight (0.25 lb/100 lb). A similar feeding pattern was observed when feeding hay out of storage racks (**37**).

The duration of grazing can be influenced temporarily by severe weather, blood-sucking insects, disturbance by potential enemies, and similar events. Most often, however, the shortened eating period will afterwards be made up for by an increased speed of feed intake. This means that horses adapt to the situation by a change in behavior for the purpose of self-preservation. A different situation arises in cases of chronic diseases, water deprivation, dental disease, or diseases of the tongue, pharynx, stomach, and intestines. Under these circumstances, feed intake can be reduced or cease entirely. Feed intake is further reduced in cases of severe exhaustion or overheating (following racing or foxhunts and with high ambient temperatures). Stimulating effects on appetite, on the other hand, are exerted by eating in a group (social stimulation by companions) and familiarity with the type of feed, the environment, and the carer.

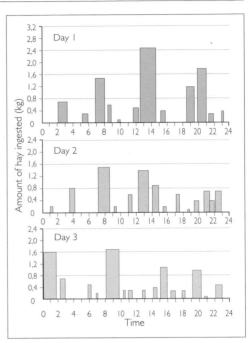

37 Rhythm of hay intake with *ad libitum* feeding from storage racks (according to Pirkelmann 1991).

Regulation of feed intake is a central event (controlled by the feed intake center in the hypothalamus) but it is also influenced by signals from the periphery. Under natural conditions, these regulatory mechanisms are very effective. It appears, however, that they may not function properly when feeding greatly diverges from normal, as is the case with large amounts of concentrated feed, long intervals between meals, and an inadequate time spent on chewing. Specific investigations of this subject in horses, however, are lacking. Knowledge derived from other species shows that the need for feed intake is signaled constantly by the feeding center. This mechanism has to be inhibited in order to interrupt feed intake. The decisive signal for the termination of a meal in horses is most likely the satisfaction of the chewing urge or fatigue of the chewing musculature. Stomach fill is inconsequential, as the horse does not possess stretch receptors that would signal a termination of feed intake with excessive stomach fill.

EATING TIMES

Horses eat during the day as well as during the night. The main feeding times, which last for several hours, usually occur during dawn and from dusk until midnight. In the late morning and throughout the afternoon, additional smaller meals are inserted. These will be abandoned only during very hot weather and with a great plague of insects. Free-roaming equids further reduce their grazing periods during cold and wet weather. However, horses will rarely interrupt their feed intake intentionally for more than 3 or 4 hours at a time. In general, few hours pass without at least a few bites of feed being ingested. The structure and function of the equine digestive tract is adapted to this eating behavior with long feeding times and continuous feed intake. Each greater divergence from this behavior can therefore represent a health hazard and result in a gastrointestinal abnormality, i.e. colic.

EATING POSTURE AND EATING TECHNIQUE

Horses usually eat with the head held low while moving at a slow pace. The sequence of steps during grazing corresponds to that at a walk, i.e. one front hoof is placed further forward than the other in order to allow the head to reach the ground. Grasses are initially manipulated with the horse's lips and then bitten or ripped off by the incisors with a brief head jerk. Loose feed particles such as grain reach the mouth through movements of the lips and tongue. Solid feed, such as tree bark, twigs and beet, is gnawed at or bitten off directly with the incisors. The tongue is then used to move feed to the molars where it is ground by a sideways motion of the lower jaw. During the chewing period, the head is often raised in order to observe the environment. Under natural conditions, horses eat relatively slowly and chew carefully. Unpleasant tasting plants and objects taken up by accident are dropped immediately. Swallowing of foreign bodies, therefore, occurs only rarely.

Depending on the type of feed, the number of chewing movements of an average sized adult horse lies between 40 and 80 per minute. The time needed to ingest different types of feed differs depending on structure and consistency. On average, considering that significant differences among individuals exist, an average sized adult horse with healthy teeth needs about 40–50 minutes and approximately 3,500 chewing movements to ingest 1 kg (2.2 lb) of hay or straw, while it only needs about 10 minutes and 800 chewing movements to ingest 1 kg (2.2 lb) of oats. Smaller horses and ponies generally require more time because they have a smaller chewing surface.

SOCIAL FACTORS

Under natural conditions, horses prefer to eat simultaneously with others. Frequently, a few group members will begin to eat and the others subsequently join them. Their rank-dependent distances are maintained during grazing. In general, the distance between horses will be at least 1 m (3 ft). Only very well acquainted horses will graze immediately side by side.

- Eating behavior as well as structure and function of the equine gastrointestinal tract have remained unchanged throughout the process of domestication. Consequently, horses require a continuous intake of small meals throughout most of the day.
- The horse's eating need will only be satisfied with an adequate number of chewing motions. In order to achieve these, a horse has to have access to feed for at least 12 hours of the day.
- Simultaneous feed intake together with companions represents natural equine feeding behavior.
- Synchronous feed intake requires that rank-dependent social distances be maintained.

Implications for management and handling

APPROPRIATE FEEDING TO SATISFY NUTRITIONAL AND BEHAVIORAL NEEDS

Appropriate feeding of horses has to satisfy nutritional as well as behavioral needs. Horses therefore have to receive feed containing sufficient energy, nutrients, and fiber, as well as vitamins and minerals, but feed also has to be selected in order to satisfy the eating and chewing needs. For this reason, the common feeding practice of giving only two meals a day, especially if they are relatively low in bulk, is not appropriate. As a general rule, and independent of the horse's breed and use, maintenance requirements should be met exclusively with roughage to which vitamin and mineral supplements are added. Only that portion of the nutritional requirement that cannot be met by feeding of roughage and grass should be supplied in the form of concentrate. Pasture access throughout the day is ideal because it most closely resembles natural feed intake. If this is impossible to provide, horses should have access to feed for at least 12 hours per day, but preferably throughout the entire day. As mentioned before, horses will then split most of the total amount of feed into about 10 meals per 24-hour period. If rationed feeding is practiced, the total amount of feed given should be divided into several meals spread out over the 24-hour day. Horses that are fed mostly concentrated feeds will finish their ration quickly and will spend most of the day without feed intake, which goes against their natural behavior. Substitute behaviors such as wood chewing, increased licking, and so on, are then preprogrammed. Inadequately short feeding times and/or lack of roughage and the resulting frustration are an important predisposing factor for the development of behavioral abnormalities (p.26).

FEEDING DEVICES

As horses mostly take up grass from the ground, they naturally hold their heads in a lowered position for more than half of the day. This posture favors the flow of saliva and is of advantage for the development of a strong back. For this reason, feeding installations should allow feed intake in a natural body posture. Roughage can be offered on the ground or, preferably, from the clean barn aisle floor that is accessible through bars (set 30–35 cm (12–14 in) apart). The latter provides an additional space gain because horses can reach through the bars into the barn aisle (p.80). Mangers that are installed close to the ground are also suitable as long as they are constructed in a manner that prevents injury from occurring (distance between bars at most 6 cm (2.4 in)). Horses are then occupied with feed intake for a longer time, less feed is lost and the risk of parasite reinfection via manure-soiled bedding is decreased (**38**). Mangers should not be installed too high. For large-breed horses, feed should be placed at a height of about 50–60 cm (19–24 in) (0.35 × wh). When using feeding gates and feeding stalls, it has to be considered that they do not allow the usual eating stance with the forelegs set apart. Feed should therefore be positioned at a height of about 20–30 cm (8–12 in) above ground to prevent the horse from putting too much strain on its forelegs.

Automated feeding devices have been evaluated and proven in a practical setting. These allow distribution of concentrate in small portions over several meals throughout the day, and are now available for individual as well as group management situations. In addition to the advantage that the carer is no longer bound by a feeding schedule, these devices are also preferable from a standpoint of nutritional physiology. From an ethological viewpoint, these systems also offer advantages as long as they do not create additional feed-related aggression. For this reason, stationary devices that allow synchronous eating are preferable for management of horses in individual stalls compared to computer-controlled feeding wagons that distribute feed consecutively. In group management situations, all horses usually use one feeding station and only asynchronous eating is possible. Preventive measures that avoid an increased occurrence of social confrontations are discussed in the following section.

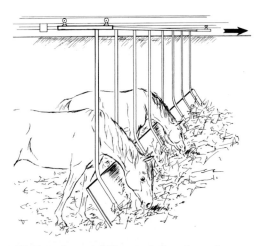

38 The rolling rack (FAL system) allows horses in group management systems to consume roughage under hygienic conditions all day long. The rack is anchored on rails, which results in a slight pendulum motion, and is pushed against the feed trough by the animals: bar distance 30 cm (12 in), total width max. 350 cm (11.5 ft).

Tips for the feeding of "easy keepers"

Slow down feed intake
Eating time can be lengthened by up to 2 hours without increasing feed intake by use of special feeding devices such as economy racks (**39**). With this system, which can be installed in individual stalls as well as in feeding areas within group paddocks, closely spaced (approximately 5 cm (2 in)) bars hinder feed intake and therefore slow it down (Table 4).

Lower nutrient/energy content
For easy keepers, the energy supply per horse should be reduced by about 10% from the usual recommendations. One can achieve this by offering an increased amount of less palatable, low-energy feed such as late-cut hay and straw, or by mixing these feeds with more palatable ones (**40**). Because of the risk of impaction colic with excessive straw feeding, it is recommended to increase the amount of straw in the ration slowly and to alternate straw rations with other feeds such as hay or grass throughout the day. With these initial precautions, straw can soon be offered *ad libitum*. With particularly sensitive horses, it is advisable to limit the amount of straw offered to 0.5 kg/100 kg bodyweight (0.5 lb/100 lb) per day. The upper limit for straw feeding in any horse is 1.2 kg/100 kg bodyweight (1.2 lb/100 lb). Similar measures apply when feeding late-cut, coarse, and straw-like hay.

Partitioned pastures or follow-up grazing
It is advisable to partially cut down pastures intended for easy keepers; however, they should not be cut too short. Partitioned pastures are ideal (**41**). In the easiest case, a small new portion is added to the pasture each day by means of an electric fence. In this way, even easy keeper horses can be treated appropriately by giving them access to fresh grass every day.

Table 4 Eating time and speed of ingestion when using the economy feeder with different bar distances (Pirkelmann 1991)

Bar distance (mm)	Measuring period (days)	Consumption per day (kg)	Eating time per day (hours)	Speed of ingestion (g/min)
165	5.5	7.4	4.9	25
55	6.7	7.7	7.5	17
55	4.2	5.9	7.4	13

PROBLEM – THE "EASY KEEPER"

Many pony and draft breeds appear to digest feed better than most of the larger horse breeds. They are therefore commonly denoted as "easy keepers". The reason for their higher weight gain is not superior digestion but the comparatively small energy expenditure for maintenance. This mostly has to be attributed to better skin insulation (dense hair coat, subcutaneous fat) and to behavior (quiet temperament). Even on pastures with average plant growth, these horses easily get too fat because their feed intake remains the same independent of nutrient supply. They also gain weight when fed roughage as soon as hay and straw are available to them for extended periods of time. In practice, one attempts to prevent excessive feed intake by limiting the duration of feed intake. Many animals therefore only have feed available for few hours of the day. This feeding regimen is not appropriate! Digestive and, most importantly, behavioral problems originate with this practice. The correct approach is to decrease the nutrient and energy supply without cutting back on eating time. The most important objective with any feeding regimen has to be the satisfaction of the horse's chewing need. The only way to satisfy this is by a sufficiently long duration of feed intake.

39 The adjustable guard in the economy rack ensures slower feed intake.

STRESS-FREE FEEDING

Feed intake without conflict is only possible if horses have the opportunity to maintain their rank-dependent social distances. Current knowledge suggests that an individual stall provides an adequate individual distance from the neighboring horses in order to allow undisturbed eating. A sufficiently large stall, i.e. an area of at least $(2 \times wh)^2$, is a prerequisite. There are horses, often those that are "highly bred", that claim an especially large individual distance for themselves. These horses can be recognized by their frequent kicking against stall walls, biting of bars, and similar behaviors. An answer to this problem is to provide an even larger stall or to put these horses at the end of a row of stalls where only one direct neighbor is present.

In a group management situation, it is especially difficult to feed in a manner that will allow everyone, including the horse of lowest rank, to satisfy their nutritional requirements and eat without stress. Based on their inborn social behavior, higher-ranked horses are always allowed to eat first in a group situation. These horses can become so dominant and possessive of the feeding troughs that other group members can only eat in fear and under stress or not at all. For this reason, at least one eating space has to be available per horse. Furthermore, bottlenecks at feed troughs have to be avoided and sufficient space for lower ranked

40 For "easy keepers", which are designed to have straw mixed in with their hay, the front guard is recommended as it prevents a separation of hay and straw.

41 With the help of pasture partitioning, fresh grass can be offered daily in adequate rations.

animals to get out of the way must be available. In addition, distribution of feed should occur rapidly and the dominant horse should be fed first and in the space it chooses for itself. For the other members, the chosen eating space, which is determined by rank order, bonding, and toleration, should also be maintained.

Feeding stalls have proven useful for the provision of roughage and concentrate in group management situations (**42–44**). They have the advantage that all horses can eat simultaneously, in accordance with their natural behavior. Conflicts and unrest caused by feed-related aggression are then avoided. As a prerequisite, one stand per horse must be available. It must not be wider than the width of a horse (approximately 80 cm (31 in)) and must be sufficiently deep (1.8 × wh) because otherwise, horses can be edged out by others. The separating walls should be closed all the way to the floor in the lower portion of the stand but should be transparent in the upper portion or have slits that allow horses to see each other. If these walls are solid and do not allow visual contact between the group members, lower ranked animals will often feel insecure. They become restless, eat hastily and frequently leave their stall in order to look for the other horses.

Computer-operated feeding systems have to be viewed positively for use in group management situations not only from a standpoint of nutritional physiology but also because they stimulate horses to move about, which has health and ethological advantages. However, caution is indicated, as horses can only eat one after the other and not simultaneously (**45**). This is not in accordance with their natural eating behavior. Without adequate precautions, excessive unrest, edging out of others, redirected aggression, or even serious fights are preprogrammed. It is, therefore, very important to have additional feeding racks for roughage or at least straw, so that horses not entitled to use the automatic feeder can substitute this feed. Furthermore, the area around the automated feeder has to be designed very generously in order to give horses opportunities to get out of the way. A device of this sort should be planned by experts in order to be sufficiently safe and appropriate for horses.

FEED-RELATED AGGRESSION AND FEED SLINGING

Feed-related aggression arises whenever only one or a few sources of feed are available. This behavior is not shown to the same extent under natural conditions, where the table is laid evenly for all horses. Even here, though, it is a requirement that horses are able to keep their social distances. When feeding horses, it is therefore necessary to ensure that all animals keep a sufficient distance from each other, that the environment is calm enough, and that all horses have sufficient time to eat. Feed-related aggression is usually at its maximum prior to concentrate feeding. Among other things, this results from a greatly increased level of excitement during the expectance period. One should, therefore, try to take the tension out of the situation from the beginning and, whenever possible, offer hay prior to feeding concentrate. This measure is also preferable from a standpoint of nutritional physiology (saliva production, layering of feed within the stomach, passage through stomach and small intestine). Feeding concentrate 10–15 minutes after the roughage is recommended.

Feed tossing or hasty eating generally also occur in conjunction with an increased level of excitement. One can avoid this problem by having sufficiently large feed troughs that allow the feed to be spread out in a thin layer. Troughs with a bulging upper rim of about 70 cm (26 in) length, 35 cm (14 in) width, and 20 cm (8 in) depth have proven useful. Ridges 3–4 cm (1–1.5 in) wide at the bottom of the trough can additionally slow down feed intake. Mixing of concentrate with finely chopped hay or straw is also very effective.

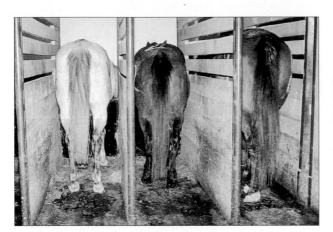

42 Sufficient depth and horizontal slits, which allow visual contact, increase the feeling of security for subordinate horses in feeding stalls. Rounded corner posts decrease the risk of injury during entering and exiting.

43 Feeding stalls that are not facing the wall and allow observation of the environment are optimal.

44 Safe and horse-friendly design of a chest barrier in a feeding stall.

45 Patient waiting in line at the automatic feeder is desirable but is the exception rather than the rule.

FEED SELECTION MUST BE LEARNED

Feed selection is not an inborn behavior. The foal primarily learns to choose appropriate feeds by imitating its dam. Pasture access together with other horses is, therefore, necessary in order to learn which plants are edible and which are not. A foal that has been raised in a stall and has only had access to a paddock devoid of natural vegetation during its development, will always have problems selecting proper feeds in an outdoor environment. Learning to avoid non-edible plants later on in life is only possible if adverse reactions such as gastrointestinal pain occur during or immediately after their intake. If some time passes until the feeling of illness develops, the horse is not able to associate this with the feedstuff. The majority of intoxications, however, do not occur in pasture, but rather during trail rides and while leading the horse outside, when the animals only have a short time to grasp at plants. The risk is increased particularly in gardens and parks because the decorative plants grown there are often poisonous. Furthermore, these plants are not part of the horse's natural environment and, due to a lack of experience, lack a repelling effect. Horses that only rarely have access to pasture are also in danger because they will initially eat the desired green feed very rapidly without being very selective. Caution has to be further exercised with heavily grazed pastures. In these situations, earth and sand are sometimes taken up in increased amounts and can result in intestinal obstruction.

A different issue is intoxication due to feeding of roughage, mowed, or conserved green feed. In these cases, the cause is not a lack of feed selection on part of the horse but rather their inability to select out toxic plants and the altered taste of these plants. For example, horsetail, bracken fern, Adonis, ragwort, and meadow saffron lose their repelling effect but not their toxicity in hay. The same is probably true for silage. Horsetail and bracken fern, for example, retain their toxic effect in silage, while the toxic content of buttercups is degraded only partially.

Signs of intoxication with poisonous plants

- Horsetail: inappetence, excitability, slowing of heart function and overall weakness (inactivation of vitamin B_1).
- Bracken fern: see horsetail.
- Adonis: irritation of the oral and gastric mucosa, disturbance of cardiac function.
- Meadow saffron: loss of appetite, heavy salivation, colic, shortness of breath (Meyer 1995).

Future eating behavior is greatly influenced by adaptation to certain feedstuffs during upbringing and use of the horse. If horses are fed extreme amounts of concentrate early on, it is possible that they will later have difficulty adapting to extended eating times. According to observations by Schäfer (1991), some high-performance horses did not easily adapt to the increased length of time required for feed intake in pasture or with roughage feeding after termination of their careers. The horses did not eat enough and lost weight. Another possible reason for this behavior may be fatigue of the untrained chewing musculature.

FEEDING AND BEHAVIORAL PROBLEMS

With horses that do little daily work, it is generally advisable to increase the proportion of roughage or pasture time and, in exchange, decrease the amount of concentrate, which is high in energy but does not keep horses "busy" for a long time. So-called temperament problems such as bucking, rearing, or bolting will then often subside without further need for correction.

Insufficient satisfaction of the eating needs is often part of the reason for behavioral problems

- Insufficient eating times predispose to substitute activities such as wood chewing and excessive licking.
- Frequent frustration caused by insufficiently long eating times predisposes to future behavioral problems such as cribbing or weaving.
- Feeding mistakes made during raising and management can lead to an alteration of normal eating behavior. Impaired feed selection is one possible result.
- Increasing the proportion of roughage while decreasing the proportion of concentrate in the diet effectively can prevent problem behaviors such as bucking, rearing, and bolting.

Drinking behavior

Natural behavioral patterns

DRINKING PROCESS AND WATER REQUIREMENT

Horses are suction drinkers. To take in water, they tightly close the upper and lower lips and only leave a small opening. When exercising suction, they thereby establish negative pressure. Due to the resulting vacuum, water can be swallowed in long swigs. During water intake, horses hold their head in a horizontal position relative to their downward stretched neck. Even domesticated horses frequently interrupt water intake in order to observe the environment. Prior to drinking and on their way to the water source, many horses will already exhibit tongue and chewing movements. Following drinking, most horses exhibit further chewing movements and will drip some water from their mouths.

Foals first have to learn how to drink water as the process differs from that of suckling. In the beginning, many foals will lick or nibble at the water surface or submerge their muzzles and nostrils. During the first months of life, foals take in only small amounts of water because they can satisfy their fluid requirements by suckling. An increased intake of water during this time could indicate inadequate milk production by the mare.

Sufficient water intake is of utmost importance for normal digestive function and metabolism, as well as thermoregulation. The required amount of water is dependent on the animals' physiologic status, their level of performance (degree of sweating), the type and composition of their feed, and the ambient temperature. Water intake will be increased during pregnancy and lactation, and after hard work, as well as after the ingestion of feedstuffs with a high dry matter content (roughage). Individual and breed-specific differences also exist with regard to both drinking frequency and the amount of water that is taken in. Przewalski horses, for example, require less water than domestic horses. Similarly, horses with an origin in countries with a dry climate (Arabians) drink comparatively less.

DRINKING FREQUENCY AND WATER QUALITY

In the wild, the water source is usually visited only once daily or at least every other day. The longest distance to a water source in which feral horses have been observed is approximately 20 km (12.4 miles). If water is available *ad libitum*, however, horses will generally drink smaller amounts several times during the day and night. With high ambient temperatures, they will drink once or twice per hour. With very cold outside temperatures, on the other hand, the water source is visited only about three times a day. Stalled horses will take in approximately 90% of their total water requirement immediately prior to or after meals. In free-roaming equids, on the other hand, a daily rhythm of water intake has not been observed. They will visit the water source at all times during the day and night. With drinking, as well as eating, social facilitation appears to occur. Most often, therefore, the entire band will visit the water source together.

- Water is indispensable for all metabolic processes and vital functions. Water deprivation can be recognized by digestive disturbances (impaction colic), decreases in performance, decreased feed intake, and sunken flanks.
- Water requirement for a 500 kg (1100 lb) horse per day is dependent on its level of work:

No work	15–25 l (4–6.6 US gall)
Light work	25–35 l (6.6–9.2 US gall)
Hard work	35–50 l (9.2–13.1 US gall)
Lactation	40–50 l (10.5–13.1 US gall)

Horses prefer clear sweet water but, under certain circumstances, will also drink brackish or even slightly salty water. Free-roaming equids utilize water sources such as creeks, rivers, lakes, ponds, puddles, wallows, and snow. In very arid regions, they will eat succulent plants to satisfy their water requirements.

Implications for management and handling

WATER REQUIREMENT – WATER DEPRIVATION

The drinking behavior of horses in the wild cannot be directly applied to our domestic horses. In contrast to free-roaming horses, domestic horses are ridden or have to pull carts, and therefore perform additional work. Also, sport and pleasure horses receive mostly very dry feedstuffs such as hay and straw, which increase their water requirement. Domestic horses should therefore have access to clean fresh water at all times.

Water quality and taste will determine if a lot, a little, or no water at all is consumed. For example, horses will not drink water that is contaminated with manure, with the result that they may spend up to 3 or even 4 days without any water intake. Lack of water is recognizable by digestive disturbances (impaction colic), a decrease in performance, decreased feed intake, and sunken flanks. Watering appliances should therefore be checked daily to ensure proper function and cleanliness.

REQUIREMENTS FOR WATERING APPLIANCES

A number of different types of waterers are commercially available nowadays. If horses are given the choice between a device operated by tongue pressure, or a trough or swimmer waterer, they will usually prefer the latter type because it allows the natural drinking process by suction.

The following are required for any watering device:

- Water pipes and the basin itself must be protected against freezing. This is a prerequisite for horses kept outside year-round.
- The waterer should not be installed too high because it requires the head and neck to be bent too much and might impair proper swallowing.
- It should be possible to turn off the water supply. This can be useful in certain situations, such as with very sweaty horses immediately after exercise, which should not drink for a short period of time.
- Pressure regulation is of benefit, as horses will drink cold water significantly slower than temperate water.
- The feed trough should not be positioned immediately next to the waterer because many horses tend to soak their feed prior to eating. Consequently, they produce less saliva and chew less, which impairs feed utilization. Furthermore, the feed trough and water will become dirty and unhygienic. At worst, the intake of leftover feed particles and fermented feed may lead to health problems (colic).
- In group management situations, it is advisable to position the water supply at the maximum possible distance from the feed supply. The minimum required distance is (2 × horse body length) + 1 m (39 in).

- Horses are suction drinkers. They prefer water sources that allow this drinking technique.
- Stalled domestic horses, but also those in pasture full-time, must have access to water at all times. As a minimal requirement, water has to be offered three times daily in unlimited amounts.

Resting behavior

Natural behavioral patterns

Aside from eating, horses spend most of their day resting. In adult horses this occupies about 5–9 hours of a 24-hour day. As the classical flight animals, they rest polyphasically, which means that their resting periods are divided into many short intervals and are distributed throughout the day. In general, horses doze standing; deep sleep in lateral recumbency only occupies a very short portion of the resting time. The duration of sleep per sleeping period averages 20 minutes in an adult horse.

TYPES OF RESTING
When resting standing, horses show the so-called "dozing face" with semi- or fully closed eyes, a loosely hanging lower lip, and ears turned sideways. They exhibit a typical posture: the front legs are generally in a parallel position, head and neck are lowered, the rear legs shift weight, and the tail hangs loosely. Due to a special design of the musculoskeletal apparatus (passive stay apparatus), horses can stabilize their extremities and are able largely to relax their muscles in a standing position. Newborn foals have to acquire the ability to rest in a standing position while shifting weight from one rear leg to the other. In many cases, one can observe this behavior from the 3rd or 4th week of life. Extended dozing in a standing position, on the other hand, is unusual for foals and may indicate disease.

When resting in recumbency, horses position themselves in a sternal or lateral recumbent position. In sternal recumbency, the horse lies on its abdomen and sternal region. The hindlegs are tucked under the body on one side and the forelegs are folded under. Sometimes, hind- or forelegs are also extended sideways or forward. The head is carried freely or the muzzle rests on the ground. They exhibit the "dozing face" but the eyes are frequently closed tightly. This resting position can particularly be observed in older foals, young horses, and also in mares in advanced pregnancy. In lateral recumbency, the horse rests flat on its side with the head, neck, and body touching the ground. Fore- and hindlegs are most often extended. The eyes are kept shut while sleeping, the mouth is opened slightly, and unintentional movements or sounds can occur. Lateral recumbency occupies a relatively short time period during the day compared to the sternal position. Although horses can rest in this position for an hour or more, on average the time is much shorter. Foals up to 3 months of age spend 70–80% of their time lying down, most of this time in lateral recumbency.

RESTING INTENSITY
Adult horses spend most of their resting periods (about 80%) in a standing position. In this posture they generally do not sleep, but merely doze. Dozing is the least intense way of resting. It is a quasi sleep/wake condition, as can be proven by measurements of brain activity and muscle tone. For this reason, horses exhibiting this type of resting are immediately ready to react to any kind of interruption. During dozing, one can observe skin and muscle twitching, slow tail lashing, and ear movements.

To sleep, horses generally have to lie down in sternal or lateral recumbency. This knowledge is based on electroencephalograph (EEG) measurements and measurements of the muscle tone performed by Ruckebusch and Dallaire (1972, 1973). Two sleep stages can be differentiated based on their characteristic EEG images: non-REM sleep (non-rapid eye movement) including the stage of slow wave sleep, and REM sleep (rapid eye movement). During slow wave sleep, the muscles are relaxed and heart and breathing frequency are slowed significantly. In horses, this type of sleep is particularly prevalent in sternal recumbency (**46**) but can occur while standing (Houpt, 1998).

46 Non-REM sleep serves the purpose of bodily regeneration and is observed primarily in sternal recumbency.

Horses are not as easy to arouse from this sleep stage as they are from dozing; however, they are still ready to flee relatively rapidly. REM sleep is probably only possible when the horse is lying down, particularly when it is in lateral recumbency (**47**). The muscles are then relaxed completely and heart and respiratory frequency are irregular. During REM phases, which have been associated with dreaming, horses not only show rapid movement of the eyes but also twitching of the ears and extremities. Unintentional sounds such as moaning and whinnying can also be heard. It can often be difficult to wake horses from this sleep stage, while at other times it can be very easy.

According to current knowledge, non-REM sleep is important for bodily regeneration. REM sleep likely also has an important function. It is assumed to be of relevance for the psychological well-being of animals. In some people, experimental permanent deprivation of REM sleep resulted in decreased intellectual abilities and psychological disturbances. Experimental deprivation of REM sleep for 2–3 weeks in rats resulted in death. When sleep was withheld entirely, the first rats died after only 1 week.

ACTIVITY RHYTHM
Horses have several resting periods during the day as well as at night. However, a significant increase in the number of resting periods with darkness is observed. In adult horses, episodes of deep sleep are usually seen between midnight and dawn.

The timing and duration of resting periods depend on several factors such as season, availability of feed, weather conditions, age, and gender.

In free-roaming horses, resting behavior is determined particularly by the availability of feed. If plenty of feed is available, more time can be spent on resting and other activities. If feed becomes scarce, on the other hand, resting is minimized. Heat and insect plagues usually prompt horses to increase their resting periods in the middle of the day. If possible, they retreat to shady areas. When choosing a resting place, avoidance of blood sucking insects is of greater importance than protection from high temperatures.

Age is a decisive factor for resting behavior. In general, younger horses, up to 3 years of age, rest significantly more than older animals.

RESTING AREAS
Horses will only lie down in a familiar environment. Free-roaming equids therefore have special resting areas. These have to satisfy their need for security. Areas that supply adequate sight and allow scents to be picked up easily are often preferred. A dry surface is also very important. Wild equids therefore prefer plains with short grass. Horses do not like to lie down in rain or wet weather, and prefer to doze standing. In strong winds or rain they also tend to seek protection under trees, bushes, and other types of cover. Horses appear to dislike wind blowing into their faces.

47 REM sleep is probably significant for psychological well being. According to current knowledge, horses can only achieve it in lateral or sternal recumbency.

If possible, they will position their rear end towards the wind.

Special resting areas are not usually sought for shorter resting periods, which each horse intersperses individually through the day. Resting areas are only visited for longer resting periods. Horses will visit these areas as a group, which is attributed to social facilitation. In the wild, not all horses will lie down at the same time, but instead some will doze standing and are always ready to react next to their recumbent companions. In this manner, the group remains on alert, which is very important for flight animals, and the recumbent horses can refresh themselves without disturbance.

RESTING DISTANCE
It can generally be observed that the individual distance of horses is reduced during resting periods while rank relationships are maintained. Horses that are very familiar with each other will sometimes lie down close to each other and at times even have bodily contact. Young foals rest immediately adjacent to their dams.

During dozing, horses will also form groups more closely together. With heavy insect plagues, animals that are friends with each other stand adjacent to each other, nose-to-tail, in order to ward off annoying flies with their tails. Horses with a very large personal individual distance tend to stay away from the group at an even greater distance than usual for sleeping purposes. This can especially be observed with highly bred warmbloods and thoroughbreds.

Implications for management and handling

It is known that all mammals sleep. How much sleep a horse requires is unknown, but sleep is definitely essential for life. According to current knowledge, REM sleep can occur in horses only when they are lying down (Houpt 1998). If horses are hindered from lying down, decreased psychological performance might result. Bodily regeneration will definitely be impaired if horses are not, or only rarely, given the opportunity to lie down.

IS SUFFICIENT SPACE GOOD ENOUGH?
A lack of space can be the reason for disturbed resting behavior. A stall should therefore always be big enough to allow lateral recumbency without any problem. This will be the case with a measurement of $(2 \times wh)^2$. In a group management situation, a sufficiently large resting area (barn with loose housing: $n \times (2 \times wh)^2$; run-out shed: $n \times (2.5 \times wh)^2$; source = German Federal Ministry of Nutrition, Agriculture and Forestry) does not appear to be sufficient to allow all horses to lie down and rest equally. From personal investigations (Zeitler-Feicht et al., 1999), it is known that even in well integrated groups, higher-ranked horses will repeatedly disturb lower-ranked horses that are lying down. It was determined that the total recumbency time during a 24-hour period averaged 7.8% for dominant horses, but was only 2.8% for subordinate horses. The frequency

- Horses divide sleep into multiple, short episodes (readiness to flee).
- Horses rest standing as well as in recumbency. In order to REM sleep, they have to lie down.
- Horses will only lie down in a familiar environment that satisfies their need for security.
- Horses prefer dry ground to lie down.
- During resting, horses will group more closely together while maintaining their rank-dependent social distances.

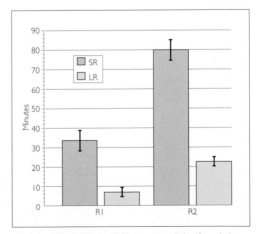

48 Subordinate horses (R1) may spend significantly less time in sternal recumbency (SR) and lateral recumbency (LR) within a 24-hour day than dominant horses (R2).

of lying down, however, was approximately equal, which shows that subordinate horses have as much need to rest in recumbency as dominant horses do. It should also be noted that a covered resting area takes on a central position during the cold season. During the studies, horses almost exclusively lay down in this area. Outside, on the other hand, resting was not observed at all, although it has to be considered that the ground (deep, wet natural ground or paved) was certainly the decisive factor for this behavior. The results of this study led to the recommendation to include additional features such as dividers and screens in the resting area when managing horse groups. It also appears useful to design the resting area as an exclusive resting area and to use shavings instead of straw as bedding. This recommendation is based on the fact that with straw bedding, the resting area also becomes an attractive feeding area. This results in unrest, and if the occupational density is sufficiently high, lower-ranked horses will not even attempt to lie down and rest. A practical alternative is to put up several feeders for straw in the exercise and feeding area. Additional resting areas such as sand lots within the exercise area or an additional covered, but openly designed area that horses can use instead of the resting area when the weather is bad, can further improve the situation for horses of low rank.

THE "HORSE BED"

Not only the size of the resting area itself, but also the nature of the ground surface is of great importance for resting and lying down. Horses unequivocally prefer dry ground. On a muddy surface, they will only lie down hesitantly or not at all, unless of course they feel the need for a "mud bath". Resting times will also be shortened when the bedding is wet. Furthermore, horses avoid hard or slippery surfaces when lying down. The latter probably has to do with potential difficulties when rising. The surface of the resting area should therefore always have good traction. This will be achieved naturally in pasture or on natural, porous earthy ground. In the barn, the bedding has to provide safety when lying down and rising.

PASTURE HUTS ARE NOT SLEEPING AREAS

Stall confinement generally contradicts the horses' natural resting behavior because they originally are flight animals and want to be able to observe their environment at all times. Usually, however, horses learn from an early age to adapt to the conditions under human care and they feel safe and protected even in a barn. It is not uncommon to see horses in their stalls sleep in lateral recumbency during the day, and sometimes they sleep so deeply that they do not even notice the observer. On pasture, however, their natural instinct develops fully again and they prefer to sleep out in the open and not in pasture huts. Huts are popular dozing areas, however, and are mostly visited to avoid insects. In domestic horses, individual animals staying awake while the others sleep can be observed in stalled horses as well as horses at pasture. It can therefore be concluded that management of horses without sufficient visual, olfactory, and auditory contact with other companions will impair their ability to relax and reinvigorate.

Resting behavior of horses can be disturbed if:

- The resting area is too small.
- The ground surface is too moist, muddy, or slippery.
- The need for security (visual, olfactory, and auditory contact with companions and the environment) is not satisfied.
- They are prevented from lying down by dominant animals or they cannot avoid the others.
- A medical problem exists. Lack of sleep can potentially result in impaired bodily regeneration and psychological recovery.

Locomotion behavior

Natural behavioral patterns

Horses are not territorial. In the wild they live in home ranges, which can sometimes overlap considerably with those of other horse bands. A prime condition for this type of cohabitation is the availability of essential resources. These primarily include grazing areas, watering places, and sleeping areas, as well as possibilities for rolling and scratching, which can be located at varying distances from each other. In general, horses of a group visit these areas together because many activities are based on social facilitation.

EXERCISE DURATION

The daily distance covered by free-roaming horses depends primarily on feed growth, on the number and the location of water sources, and on climatic conditions. Under normal conditions, horses cover a distance of about 6–11 km (3.7–6.8 miles) daily. This data, however, was derived from observations restricted to New Forest ponies, Camargue horses, and Mustangs. It cannot be excluded that, given the same conditions, breeds with higher general exercise levels, such as Arabians and thoroughbreds, would cover greater distances. As long as sufficient feed is available, all equids are relatively stationary. If, in addition to feed, sufficient watering places are available, they rarely move more than 2–2.5 km (1.2–1.6 miles) daily. In arid areas, however, longer distances often have to be covered in order to reach the next water source. From observations in feral horses in Montana, for example, it is known that their resting areas are located up to 16 km (10 miles) away from the next water source. In

this case, the animals are forced to walk great distances, because they usually require water at least every other day. Free-roaming equids migrate over longer distances in the course of the year, which is attributable to a change in climatic conditions and, as a result, feed growth. Daily weather changes also influence locomotion behavior. In windy, cold, and rainy weather, horses, especially youngsters, have an increased preference for movement.

Aside from environmental factors, exercise duration and speed depend on age, gender, and group structure. In general, the proportion of total movement represented by trot and canter is larger in young animals and stallions than in adult mares (**49**). Consequently, harem stallions move more than mares, and stallions in bachelor groups more than harem stallions. In addition, running and fighting games take place particularly frequently among youngsters. These differences in locomotion behavior are attributable to differences in the motivation for certain activities between horses of different age and gender.

GAITS

The main gait of horses under natural conditions is the walk. Aside from grazing, during which slow movement occurs and which occupies 60% of a 24-hour day, all wanderings of horses mainly take place at this gait. During these wanderings, horses move on trails that, depending on the nature of the ground, are approximately 30 cm (12 in) wide, such that each horse virtually follows in the footsteps of the one in front. This walking like a "line of ducks" has safety purposes because the dominant mare leads the group. She knows the trails and the ground conditions and the other horses can trust her experience. The harem stallion usually moves at a distance of several meters (several yards) parallel to the herd or represents the tail end of the group. It is his job to drive the herd forward, to keep it together and, if necessary, to defend it. Because herd size is usually small, all animals have visual, olfactory, and auditory contact with each other. In addition, the trails most often zigzag, which further improves visual contact between the group members.

Under free-roaming conditions, faster gaits are usually exhibited only temporarily during play, in massive conflict situations, or during flight. Backing, sideways movements, turning, rearing, and kneeling are also part of the normal repertoire of movements. They can be observed especially

49 Under natural conditions, horses canter only for short periods of time.

in the course of social interactions as well as during ritualized fighting. Jumping across obstacles is generally only observed in desperate situations.

NEED FOR EXERCISE AND EXERCISE REQUIREMENT

These two terms have to be differentiated. The need for exercise represents the emotions and tendencies of a horse and is aroused by various endogenous (e.g. hunger) and exogenous (e.g. approaching predators) stimuli. For this reason, the availability of essential resources has a significant influence on whether and how much a horse moves. Under natural conditions, horses invariably have to move more in order to satisfy their need for feed, quench their thirst, and find protection from insects. It is the exception for all resources to exist in close proximity within the activity radius, and for grass to be present in abundance. If this is the case, however, even horses in the wild show little tendency to move. This behavior is useful because the "fat times" have to be taken advantage of to replenish one's body reserves. Another important stimulus for movement is the presence of companions. Depending on age, gender, and group structure, horses exhibit different degrees of motivation for fighting and running games, for the search for sexual partners, for exploration, and so on. The need for exercise also varies depending on breed. Arabians, for example, even more so than thoroughbreds, are horses with a lot of energy that like to run a lot, while draft horses have a significantly lower need for exercise. The role of feeding should not be underestimated either. In general, the need for exercise will be increased with feeding of too much high-quality feed.

Exercise requirement, on the other hand, denotes the amount of exercise that is necessary to keep a horse healthy, or in other words to maintain the functionality of its physiology and morphology (e.g. circulation). The exercise requirement is the result of the horse's evolution into a flight animal. The musculoskeletal apparatus, the heart and circulatory system, all organ systems, have adapted to this manner of movement for millions of years. Only since domestication has it no longer been essential for the horse to walk long distances daily. But this time period is very short compared to evolution, and therefore does not alter the exercise requirement of horses considerably. Even today, movement over several hours at a slow walk is an important requirement for a horse to remain physically and psychologically healthy during its lifetime.

- Under natural conditions, horses move at a walk for about 16 hours a day. Faster gaits are rarely exhibited.
- Need for exercise and exercise requirement:
- The need for exercise requires a stimulus to be activated (= subjective).
- The exercise requirement results from the phylogenetic development. Accordingly, the horse is adapted to slow, continuous movement for 16 hours per day (= objective).

Implications for management and handling

EXERCISE-PROMOTING MANAGEMENT

The only situation in which horses encounter largely natural exercise conditions is in a social group and with pasture management. For this reason, horses should be given access to pasture whenever possible, either throughout the day or for at least several hours daily. With the management practices that are common nowadays, the horses' exercise requirement is generally met in a grossly insufficient manner. Stall confinement is still the most popular form of management. Without access to a run, horses are sentenced to standing in one place for at least 23 hours a day, if not more. Studies by Rodewald (1989), as well as recent interviews by Beyer (1998) in 56 boarding facilities with more than 2,300 horses, confirm that more than 95% of horses are ridden or driven for less than 1 hour per day. The increased occurrence of "stocked up legs" is not the only signal that this type of management results in physical damage. Access to a pasture without vegetation and without further stimulus for movement will not solve the problem, however. Under these conditions, horses will also spend most of their time standing rather than moving (50).

It is useful to take note of the natural exercise behavior of horses when designing management systems. Exercise stimuli have to be provided to motivate horses to walk (51). An optimal system is the run-out shed with separate functional areas, also called a multi-room barn. The basic concept for this management system is based on different, spatially separated areas designed to meet the horses' varying needs. Similar to the situation in the wild, only on a much smaller scale, horses in this type of management system have to move in order to satisfy their different needs such as eating, drinking, and resting. The decisive factor for an increase in exercise in these systems is the feeding frequency. The higher the frequency, the more the horses will walk. In an experiment performed by Frentzen (1994), Haflinger horses that were fed six times daily covered an average distance of 4.8 km (3 miles) per day, which took care of a large part of their daily exercise requirement (Table 5). It is also useful to design the different functional areas such that distances between them are as long as possible, because the further the functional areas are apart from each other, the further the horse will have to walk to satisfy all its needs. A generously sized area will further prevent concentration of animals in preferred areas and

50 Horses in pastures devoid of vegetation or other stimuli for movement spend most of their day standing.

51 Long distances between the different functional areas are a natural way to stimulate horses to walk for several hours per day.

Table 5 Daily distances covered by horses in different management systems
(Rehm, 1981; Rodewald, 1989; Kusunose *et al.*, 1985; Frentzen, 1994)

Management system	Distance
Near-natural management	6–17 km (3.7–10.6 miles)
24-hour pasture access	8.4 km (5.2 miles)
Run-out system with division into functional areas	4.8 km (3 miles)
Day pasture	3.5 km (2.2 miles)
Run-out system without division into functional areas	1.8 km (1.1 miles)
Individual box stall	0.17 km* (0.1 miles)

*539 steps total: 39% sideways, 32% turning, 20% straight forward, 9% backwards

thereby decrease the risk of confrontations. In a box stall, only minimal movement is possible. In addition, this is less of a forward movement than walking around in circles, which may put excessive strain on the extremities (Table 5). Outside stalls with paddocks are the only variant of box stalls that not only allow, but also encourage, movement to a certain extent. For example, the horse will be prompted to move in and out of its stall by its neighbor's behavior, the weather, or an unusual sound. Significant improvement can be gained by transforming an outside stall into a paddock stall according to recommendations made by Ullstein (1996). This exercise-stimulating variant is also based on a division into different functional areas as has been described for the run-out shed. One must be clearly aware that stall confinement, even with an attached paddock, will never satisfy a horse's exercise requirement. Management in a group generally allows more exercise, but only a run-out system with an exercise-promoting design and division into different functional areas will result in movement over several kilometers per day.

COMPENSATION FOR AN EXERCISE DEFICIT

Under optimal conditions, horses will have access to pasture in the company of others throughout the year for at least several hours per day. New riding establishments should only be permitted if this requirement is met. If only pastureland without vegetation is available, it should be designed to be suitable for all weather conditions or should at least in part be surfaced. The ground surface in the entire enclosure must have enough traction to provide secure footing. From this standpoint, sand and sand mixtures are suitable; however, the risk of colic from accidental ingestion of sand during feeding needs to be considered. To prevent this it is recommended that the horses be offered hay and straw in racks located in vegetation free areas. Horses also prefer to play on sand. Mud, on the other hand, is usually avoided for running purposes. Daily access to pasture, however, merely provides an opportunity for exercise; in no way does it condition horses to be able to withstand several hours of weekend trail riding after having been stalled with access to pasture all week.

Hot-walkers or treadmills are a valuable aid in meeting daily exercise requirements. They are not, however, a replacement for free roaming in a pasture or paddock or for daily work. Most horses get used to these installations quickly,

their endurance improves, and their musculature becomes stronger. However, walking in circles around a hot-walker puts more strain on joints and tendons than walking in a straight line. The maximum time spent on a hot-walker should therefore not exceed 30 minutes in young horses and 45 minutes in older, conditioned horses. In this context, treadmills have to be regarded more favorably because movement in a straight line allows even foot placement.

One should seek additional alternatives during daily handling in order to cover the horse's exercise requirement. For example, one can teach the horse to be ponied and have it accompany a reliable second rider on additional rides (**52**). Having someone "share" the horse, even if it is only for pleasure walks, can also help considerably. It is not a good idea, however, and may even be dangerous, to take the horse from its stall and, without an appropriate warm-up program, simply "let it run around for a bit" in

52 Ponying is one way to compensate for a lack of exercise. (To be taken on trail rides, dogs should be well trained to obey perfectly in any situation.)

the arena. If this is done, the risk of strains and injury is especially high. In addition, 10 minutes of jumping around, bucking, and galloping will at most vent the horse's need for exercise but will in no way satisfy its exercise requirement.

WHICH TYPE OF EXERCISE IS APPROPRIATE FOR HORSES?

Appropriate exercise is exercise designed according to natural living conditions. Under free-roaming or pasture conditions, daily exercise is spread out over the entire 24-hour day and mostly occurs at a walk, with faster gaits being the exception. Exercise regimens of many stalled horses, however, represent the exact opposite. These horses spend most of their time standing, and exercise is often limited to 1 hour but is proportionately faster. In practice one can often hear the statement that intense work adequately meets daily exercise requirements. Under these conditions, however, not only the proportion of trotting and cantering increases but also the distance covered daily. Not uncommonly, horses have to cover a longer distance within an hour than they usually would in an entire day if they were living freely outside. Highly concentrated exercise in this manner cannot compensate for a lack of slow movement spread out over a long period of time. A common result is excessive loading of the musculoskeletal apparatus as well as problem behavior because – despite everything else – the horse's need for exercise remains unsatisfied with this type of short, intense work.

The "day off", a day on which the horse never leaves the stall, is designed exclusively for human benefit. It offers nothing but disadvantages for the horse's health and psyche. It can of course be reasonable, e.g. after a very strenuous event, to give the horse a day off work. This does not mean, however, that it is not allowed to move at all. Days off should rather include a quieter form of exercise such as pasture turnout or a trail ride at walking speed.

CONSEQUENCES OF A LACK OF EXERCISE

The high proportion of lameness among all diseases is undeniable proof that the musculoskeletal system of horses is exposed to severe strains: about 35% of insurance premiums for horses are paid off yearly due to incurable diseases of the musculoskeletal system. Inappropriate and insufficient exercise is frequently also the cause of secondary diseases such as digestive disturbances, cardiac and circulatory system failures, as well as respiratory problems; it can also impair the natural hoof mechanism. For growing horses, exercise is especially important. Sufficient exercise allows bone growth and development to adjust to future challenges. Among other factors, an exercise deficit during the upbringing of a horse predisposes to premature excessive wear.

Less obvious, because the causative factors have often occurred in the past, is the fact that insufficient exercise predisposes to behavioral problems. In other words, the less opportunity for exercise a horse is given and the higher this horse's need for exercise, the higher the likelihood of a behavioral disturbance. Stallions, which are often kept in stalls throughout the entire day and only have limited access to a run, are therefore particularly predisposed. Not only does the quantity of exercise matter, the quality is also important. McGreevy and Mitarbeiter (1995) discovered that dressage and racing horses tend to have behavioral problems more frequently than horses trained for endurance rides.

Lack of exercise is a well known cause of problems arising during handling and use of horses. Many temperament problems arise from it. Explosive discharge of a built-up need for exercise after long hours of standing in a stall is absolutely natural and should be regarded as normal behavior. Appropriate management and sufficient opportunity for daily exercise are the best prevention in this case. The final conclusion has to be that the horse's physical and psychological well being strongly depend on the opportunity for daily exercise.

- Appropriate management offers horses the opportunity for exercise. Stabling quarters should be designed to provide stimuli for movement.
- Quantity as well as quality of exercise has to be tailored to the horse's needs. Exercise which is too brief, but also that which is too intense, can cause health problems and behavioral disturbances:
- Insufficient exercise predisposes to future problem behavior such as cribbing and weaving.
- Exercise that is too intense can lead to psychological overburdening and result in problem behavior.
- Lack of exercise is a frequent cause of temperament problems during handling and use.

Elimination and marking behavior

Natural behavioral patterns

While elimination of manure and urine primarily serves to eliminate end-products of metabolism, it also gives horses the opportunity for intra-species communication. Stallions in particular can be observed to defecate and urinate on top of another horse's eliminations. This behavior is denoted as marking or documentation.

According to Klingel (1972), marking in non-territorial equid stallions (plains zebras, mountain zebras, domestic horses) represents a relic of their original territorial behavior, which is well known in Grevy zebras and wild donkeys. Tschanz (1979), on the other hand, interprets defecation on top of another horse's eliminations as a non-ritualized signaling act. For this reason, it should be denoted as documentation rather than marking.

DEFECATION AND URINATION

In order to defecate, the horse's body posture is changed only slightly. It is similar for both genders: the tail is lifted, the head and neck are lowered a little, and the back is arched slightly. Defecation usually occurs with the horse standing, but due to external circumstances or under human influence, it can also occur while the horse is moving. Frequency of defecation depends on age, gender, and feed among other factors. Foals defecate less frequently than adult horses and stallions more than other horses, which is attributable to marking behavior. Under natural conditions, horses defecate approximately 8–12 times distributed evenly throughout a 24-hour day. Defecation is socially facilitated, i.e. when one horse defecates, others will frequently follow.

Urination, which can only occur standing, requires horses to put their forelegs forward and take on a stretched out posture, the hindlegs are spread and bent slightly. In mares, the hindlegs are usually spread, while stallions stretch them out backwards. Horses seek soft ground to urinate on in order to avoid urine splashing against their legs and abdomen. Amount and frequency of urination depend on the amount of water intake via feed and water, as well as the type and amount of exercise. On average, horses urinate every 4 hours. Foals urinate more frequently than adult horses, and stallions more than other horses due to their marking behavior. A special variation of urination is the urine squirting of mares, which often occurs in combination with hindleg kicking, tail lashing, and squealing. It can be observed mostly during mare fights and as defense against the driving stallion, and it is a clear signal for intra-species communication.

Consistency, size, color, and amount of feces are primarily dependent on feeding, but individual and breed-dependent characteristics and influences of the autonomic nervous system are also significant. Every rider at horse shows knows that nervous and scared horses will eliminate unformed manure. Urine squirting of mares is caused by great excitement and can therefore also be evoked in a variety of fear-inducing situations.

DEFECATION AREAS

Free-living horses occupy home ranges and are not as stationary as, for example, pigs. In the course of evolution, therefore, it was never necessary for horses to develop behavioral patterns with regard to defecation and urination, which would help to prevent transmission of parasites and other infections. Consequently, horses have no natural manure avoidance behavior. In the wild, however, they still prefer certain areas for defecation, for example the vicinity of trails. Accumulation of feces in these areas primarily serves as an olfactory marking of the terrain, and provides information about the eliminating horse. Domestic horses in pasture also primarily defecate in certain areas. As a consequence of our spatially restricted pastures, this leads to the formation of elimination zones or rank spots. Horses do not graze such areas as long as they retain a smell of excretions, so the grass will grow up very high. Because in the course of domestication horses have always been kept on restricted pastureland, it is assumed that this behavior represents a type of adjustment process. It definitely shows that, when given the opportunity, horses attempt to avoid the odor of their own excrements near their feed. A positive side effect is that this behavior helps to minimize the risk of reinfection with endo-parasites.

MARKING

In general, adult stallions are the only horses which show a distinctive marking behavior. On occasion, however, it can also be observed in young animals and mares. Marking of eliminations follows a characteristic procedure: smelling the other horse's defecation and urination area, stepping forward, elimination on top of the present feces (**53**) or urine, stepping backward, smelling the area, walking away. Frequently, the olfactory investigation is accompanied by flehmening or pawing. The tail is lifted high during defecation, which likely has a signaling function.

All horses show interest in their species-specific eliminations and sometimes very intensely smell their own and those of other horses. In the past, manure was therefore called the horse "mail" and it was correctly assumed that chemical messages were transmitted via the eliminations (**54**). It is now known that feces and urine contain pheromones that provide olfactory information about the physical condition of the eliminating horse. For example, stallions recognize the readiness of mares to breed by smelling their urine. This exchange of information also serves to explain the behavior of stallions that prefer not to eliminate feces in their own stall but instead push it through the bars into their neighbor's stall or wait until they are taken outside. This behavior is believed to be aimed at transmitting the "message" of the stallion's presence to other horses. It is often incorrectly interpreted as particular cleanliness.

In stallions, elimination behavior is further combined with dominance behavior. It serves to settle dominance issues without fighting. According to Tschanz (1979), attention to certain rules is necessary to achieve this: to not cover the manure of another stallion means to recognize his dominance and vice versa; the dominant stallion has the right to be the last to cover the excretions of other stallions. If this is not accepted by the subordinate stallion, a fight ensues. Eliminating or not eliminating feces on top of those of a rival therefore suffices to settle rank order in this case.

- Horses do not like the smell of their own excretions. On pasture, they therefore differentiate between eating zones and elimination zones.
- Horses seek soft ground surfaces for urination, hard ground is avoided.
- Manure is the horses' "mail". It contains olfactory information about the physical condition of the eliminating horse.

53 Stallions prefer to urinate on top of mares' manure.

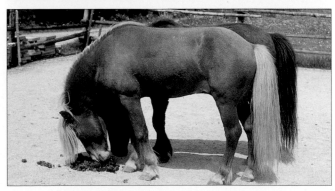

54 Manure is the horses' "mail".

Implications for management and handling

Unlike the situation on pasture, the stalled horse does not have the opportunity to differentiate between eating and elimination zones. In general, it has to eat and rest in direct proximity to its excretions. As shown by their natural behavior, both appear to be uncomfortable for horses. Additionally, health risks may ensue unless the bedding is kept meticulously clean.

FEEDING WITHOUT CONTACT WITH MANURE

It is common practice to feed hay off the stall ground and to supply straw via the bedding, which may be soiled with excrements to a varying degree. While horses get used to eating in direct proximity to their excretions, it is much healthier to offer roughage in feeders. These should be installed close to the ground and not too high, in order to allow a natural eating posture. Bars of the feeder should be no more than 6 cm (2.4 in) apart to avoid injury, as horses can otherwise step into them and catch their hooves. Feeding gates (**55**) are of particular value as they allow roughage to be offered from the barn aisle. They not only allow feed to be offered hygienically, but also carry a lower risk of injury than feeding racks. The feeding gate should be closed off towards the neighboring animal to prevent horses from reaching into the neighboring stall or inlet (paddock) with their heads. Dangerous accidents have occurred in this manner when horses have got their heads caught. As young horses are especially curious, agile, and sociable, it is recommended to close off every other row of the feeding gate for them.

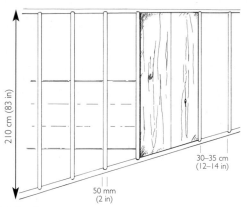

55 Feeding gates allow feed to be offered hygienically. They should, however, be closed off towards the neighboring animal to prevent it from getting its head caught from the outside and injuring itself.

For paddock management, there are several ways to minimize contact with excrement during eating. For example, one can offer roughage exclusively in feeding stalls or install additional eating spaces for straw feeding (horse to eating space ratio =1:1) outside the resting area (**56**). Horses will prefer these to eating soiled bedding from the resting area.

RESTING AND ELIMINATION AREAS

Horses prefer to lie down on a dry, soft ground surface. Given the choice between bedded resting areas and those without bedding, they will always choose the former, and prefer straw to shavings. Management without bedding results in dangerous air conditions (ammonia). In

56 Installing a feeding rack within the paddock allows feeding of hay and straw without contact with manure. An additional great advantage is that horses are encouraged to spend most of their time outside.

addition, horses kept under these conditions will decrease their relaxing resting times in sternal or lateral recumbency or abandon them entirely, and instead doze increasingly in a standing position. Ubbenjans (1981), among others, came to this conclusion. From comparative studies, she found that surfaced areas (cement, pavement) as well as areas covered with plastic or rubber materials must not be used in horse management without bedding.

Bedding or other soft and absorbent surfaces are also necessary for elimination of urine. Horses urinate only reluctantly on hard surfaces. Male horses in particular will often retain urine for hours until they have found an appropriate location. Obviously, splashing of urine against the abdomen is perceived as uncomfortable. This is an additional reason for the absolute requirement for a bedded area in individual stalls as well as group management, unless horses have permanent access to a run with a natural surface such as sand or grass. The behavior described above can be easily observed in draft horses that are used exclusively on paved roads. These horses will frequently retain their urine until they are returned to their stall. When working his horses for several hours on asphalt, therefore, a knowledgeable horseman will always have a handful of shavings available to provide padding for his horses to urinate on.

PASTURE HYGIENE – A MUST

On pasture, horses eliminate feces in certain areas. Only stallions show directed placement of feces on top of other horses' eliminations, while young horses, mares, and geldings mostly defecate in the proximity of other eliminations. As a result, roughs of increasing size develop, which are particularly noticeable in stationary pastures. Over time, more and more grazing area is lost in this manner. Remedies for this situation are regular collection of feces, simultaneous or alternate grazing with cattle or sheep, additional cutting of grass, and appropriate fertilization. Mobile mini tractors, which collect manure in a vacuum cleaner-like fashion are currently being developed. The spreading of manure by machines ("dragging" of manure) is inappropriate because it only serves to distribute the manure, which horses would otherwise avoid, across the entire area. This measure also dramatically increases the risk of reinfection with parasites.

HEALTH RISKS DUE TO SOILED BEDDING

Permanently soiled bedding can result in a number of problems affecting the horse's physical as well as psychological health. First and foremost, ventilation problems in covered buildings have to be considered. The stench of ammonia in the stall is caused by poor hygiene because it originates from bacterial breakdown of feces and urine. Ammonia is an irritant for the mucous membranes of the eye and respiratory tract, and by adsorption to miniscule dust particles it is able to reach the alveoli deep within the lung. This noxious gas is considered one of the major causes of chronic respiratory disease, particularly when in combination with dust. Chemicals that bind ammonia can reduce the odor but in no way replace thorough cleaning of stalls.

Thrush is another health problem correlated with permanently soiled bedding. About one-third of stalled horses are affected by this disease, which contributes to destruction of the hoof horn in the frog region. Clean bedding and regular hoof care virtually eliminate the risk of thrush.

The danger of ongoing reinfection with endoparasites is significantly increased if horses are forced to eat adjacent to manure-soiled bedding. The same is true for pastures if, as mentioned earlier, parasite eggs and larvae have been distributed across the entire area by dragging machines.

Finally, it must not be overlooked that moist bedding can lead to behavioral changes. According to Zeeb (1997), horses decrease their resting times when the moisture content of bedding increases above 60%. Under these conditions, it should be expected that horses will, over a period of time, lose their vitality.

- From the standpoint of well-being and health, daily thorough cleaning of stalls and provision of fresh bedding is required.
- Soiled bedding results in:
- Stale air ("coughing").
- Thrush.
- Increased worm burden.
- Increased insect plague.
- Decreased resting times.

Comfort behavior

Natural behavioral patterns

Comfort behavior includes all behaviors which serve the purpose of personal hygiene. It represents a well established part of the daily rhythm of free-roaming hoofed animals. Being able to exhibit these behaviors without disturbance is very important for the animal's well-being. Solitary and social grooming are differentiated. While the latter also serves for communication between horses, the former represents true comfort behavior and is exhibited by each horse separately as needed. It includes nibbling, licking of the body, scratching with the rear hooves, and rubbing against objects, as well as rolling, bathing, and shaking.

SOLITARY GROOMING

All behaviors included in solitary grooming serve the purpose of cleaning the coat and skin and are exhibited with increasing frequency when horses are shedding. Nibbling is done with the incisors and all reachable body parts are included (**57**). The skin is rubbed against or picked at with the teeth. Licking, which is observed infrequently, is shown in particular to remove liquids. For example, one can often observe licking movements along the lips after drinking. On rare occasions, horses also lick themselves, particularly at the mouth region but also at the shoulders, the front legs, and the sides of the body.

Scratching with the anterior border or the rear hooves is preferably used at the head, especially the ears, and the upper neck region. It is done with remarkable caution and only by young horses (Houpt 1998). For rubbing, the horse rubs its head, neck, mane, or rear end against stationary objects such as trees, and fence posts. They also try to rub their backs and abdomens by walking back and forth below or across branches or fallen trees. Horses rub against group members or against themselves. One can frequently observe the so-called "grooming face" with a stretched out upper lip, which is considered to indicate a "pleasure-seeking" process and well-being. In the wild, horses have preferred rubbing areas, which they visit regularly.

Rolling is an elementary need (**58**). Well cared-for horses have the same urge to roll on a daily basis as free-roaming hoofed animals. Horses indicate their intention to roll by their behavior, which includes visual, olfactory, and sometimes even tactile investigation of the rolling area. To do this, they first walk around in several circles with their head lowered to the ground, their ears put forward, and their tail lifted. Subsequently, they may loosen the ground a little by pawing at it. They then put their legs together underneath their body, slowly bend their joints, roll over the shoulder towards one side with the rear end following this motion, and come to rest in sternal recumbency. Most often, they immediately go into lateral recumbency and begin to roll. Intense contact between the head and neck and the ground appears to be important. Rolling all the way over to the other side often requires several attempts. Rolling over the back has to be learned, while "one-sided" rolling represents inborn behavior (Dillenburger 1982). Some horses have difficulty in rolling all the way over to the other side. They therefore divide the rolling process into two phases and treat one side first, then get up, lie back down and scrub the other side.

Free-roaming horses have special rolling places. These are often devoid of vegetation, sandy, dry, and dusty. On pasture, horses will sometimes remove grass in certain spots by pawing to create rolling places. In the summer, watering places are also popular places for rolling. At times, even muddy ground is sought out. These mud baths are popular with some horses, especially during moulting in the spring and with plagues of annoying insects.

Rolling probably has an additional communicative function. This is suggested by the intense olfactory investigation of the ground

57 Horses nibble at all reachable body parts with their incisors.

prior to lying down. Furthermore, rolling appears to be infectious and often, several group members will roll simultaneously or one after the other in the same spot. The harem stallion is often the last one to roll. This results in his scent covering that of everyone else, which may serve to demonstrate his dominance.

Most perissodactyles (odd-hoofed animals) like water and can swim relatively well and for long distances. When stepping into the water, they frequently paw at it with their front legs and subsequently drink. Fear of water seems to be breed-dependent to a certain extent. Most ponies and draft horses walk into water without much concern, while Arabians are more likely to exhibit caution and refusal. All horses prefer clear water to muddy water.

Shaking generally takes place after rolling and also in response to soaking through of the hair coat. Exceptions are mud baths during times of severe insect plague, after which horses often do not shake, as the mud crust apparently has a protective function. Shaking follows the "from front to rear rule", which means that the shaking motion begins at the head from which it moves over the neck and rump until it reaches the tail head. In order to shake, horses take on a sawhorse stance. Mere shaking of the head mostly serves to ward off insects. With minor skin irritations, horses react by skin twitching of the affected region, which is effected by rapid contractions of the subcutaneous musculature. Annoying insects are also chased off by tail lashing, stomping of the legs, or kicking at the body, as well as by directed nudging with the mouth. Tail lashing to chase off insects is very important for the horse's well-being. A long tail enables horses to reach large parts of their lower body and abdomen. The tail is used very specifically to ward off insects when horses are dozing together. Horses will stand head-to-tail to each other in order to chase flies from each other's head.

SOCIAL GROOMING

Aside from the actual grooming procedure, communication is a major component of this type of grooming process. Social grooming is usually exhibited with preferred partners and presumably serves to strengthen relationships. Grooming also appears to have a calming effect. Grooming horses will frequently initiate the process simultaneously, but quite often an animal of lower rank starts the process. It indicates its intention to the chosen partner by showing its "grooming face" with the ears upright in a friendly manner and the upper lip stretched far forward. Subsequently, both horses stand next to each other, nose-to-tail, and with their incisors they begin to work systematically on each other's hard-to-reach places. Favored spots are the crest of the mane, the withers, back, and croup. Social grooming can occupy varying amounts of time. It can last for only a few seconds but also for several minutes. Sometimes, short breaks are taken or the horses change sides. Social grooming is more frequently observed in foals and mares than in stallions. It is particularly pronounced between mares and their own foals and among youngsters. Grooming frequency varies with the time of day and the season. Social grooming in horses can be observed particularly often in times of shedding and with severe insect plagues during the summer.

- Comfort behavior is a well established part of the daily rhythm of free-roaming horses.
- Increased solitary grooming such as rubbing is to be considered normal at times of shedding.
- Rolling is an elementary need. Horses prefer sandy and dry places to roll.

58 Rolling is an elementary need. Poorly groomed horses will roll more than well groomed ones. Preferred rolling areas are devoid of vegetation, sandy, and dry.

Implications for management and handling

ROLLING AREAS AND RUBBING DEVICES

A management system is appropriate for a certain species only if it meets the animals' requirements in each functional area. Solitary grooming in particular should be possible without restrictions. In contrast to tie-stalls, box stalls allow this as long as their measurements meet the minimal requirement of $(2 \times wh)^2$ per horse. The same is true for group management systems. Specially constructed places for rolling are particularly horse friendly. In run-out systems, they can be integrated into the outside area without any problem. A rolling area should have an area of about 5×5 m (16.4×16.4 ft) and should allow constant use, so it may need a roof. Sand is a very suitable surface. If special rolling areas, runs, or pastures are not available, a covered or outside riding arena can serve the same purpose as long as horses are allowed to move about freely in it at least once a day.

After hard work and heavy sweating, horses experience a particular need to roll. A good horse owner will therefore allow a horse to roll extensively when the work is done. This not only has a positive psychological effect, but also prevents the horse from rolling in its stall. Even in a stall with adequate size measurements, room is limited and there is an increased risk that the horse will become cast and possibly injure itself. Fresh straw can also evoke spontaneous rolling. Many horses give in to this need as soon as they enter a freshly bedded stall. For safety reasons, one should therefore always check on all horses after the stalls have been bedded.

Rubbing against a fixed object is another need that horses satisfy rather fervently. They practice this with any fixed objects within their reach, but special rubbing devices will save the barn or pasture constructions. In runs that are fenced in with electric fencing and do not contain trees or anything similar, these devices will definitely contribute to the horses' well-being (**59**). Wooden rubbing poles deeply anchored within the ground, or brushes as used in cattle operations, are suitable. Loose halters, which are unfortunately seen frequently, represent a great danger during rubbing. They may result in the horse getting caught, to which it may react with uncontrolled counter-pulling or panic. Some animals have died because of this negligence! Unattended animals should ideally not wear a halter. If they do, it at least needs to be made of material that will tear when pulled against strongly or it must have a self-opening mechanism.

Social grooming serves the establishment of friendly relationships among horses. In group management situations, it can be practiced without restraints. In separately stalled horses, it is also possible as long as horses get along well and the stall walls can be reduced to chest height, or if a run is available. This is one reason why small paddocks attached to stalls should not be enclosed with electric fencing.

HEALTH ASPECTS

Increased rubbing during the time of shedding of the hair coat is normal behavior. Some mares will also exhibit it at an increased frequency when they are in heat. In both cases, there is a clear time limit. If excessive rubbing is observed outside these situations, however, a medical problem is frequently present. For example, extensive rubbing of the tail head can be caused by endoparasites. Frequently, pinworms (*Oxyuris equi*) that inhabit the large colon are the cause. The female parasites leave the colon, migrate to the horse's anus, and deposit their eggs there, which elicits intense pruritus (itching). Increased rubbing is also shown with infectious or allergic conditions. A well known example is summer eczema. In isolated cases, behavioral causes can also be present. In any case, these signs should prompt the owner to consult a veterinarian.

Rolling can usually be interpreted as a sign of comfort and it is an indication that the horse is feeling well. It can, however, also indicate pain in the abdominal region in cases of colic or prior to foaling. In these situations, however, horses will usually exhibit a changed overall behavior. A further indication of a medical problem can be the absence of shaking after rolling, because shaking is often abandoned due to pain.

- Appropriate management allows the unrestricted exhibition of comfort behavior.
- Excessive rubbing, licking, or chewing often indicate a skin condition associated with pruritus (itching). In isolated cases, a behavioral problem may be present.

59 Paddocks and run-out systems with electric fencing should be equipped with scratching devices such as brushes.

Play behavior

Natural behavioral patterns

A good definition of playing is that of "a pleasurable activity without purpose that is undertaken for its own benefit". It is, however, much more. In play, young horses optimize their coordination of movements and simultaneously practice social behavior. It serves to practice the behaviors that are important in adult life, and allows youngsters to gain new experiences. Play further enhances physical and psychological health. It is only shown in the "relaxed zone". The feeling of security required for playing is provided by the dam for her foal, and by the herd or companions for adult horses.

As is the case in all higher mammals, curiosity and the drive to play are much more strongly developed in juvenile perissodactyles than in adults. Seventy-five percent of the activity of foals represents play, but even older horses can be motivated to play. Domestic horses play more than free-roaming equids. In addition to a greater need for exercise due to spatial restrictions, they probably play more because they are in the care of humans and are provided with sufficient feed and are protected from predators. This not only provides the time but also the security needed for playing.

Horses are particularly fond of playing with social partners, but also play by themselves. The latter, also called solitary play, is seen particularly in very young foals and in horses kept by themselves. It mostly consists of running games, during which the horse trots, gallops or bucks

wildly while snorting boisterously, and often with exaggerated movements. During the first 3–4 weeks of life, foals play almost exclusively by themselves. They jump and hop around their dams, nibble and touch them. This helps youngsters to develop a notion of space and individual distance, and it helps to coordinate and practice inborn movements. Solitary play with an object (branches and so on) also occurs. It serves the acquisition of knowledge about different objects with all the senses.

The characteristic of social play is the search for a partner and subsequent encouragement to play. Horses achieve this by nudging, pinching, light biting, head swaying, and circling with "exaggerated jumps". The intention to run, for example, is indicated by lifting the tail high (**60**). Any horse understands this signal and every horse nearby that is willing to run will

60 An elevated tail head has a signaling function during social running games.

become stimulated. Often, the entire herd will be enticed and, for a few minutes, a wild chase ensues with everyone snorting, kicking, bucking, jumping, rearing, and leaping. Chases, which include attempts to bite one another in the rear end, or races with role reversal, are also very popular. Fighting games include all components of the future stallion fight with rearing, front leg striking, nipping, biting of the head and crest, "kneeling down", circling, chasing, rear leg kicking, and many more. Colts will start to show fighting games by 4 or 5 weeks of age, while fillies prefer running games and social grooming. Furthermore, colts will exhibit playful sexual behavior from the first week of life in the form of mounting the dam and other foals. Even fillies, although much less commonly, will show playful mounting of others.

Is it a fighting game or a real fight? Several characteristics can be used to distinguish the two. Playfulness is recognized from the horses' facial expression. There is no threatening expression, but instead, the mostly upright ears signal a positive, friendly attitude towards the playing partner. The serious component is missing, i.e. injuries are avoided, unless they occur accidentally, and, in addition, partial actions can be mixed deliberately such as mutual chasing with role reversal.

> Play is a certain sign of well-being. Characteristics of play are:
> - Lack of threatening facial expression.
> - Lack of intention to injure the other horse.
> - Role reversal.

Implications for management and handling

RAISING OF FOALS

Foals need companions of similar age in order to develop normally. Young stallions additionally need companions of the same gender, as the tender "girl's play" cannot replace fighting play. Most often, two foals that are friends will play together. For this reason, youngsters should be kept in larger groups. If no playmate is available, as is the case with foals raised by themselves, aberrations in social and particularly sexual behavior are to be expected.

Human beings can neither replace nor are they adequate playmates for foals! For children in particular, but also for adults who do not recognize the turning point, seemingly amusing

foal play can become dangerous very rapidly. Young stallions and geldings, for example, tend to pinch playfully when saying hello. If this behavior is rejected by simply tapping them on the muzzle, saying "No, no" with a smile or offering them a carrot as a distraction, one encourages these biting games, even if unintentionally. An appropriate corrective measure would be to administer a quick and short but distinct slap on the muzzle, preferably supported by vocal correction such as a stern "No". This correction has to occur immediately prior to or during biting. In a similar fashion, mares correct their foals by a distinct pinch into the rear if the foals' teeth nip the udder during nursing. The foal quickly learns to associate biting with punishment as long as the latter is carried out at the correct time. Following the correction, one should immediately be friendly towards the foal again, in order to avoid fear of humans developing.

PLAY IN THE HORSE'S EVERYDAY LIFE

Play is a sure indicator that the horse is feeling well at that particular moment. If an older horse is still interested in playing, this certainly indicates that it is doing well. Group management or access to common runs offer optimal conditions for social play. The agreeability among horses and their liking for each other, as well as the type of ground surface and the weather will influence type and frequency of play. Most horses have one or several preferred playmates, i.e. they do not play without an adequate partner. Male horses are generally more playful than females. Hackbarth (1998) observed up to 30 social play activities per horse per day with up to five different playmates, in a well integrated horse group kept in a "play-friendly" indoors/outdoors system (**61**). Dominant horses and geldings were observed to play significantly more than horses of lower rank and mares. In addition to cheek pinching and "halter playing", mutual chasing and fighting games can be observed in indoors/outdoors management systems as well, as long as the ground offers sufficient traction and is not too hard. Not infrequently, the sand-bedded rolling area is turned into a playground. In cool weather, running and fighting games are particularly popular, while mutual grooming is preferred early in the year when the first warm sunshine appears.

At times, however, horses also like to play by themselves with all kinds of objects. Suitable toys are branches, balls, cones, cartons, chains, and so on. The only important feature of these toys is that the material has to be injury-proof and non-toxic. Horses in stalls in particular should be given the opportunity to play in order to prevent sensory deprivation (**62**). Without an opportunity to play, many horses will find their own toys and play in the water, dig up their bedding, or play with the door lock (**63**). In short, they invent things that annoy people! This is another reason why the horse's drive to play should not be ignored, because in combination with boredom, this need rapidly results in unwanted behavior. However, even the nicest toy becomes uninteresting at some point and has to be replaced by a new one. This is also the case for branches.

- Lack of a playmate during the early years of development predisposes to future aberrant social and sexual behavior.
- Appropriate management offers the opportunity for solitary and, even better, social play.
- An unsatisfied need for play can become the cause of unwanted behavior.

61 Number of social play activities and playing partners in a run-out shed with pasture as a function of rank order (Hackbarth 1998).

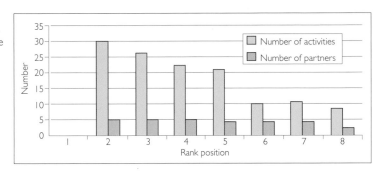

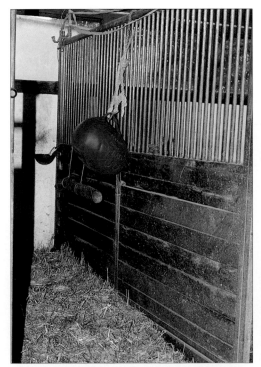

62 Straw bedding, toys, and daily pasture turnout help to improve management in individual box stalls.

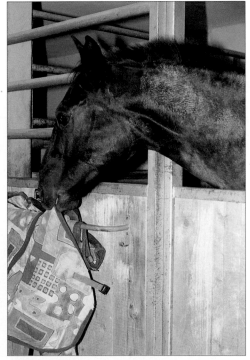

63 Lack of occupation encourages horses to find their own toys.

Curiosity and exploratory behavior

Natural behavioral patterns

Like goats and chamoix, horses are extremely curious animals, which like to explore. These behaviors are particularly strongly developed in foals. Aside from playing, curiosity and exploratory behavior are thought to be the "major drives for independent learning". Curiosity manifests in the form of ogling, sniffing, licking, and nibbling at unknown objects, as well as in testing movements such as careful tapping, pawing, and pushing. When exploring, the horse shows similar types of behavior and behavioral processes. For this reason, applied ethology does not differentiate between curiosity and exploratory behavior.

According to Tembrock (1964), curiosity and exploratory behavior can be differentiated as follows:
- Curiosity is an unfixed motor behavior and serves to acquire a species-specific "amount" of novel information.
- Exploratory behavior is orienting behavior in space and time. It is species-specific in its motor function and is directed towards species-specific stimulus patterns, which are required to complete the species' action system in space and time.

Exploratory behavior is an important prerequisite for survival in the wild. It serves to exploit new resources, helps to make new experiences in order to avoid unnecessary flight, and plays an important part in the avoidance of predators. Life in a group is advantageous, because exploration of foreign stimuli requires a certain division of labor. Subsequently, even when resting at night, some animals will always be on guard while the others relax and rest.

Visual and auditory senses are primarily used for orientation from afar. The body position typical of fleeing behavior is exhibited: the head is raised, the eyes are opened wide and directed forward, the ears are upright, the nostrils widened, the muscles tensed, and the tail lifted up high. Generally, it suffices for one group member to take this tense body posture in order to alert all others of the event in question. The horses' subsequent reaction differs depending on the type of object, the distance at which it is located, how intense an impression it makes on the animals, and how much it surprises them. Only intense or sudden stimuli will result in an immediate flight reaction with sudden lifting of the head and jumping away. In other situations, the horse will at first attempt to locate and identify the source of the stimulus by looking, listening, and picking up scent. If the situation is judged to be harmless, horses will generally carry on their previously interrupted activity. If uncertainty remains, a closer inspection follows. For this, several horses will usually team up, with a dominant animal leading the group. With abrupt movements and always ready to flee, the leader approaches the unknown object up to a safe distance, stops, secures the area, trots in the opposite direction for a few steps, stops again, and again secures the area. In this fashion, the object is approached and circled in a zigzag motion until the horse carefully comes closer. Defecation due to excitement can occur.

What follows next is known as close-up orientation. At first, horses approach the strange object carefully, still with a very tense body posture, a long extended neck, erect ears, and widened nostrils. After extensive visual inspection, which is often accompanied by snorting, the object is then sniffed at extensively. This olfactory recognition appears to be very important and obviously supplies the horse with much information about the unknown object. Sometimes, the senses of taste and touch are also utilized. Foals, in particular, explore everything with their mouth first and nibble or lick at strange objects. They then begin to investigate them by tapping and pawing with their hooves. On the other hand, older horses only use their sense of touch, apart from the whiskers, for the investigation of ground surfaces such as puddles.

- Because the horse is a flight animal, it shows species-specific behavior in being very alert and exhibiting great curiosity and exploratory tendencies.
- Curiosity and exploratory behavior serve to gain new experiences and therefore contribute to independent learning.
- Orientation from afar primarily employs the visual and auditory senses. For close-up orientation, olfactory recognition is very important.

64 A long view across the surrounding area is optimal for a horse's well-being and sense of security.

Implications for management and handling

ENVIRONMENTAL VARIABILITY

During its evolutionary history, the horse could only survive through constant alertness and exploration of the environment. Consequently, its senses and perceptive performance are designed to handle a large sensory load. It therefore requires a richly structured environment and as much contact with its surroundings as possible. Appropriate management systems will pay attention to this need. In individual stalls, horses should at least be given the opportunity to look over a half-opened door into the barn aisle in order to participate in barn events. Outside stalls, stalls with attached paddocks, or paddock management are even better suited as they provide additional environmental stimuli (**64**). Life in a closed-off stall without view or access to a run has to result in sensory deprivation (**65**). If the sensory threshold is exceeded, the horse will signal danger. The sensory threshold is lower in a horse that is kept isolated than in one kept in a group. Sensory deprivation and lowering of the sensory threshold result in a situation where each event, however unimportant, that interrupts the monotony of the day, takes on disproportional dimensions for the horse. They are startled by "nothing" or are quickly overexcited. Kicking the stall walls and

65 Horses need visual, olfactory, and auditory contact with their environment in order to feel safe and comfortable. Dark, closed-off, inside stalls lead to sensory deprivation and overexcitability.

rubbing the teeth against the bars are also signs of sensory deprivation or of the resulting overexcitement when anything happens. Some animals, however, respond to an environment without sensory stimulation by becoming dull or inert, while others will begin to find alternative activities.

One can conclude that a lack of environmental stimulation can be the cause of many behavioral problems.

It should be noted that the degree of environmental stimulation should fit the individual horse. The view from an outside stall into a jumping arena or an exercise track is not ideal for every horse. In sensitive and nervous horses, this may increase the level of excitement even further. Calmer horses, such as those with draft horse influence, remain relaxed and seem to enjoy the view. The notion that the horse needs a quiet and shielded area in order to relax is incorrect. Horses only feel secure and can relax sufficiently if they have visual, olfactory, and auditory contact with companions. To achieve this, they have to be able to observe their environment to a large enough extent (**66**).

LEARNING BY EXPLORATION

Similar to playing behavior, curiosity and exploratory behavior are particularly developed in foals and young horses. During this portion of their lives, they also have the greatest capacity for learning. The more opportunity they have during this time to explore, and the more objects and situations they get to know, the more experienced they will be in their adult life. One frequently encounters the opinion that horses cannot be worked until they are 3 years old. This is correct with regard to the preparations for riding. It is,

66 Outside stalls increase the exposure to environmental stimuli and, in addition, offer fresh air and natural light. They should, however, be designed appropriately. (In Germany, according to the requirements of the Federal Department of Nutrition, Agriculture and Forestry, *BMELF.*) In this picture, the opening is too low and the door handle is not sufficiently secure.

however, wrong if one has the goal of training a horse that is willing to learn, that is safe, and that masters a variety of situations without shying because it has got to know them from its early days onwards. One can therefore utilize the curiosity of a young horse and get it used to tractors, cows, plastic tape, umbrellas, and many more things. It is important only that the positive general attitude, on which curiosity is based, is maintained. Horses that are trained to learn early on will learn better and faster throughout their life than those that have not had the same opportunity. The jumpiness of horses differs among individuals and may also have a heritable component. Much of it can, however, be adjusted by experience and learning. With repeated presentation, horses can get used to a great variety of stimuli, even to those that occur suddenly. It is important only that they do not associate negative experiences with these stimuli. In the wild, distractions and new opportunities for learning are constantly present. We should mimic this in the management of horses and in their handling.

With increasing age, the need to explore decreases slowly, however, it will remain active forever in horses kept in an environment full of variety. One should, therefore, always try to confront the horse with new things during its training and daily work. In doing so, it is important to always allow sufficient time for the horse to explore the new situation. A calm, step-by-step approach, such as walking around the strange object in smaller and smaller circles, as horses would naturally do, can help to decrease fear. During the exploration period, tension is very high. The smallest changes are often sufficient to evoke a reaction such as backing away, snorting or brief flight. It can therefore be reasonable to dismount and lead the horse, or at least to stop, because horses can more easily recognize and assess a strange object when standing than in motion. Young horses, in particular, tend to panic if they are forced to pass a strange object. It is also important, especially in the period of close-up orientation, to allow enough freedom of the head as the visual field of horses, with their eyes located laterally on the head, differs from ours (p.195). Olfactory exploration will then complete the process for the horse (**67**).

- Horses require sufficient environmental stimuli to feel secure and comfortable.
- Sensory deprivation is a causative factor for many behavioral disturbances and unwanted behaviors of horses.
- Early learning by exploration, combined with positive reinforcement, helps to develop safe, experienced horses.

67 Horses overcome their fear of frightening objects better if they are given the opportunity for olfactory investigation.

Part C: Cause, diagnosis and therapy of problem behavior

Behavioral aberration or unwanted behavior?

Behavioral aberrations in horses have been recognized for hundreds of years. One reason may be associated with the fact that horses, as indispensable working animals for daily labor and during war times, have historically drawn the most attention in veterinary medicine. Another reason is that the horse is particularly prone to developing aberrant behavior. This is attributable not least to its large requirement for exercise and high level of sensitivity.

In earlier times, behavioral aberrations in horses were referred to as vices. This term is still used today in the hippologic and veterinary literature. It implies, however, that the horse has to be blamed for the behavior, which results in entirely incorrect considerations regarding causes, therapy, and prevention. The human being, the management systems designed by him, as well as his way of handling the horse are the causes of aberrant behavior – not the horse. Furthermore, a horse has neither virtues nor vices in the human sense because it does not consciously choose to do anything bad or good. The term vice should, therefore, be removed from the vocabulary of every horse lover and should be replaced by more neutral terms. In the following, therefore, the general term of problem behavior will be used, and it will further be distinguished between aberrant and unwanted behavior. This differentiation is important because the two may have:

- Different predisposing factors and causes.
- Different psychological and physical consequences.
- Different methods of treatment.
- Different prognoses for therapy.

Prior to defining these terms further, however, the term "normal behavior" will be explained because it represents the reference term for every type of aberration.

Definition of aberrant behavior

WHAT IS CONSIDERED NORMAL BEHAVIOR?

It is essential to recognize normal behavior, so that one can then differentiate it from aberrant or unwanted behavior. As a preliminary remark it should be noted that all higher developed species of animals possess a range of species-specific behavioral patterns, which are in themselves very consistent. This means that an observer generally has no problem assigning an individual animal to a particular species based on its movements, vocalization, and body posture. Although individual divergences from the norm occur, these are relatively minor in animals that are given the opportunity to develop without restrictions. Therefore, normal behavior can be derived from observation of typical behavioral patterns shown by horses in the wild. It has to be considered, however, that the mere description of events does not sufficiently characterize a behavioral pattern. If one wants to define normal behavior, one also has to consider the context in which the behavior occurs and the object towards which it is directed. This has already been described in detail in the preceding section.

WHAT IS A BEHAVIORAL ABNORMALITY?

The fundamental ethologist Immelmann (1982) denotes "every behavior diverging from the norm" as aberrant behavior. This definition is very broad. In trying to use it in practice, one quickly recognizes its limitations because it is almost impossible to determine at what point a behavioral variation is still to be considered normal or represents an aberration. Brummer (1978) narrows down the definition and defines aberrant behavior as "a considerable and/or lasting aberration from the behavioral norm". The definition according to Sambraus (1997a) will be used as a basis for discussion in this text. He describes the term even more strictly and denotes "with regard to modality, intensity or frequency, a considerable and lasting aberration from normal behavior" as aberrant behavior. The aberration can take on different forms. It can be divided into the following categories:

1 Behavioral patterns which are not part of the natural ethogram (e.g. cribbing).
2 Behavioral patterns which are part of the natural ethogram but:
a diverge with regard to quantity (e.g. stereotypical headshaking).
b are exhibited in a different context:
    – activities without an object (e.g. tongue playing).
    – activities directed at inanimate objects (e.g. rubbing teeth against bars).
    – activities directed against animate objects (e.g. self-mutilation).

This categorization will be further elucidated below. The explanations also serve to demonstrate that despite the limitations put on these terms, they do not only describe aberrations, but can also include normal behavior. It is therefore necessary to recognize from the beginning that the diagnosis of aberrant behavior requires extensive and well founded scientific knowledge.

Aberrant behavior belonging to the first category should be easily recognized as such. It includes behavioral patterns that are not part of the natural behavioral repertoire of horses. These are also called qualitative aberrations from normal behavior. A good example is cribbing. It is a behavior that is exclusively shown by horses kept in the care of humans. In the wild or under natural living conditions, it is never observed.

Category 2a contains behavioral patterns which are seen under natural conditions in free-roaming horses, but which differ considerably from normal behavior with regard to their duration or frequency. For example, shaking of the head to ward off insects is part of the ethogram and represents normal equine behavior. If it is exhibited stereotypically and for a longer time, however, a behavioral aberration may exist. Other considerations include diseases of the ears and photosensitive behavior. Pain caused by an incorrect riding technique or ill fitting tack as well as learned behavior can also be the cause. The latter cases represent normal, but unwanted behavior from the human standpoint.

Category 2b includes behavioral patterns, which are also part of the normal ethogram, but which are shown in a different context. To assess this, it is always also important to consider the object towards which the behavior is directed. For example, tongue movements are without doubt normal when shown during feed intake or while expecting to be fed. Tongue playing in the barn on the other hand, during which the horse moves and twists its tongue within and outside the mouth, is to be regarded as aberrant behavior because it is exhibited in the absence of an object. Feed is neither present in the mouth, nor does the horse attempt to reach feed or other objects.

An example of an activity directed towards an inanimate object is grinding the teeth against bars (**68**). If this behavior is exhibited stereotypically over a longer time period, it has to be called aberrant. There are, however, two additional forms of this behavior: rubbing against bars as an attention-seeking behavior and rubbing against bars as a substitute activity. In both cases, however, the behavior is not shown stereotypically. Possible causes are learned behavior and a high level of excitement. It is then not aberrant behavior but rather undesired or normal behavior.

Self-mutilation, which is exhibited in the form of biting at the animal's own body, represents an activity directed towards an animate object but is shown in a different context. Biting as such is a normal behavioral pattern of horses, but is usually seen as part of social confrontation. If the attacks are directed against the horse's own body, one has to refer to this as an activity directed towards a living object shown in a different context, because a social function is not present.

The identification of whether a behavior is normal or aberrant, therefore, requires both adequate scientific knowledge and careful observation of the behavioral patterns exhibited. As discussed above, each type of aberrant behavior can be assigned to one category; knowledge of the categories, however, does not suffice to diagnose aberrant behavior definitively.

Synonymous terms used in the literature for the term "aberrant behavior" include the terms ethopathy ("Aberrations of instinctive behavior as a consequence of domestication" according to Lorenz) and behavioral anomaly. The English term "stereotypy" is also used to describe aberrant behavior.

In German, use of the word "stereotypy", however, formally restricts the wide field of aberrant behavior too much, and it also suggests that only behavioral patterns shown stereotypically represent aberrant behavior. It also needs to be considered that many forms of normal behavior are exhibited

68 Rubbing the teeth against bars as a displacement activity.

stereotypically. This is true for locomotion (walk, trot, canter) as well as chewing movements or the events during breeding, where this uniformity in itself is characteristic for species-specific behavior (Sambraus 1997a). Mason (1991) considers these facts in her definition. She describes stereotypical behavior as "behavioral patterns, which repeat themselves almost identically and without recognizable function". Not all forms of aberrant behavior follow this definition, however. Based on recent research, a function is not always lacking either, because the potential stress release, for example, represents a very useful function. Luescher *et al.* (1991) therefore suggest the term obsessive-compulsive disorder (OCD), which is used in human medicine. But even this term is problematic because the compulsive behavioral patterns it describes in humans are exhibited consciously. It is difficult to determine if an animal is behaving obsessively. In the following discussion, therefore, the term aberrant behavior according to the chosen definition shall be retained.

ADAPTATION STRATEGIES

As can be derived from the previous discussion, not every behavior that diverges considerably and continuously from normal behavior, is necessarily aberrant behavior. Extreme excitement or learned behavior can also be present. It is also possible that the altered behavior results from a successful adaptation to altered living conditions of horses in the care of humans. Under natural conditions, for example, horses ingest feed for at least 12 hours per day. If their nutritional requirements are met with small amounts of roughage and large amounts of concentrate, and if they are stalled on shavings, horses inevitably spend only a few hours a day eating, and spend the rest of the time standing or dozing. In their eating and resting behavior, therefore, considerable divergence from normal behavior is present with regard to frequency. This should, however, not be considered aberrant behavior but instead successful adaptation to the circumstances. It should be noted that not all horses achieve this adaptation.

Dunking of feed in water prior to or during eating, which is common among domestic horses, is also a behavioral adaptation (**69**). Soaking appears to make the feed more palatable, and to ease the chewing effort. In this

69 Soaking of feed in water is very popular among horses. It does, however, result in unhygienic conditions within the feed trough and waterer.

instance, however, the behavior's usefulness can be better understood from the standpoint of the horse than from that of the human.

If viewed from a different angle, some aberrant behavioral patterns can also be regarded as a type of adaptation strategy. Recent scientific findings in people as well as animals suggest that during certain aberrant behavioral patterns, a reduction of excitement (decrease in heart rate) or a filtering of outside stimuli (self-narcosis) occurs. The physiologic parameters suggest that the organism attempts to adapt to the adverse situation, which is denoted as "coping". It is possible that the coping mechanism at least temporarily offers an advantage to the animal, because it enables it to bear its inadequate living conditions better. This does not, however, change the fact that mistakes made in management and handling of the animal can exceed its adaptation capacity.

WHAT IS UNWANTED BEHAVIOR?

Unwanted behavior has to be differentiated from aberrant behavior. It is defined as behavior which is in concordance with the horse's normal behavior, but results in problems during management and use. Behavioral patterns shown with unwanted behavior are therefore part of the normal ethogram. Refusal during loading will be used as an example. It is normal behavior if the horse, whose ancestors were animals of the plains, does not voluntarily enter a "dark cave" without any escape route – in this case the horse trailer – and that it vehemently refuses if it is not sufficiently familiar with the person loading it and with the trailer. The same goes for bolting and shying. These two behaviors also represent normal behavior. Horses are flight animals. To be jumpy and to flee are normal behavior for them, and were essential for survival in the course of evolution. The unwanted behaviors listed in Table 6 are therefore to be differentiated from truly aberrant behavior. It does, however, need to be considered that some of these behaviors can also represent aberrant behavior if they considerably and continuously diverge from normal behavior and other causes such as pain, fear, conditioned behavior, or rank order problems can be excluded.

Definitions
- Aberrant behavior: behavior that with regard to modality, intensity or frequency diverges considerably and continuously from normal behavior.
- Unwanted behavior: this term denotes behavioral patterns, which in the broader sense are normal but pose problems in management and use of the horse.

Table 6 Unwanted behaviors

During handling and management	Under saddle or tack
• Refusal to be caught	• Bolting[2]
• Refusal to be tied	• Going against the bit
• Refusal to be led	• Shying[2]
• Refusal to be groomed	• Herd-boundness[2]
• Problems during shoeing[2]	• Bucking[2]
• Problems during loading[2]	• Rearing[2]
• Biting[1,2]	• Girthiness[2]
• Kicking[1,2]	• Tail lashing[2]
• Tearing of blankets	• Putting the tongue out or bringing the tongue over the bit[2]
• Rubbing the teeth against objects[2]	• Headshaking[2]
• Feed tossing	• Headshyness[2]
• Pawing[2]	• Lip smacking[2]
	• Teeth grinding[2]
	• Short-strideness
	• Brushing off the rider
	• Refusal to enter the starting gate[2]

[1] Directed against objects (box walls and so on), at other horses or people
[2] Differential diagnosis: behavioral abnormality

Categories of aberrant behavior

Classification of aberrant behavior

ETIOLOGIC CONSIDERATIONS

Classification of behavioral abnormalities is shown in Table 7. As has been indicated previously, the definition of aberrant behavior also includes behavioral patterns, which occur as a side effect of various diseases. Injuries of the musculoskeletal apparatus, for example fractures of bones of an extremity, can lead to altered behavior. The horse will in this case show pain in the form of lameness. Although this behavioral reaction provides relief and will contribute to healing, it also must be considered aberrant behavior according to the definition, and has to be classified as a symptomatic behavioral aberration (category 1) (**70**). Altered behavioral patterns, which almost inevitably occur with infectious diseases of the central nervous system (equine protozoal myelo-encephalitis (EPM), rabies, and so on), also have to be classified in this category.

70 Very frequent, intensive and long-lasting tongue and licking movements due to a suppurative tooth infection. Classification: symptomatic behavioral abnormality.

Table 7 Classification of behavioral abnormalities under etiologic aspects*
(Brummer 1978; Sambraus 1997a)

Category	Origin of the aberration	Example
1. Symptomatic	Accompanying sign of an organic disease	Frequent headshaking, e.g. with an ear infection
2. Organopathologic	Inborn or acquired organ defects	Cryptorchidism
3. Domestication-induced	Alterations of the central nervous system or endocrine system	Decreased flight impetus
4. Deficit-induced	The body is lacking certain substances; the behavior, however, does not eliminate the deficit	Geophagia (dirt eating) and coprophagia (manure eating) can be caused by a mineral deficiency
5. Management- and handling-induced	Past events, elicited by frustration, deprivation or conflicts	Cribbing, weaving, misdirected imprinting, self-mutilation

*The five categories are not always strictly separable. In particular, certain circumstances can predispose to management- and handling-induced behavioral aberrations. Weaving (category 5), for example, occurs almost exclusively in warmbloods and thoroughbreds and has never been observed in heavy draft horses. The varying excitability of different breeds is a result of artificial selection (category 3).

Congenital (inborn) or acquired organ defects (category 2) can also be the cause of aberrant behavior or of so-called organopathologic behavioral aberrations (**71**). Cryptorchidism is an example of a congenital organ defect leading to aberrant behavior, while the loss of an eye is an example of an acquired defect.

Behavioral alterations can further be the result of domestication (category 3), in which case they are called endogenous behavioral aberrations. These include behavioral patterns that differ between domestic animals and the original wild form (p.19). An example in domestic horses is the decreased motivation for flight compared to non-domesticated equids.

A deficit of a certain substance can also lead to aberrant behavior (category 4). Wood chewing in horses, for example, is sometimes caused by a deficiency of trace elements (Meyer 1995); the more common cause is insufficient dietary roughage. The altered behavior does not necessarily indicate this specific deficit and does not help to remedy it.

Category 5 includes behavioral aberrations that are caused by inadequate management and inappropriate handling. These are behavioral aberrations in the true sense of the word. The following discussion will particularly concern them. Prior to diagnosing aberrant behavior belonging in this category, however, it is necessary to rule out aberrations in categories 1 through 4, because they require a different therapeutic approach.

MANAGEMENT- AND HANDLING-INDUCED BEHAVIORAL ABNORMALITIES

Behavioral aberrations caused by management and handling are true behavioral aberrations. Worldwide studies performed in recent years prove that approximately 10% of all horses show these behavioral aberrations, while this percentage can be higher or lower depending on breed, management system, and use of the horse. "Highly bred" breeds such as thoroughbreds and Arabians are particularly affected, while ponies and draft horses are less affected.

Behavioral aberrations which occur in conjunction with inadequate management and inappropriate handling are often residual-reactive. This means that even if the original cause is removed, the behavioral divergence from the norm remains. In contrast to categories 1 through 4, behavioral aberrations in this group do not occur in free-roaming horses, but only in domesticated horses or horses kept in captivity. This is attributable to the fact that under human care, a balance between the situation eliciting the behavior and the animals' inner drive is not always present. Under natural conditions, on the other hand, this is generally the case. If, for example, a horse in the wild feels the need to eat, it can always search for food and it will always, even under the most meager conditions, find something edible (**72**). This opportunity is not always given under our management conditions. A horse subjected to rationed feeding will after a short time not have any feed left, and it will have to wait for several hours until the next feed. Under these circumstances, aberrations from the balanced situation can arise and they can be severe enough to exceed the horse's capacity for adaptation. A possible result is the escape into aberrant behavior (**73**). For this reason, behavioral aberrations caused by management and handling mistakes also are relevant under animal welfare aspects.

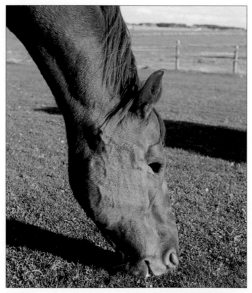

71 Behavioral alterations caused by loss of an eye are among the organopathologic behavioral abnormalities.

Classification of management- and handling-induced behavioral abnormalities

In ethology, behavioral aberrations resulting from mistakes made in management and handling are assigned to certain functional areas. This has a certain didactic value and it also emphasizes the fact that most behavioral aberrations are found in easily activated functional areas such as eating and locomotion behavior. This classification should not, however, suggest that a behavioral aberration is caused by a deficit in the corresponding functional area. Cribbing, for example, which has to be assigned to the functional area of eating behavior, is therefore not necessarily caused exclusively by deprivation in this functional area. Many other reasons for this aberration exist (p.138). The classification in functional areas in the following discussion is meant to provide an aid to help the reader gain an overview of the different behavioral aberrations. Table 8 summarizes the most important behavioral aberrations.

> Behavioral aberrations due to management and handling mistakes are often residual-reactive, which means they remain present despite correction of the causative factors.

Table 8 Management- and handling-induced behavioral abnormalities

Functional area	Behavioral abnormality
Eating behavior	Cribbing Tongue playing Excessive wood chewing[2] Rubbing the teeth against bars and bar biting[1]
Exercise behavior	Weaving Stall walking, fence walking, figure-eight walking Excessive pawing[1] Stereotypical kicking against stall walls[1]
Social behavior	Abnormal social imprinting Self-mutilation Heightened aggressiveness[1]
Comfort behavior	Stereotypical tail rubbing[3] Stereotypical headtossing or shaking[1,3]

Differential diagnosis:
[1] Unwanted behavior
[2] Deficit-induced behavior
[3] Symptomatic behavioral abnormality

72 Under natural conditions, horses can always find something to eat and satisfy their chewing need as these wild horses are doing on a plateau in Sardinia.

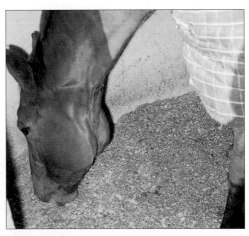

73 The chewing need of horses kept in stalls bedded with shavings and fed in rations often remains unsatisfied. Aberrant behavior such as eating of shavings is a potential consequence.

Causes and triggers of problem behavior

Behavioral aberrations

WHEN DOES A BEHAVIORAL ABERRATION BECOME MANIFEST?

Behavioral aberrations due to management and handling mistakes do not manifest immediately. The causative and predisposing factor in their original development is an environment which insufficiently meets horses' requirements. Mistakes in this area are frequently made unknowingly because – often with the best intentions – one uses human needs as a guideline. For this reason, evolution and the ethogram were discussed in depth in the first part of this book and the essential requirements of the horse were highlighted. The close relationship between the individual management systems and the occurrence of behavioral aberrations has by now been proven unequivocally. Scientific studies from Canada, Great Britain, Italy, Sweden, and Germany have been published in recent years, which demonstrate that lack of social contact, insufficient exercise, lack of roughage, and lack of environmental stimuli and opportunity for play can lead to deprivation, frustration, and conflict in the horse. The resulting emotional build-up in return lays the groundwork for future behavioral aberrations (p.26).

The type and use of the horse plays an additional role. Dressage and race horses show behavioral aberrations more frequently than those used for endurance competitions. A definitive association between the development of behavioral aberrations and use of the horse is, however, not possible because aside from educational and training methods, management of horses in these performance categories also frequently differs from that of others.

It is possible that there is a genetic predisposition for the development of behavioral aberrations in the form of a recessive inheritance (Vecchiotti and Galanti 1986; Marsden 1995), although it is not proven. Thoroughbreds, Arabians or other highly bred breeds are particularly susceptible, while draft horses and ponies are less predisposed, and it is possible to show that certain stallion lines are affected with significantly increased frequency. A genetically based predisposition could also offer an explanation for the observation that only certain horses react to deficits in management and handling with behavioral aberrations, while others do not, although they are exposed to the same conditions.

CAUSES AND TRIGGERS OF BEHAVIORAL ABERRATIONS

Causes of the first-time occurrence of a behavioral aberration are most likely drastic experiences in a negative sense (Radtke 1985; Sambraus and Rappold 1991). Proven examples of such an "initiating trauma" are: abrupt weaning from the dam, sudden commencement of intense training, overly demanding training, drastic management changes (transfer to a box stall following previous group management with access to pasture), temporary isolation or extended stall rest due to disease. These abrupt changes for the worse have particularly far-reaching consequences if they occur during juvenile development.

Behavioral aberrations

Predisposition
- Inadequate management.
- Inappropriate handling.
- "Highly bred" horses.
- Genetic predisposition.

Causes
- Drastic negative experiences.

Triggers
- Activities in the environment, which are associated with an increased level of excitement in the horse.

The cause for the first-time occurrence of a behavioral aberration must be differentiated from the actual trigger. The latter denotes events which trigger exhibition of a behavioral aberration in a horse that has already developed it. In particular, triggers are events that are associated with an increased level of excitement in the affected horse, such as feeding, barn work, people traffic, saddling, grooming, and so on. At night, when everything is quiet, behavioral aberrations are rarely observed, although some behavioral aberrations such as stall walking and cribbing do occur in the absence of people (Houpt 1998).

Unwanted behavior

PREDISPOSITION

Unwanted behavioral patterns are usually, as Zeeb (1997) said, "harm-avoiding reactions". Their occurrence is, just as that of behavioral aberrations, influenced by certain predisposing factors. For certain characteristic features such as need for exercise, flight motivation, fearfulness, and excitability, for example, evidence of heritability exists.

In order to identify the cause of a behavioral aberration, it is therefore helpful to assess the horse according to its character traits (p.20). Generally, "highly bred" sensitive horses tend increasingly towards panic and overreaction, while those with draft horse influence primarily show behavioral patterns based on stubbornness and laziness. Conformational deficits can also predispose to unwanted behavior. One has to recognize these and accept the horse within the limits of its abilities, or find an alterative use for it. Horses with conformational deficits are frequently unable to perform as they are asked to (**74**). They are therefore overwhelmed in a certain sense. The avoidance behavior they show is often mistakenly interpreted as refractoriness. For example, horses with a short back are predisposed to tenseness of the musculature if they are ridden intensively in a dressage-type manner without having been adequately warmed up. One way to show their pain is by bucking.

Management deficits in particular predispose to unwanted behavior. High concentrate feeding, lack of exercise, lack of social contact and a non-stimulating environment virtually provoke temper problems such as bucking, rearing, and bolting. This was discussed in detail in Part B.

CAUSES AND TRIGGERS OF UNWANTED BEHAVIOR

Fear (**75**) and pain are the major causes of unwanted behavior. Aside from diseases, the latter is caused by an improper riding technique or improper influence during driving, or by equipment deficits. Pain, for example, can be caused by an ill-fitting saddle, a "harsh" bit or a hard hand, or by improperly fastened side reins. Horses can only communicate this pain with the language of "movements and reactions". If, for example, a horse causes problems during bridle placement or frequently shakes its head, this can be a sign of tension of the neck muscles. If it ventroflexes during saddling, walks off to the side or splints its back, pain in the back region has to be considered. An alert horse owner can detect pain by observation of the horse early on and can altogether avoid development of unwanted behavior by timely treatment.

74 Horses with physical deficits are predisposed to unwanted behavior if they are asked to perform tasks that exceed their physical capabilities.

75 Flight or an attempt to flee in frightening situations is normal horse behavior. Fear is one of the main causes of unwanted behavior.

Fear is the inborn reaction of the flight animal horse to unknown situations. It is enhanced by conflict situations, deprivation, bad experiences and pain. Furthermore, a close correlation to rank order exists. If protection by a higher-ranked animal or by the "dominant animal" in the form of the human being is missing, fear in horses is preprogrammed. For this reason, animals of low rank are particularly fearful, even more so if they are without a leader. Sensitive horses, in particular Arabians, frequently react with panic-like fear if they are given no possibility for escape. They react similarly when they are asked to perform tasks that they do not understand. In this sense, handling methods based on cognitive learning exhibited by humans overwhelm the animals' learning capacity. Typical reactions shown by fearful horses are herd-boundness, bolting and shying. If one tries to hold them back with force, the fear-induced excitement will unload "upwards" in the form of bucking and rearing.

Rank order problems play a role in almost all unwanted behaviors. A horse will always attempt to establish a rank order and, if the human being allows it, will take on the dominant position. The question of rank will then be dealt with in a horse manner, which includes means such as biting and kicking that are extremely uncomfortable for the human being or are even perceived as malicious. For the horse, however, they are tried and tested measures according to its inborn behavior. Rank order problems can arise due to ignorance or ignoring of horse-specific behavior, insufficient expertise in handling of horses, or due to mistakes made during basic training of the horse. Continuous repetition of the same exercise can also lead to unwanted behavioral patterns. Particularly for horses of high rank that are quick at learning, traditional training methods will quickly become too undemanding. Typical problems observed in horses with unresolved rank order issues or in those dominant to the human are unwillingness to be led or caught, biting and kicking directed against the person, and other directed defense reactions.

Ignorance of the learning behavior of animals or thoughtlessness and negligence often result in a virtual training of unwanted behaviors. If, for example, a horse withdraws its hoof during shoeing and receives a carrot, with the intention of providing a distraction or to calm the horse, this represents exactly the wrong time point. The horse is being rewarded for withdrawing the hoof and it will consequently repeat it the next time. The same goes for kicking against stall walls, rubbing against bars and pawing if the cause is attention-seeking behavior. Even the approach and scolding is rewarding because the horse receives attention. A horse generally learns very quickly to prevail in its behavior if the human allows it.

The trigger of unwanted behavior is the recurrence of the same situation or similar circumstances that originally caused the behavior to occur. Predisposing factors can have an enhancing effect.

Unwanted behavior

Predisposition
- Inadequate management.
- Physical deficits.
- Individual character traits.

Causes
- Pain.
- Fear.
- Unresolved rank order.
- Learned behavior.

Triggers
- Recurrence of the situation.

Diagnosis of problem behavior

Approach

For anamnestic purposes, it is useful to make a checklist and use it to accumulate all relevant information (Table 9). This way, one also has a constant reminder of the data that have yet to be collected. The anamnesis could, for example, take place as follows:

During an in depth conversation, information about the aberrant behavior is collected. At first and without making any judgement, one takes down the description of the horse's behavioral pattern given by the owner or another person familiar with the horse. Detailed questions are essential for the detection of causative factors. These include:

Table 9 Diagnostic approach to problem behavior (behavioral aberrations and unwanted behaviors)

1. Description of the behavioral pattern	• Without judgement. • Directed questions.
2. Previous history	• Raising. • Training. • Use. • Management.
3. Current management and use	• Management system. • Feeding. • Other management factors. • Daily use.
4. Health status and diagnosis of pain	• Clinical diagnosis (veterinarian). • Diagnosis of pain by palpation. • Evaluation of possible painful influences (equipment, riding style and so on).
5. Evaluation of the horse	• Conformation. • Character.
6. Personal evaluation	In the barn by observation, if indicated with the help of a video camera. During exercise under the following circumstances: • Without human influence. • In hand. • At work with the owner/handler. • At work with an expert.

- Since when did the conspicuous behavior exist?
- How does it manifest itself?
- What is its progression?
- Under which circumstances did it first appear?
- What elicits it now, what influences it?
- Does it impair use or health of the horse?
- Which therapeutic attempts have already been made, by whom and with what success?

Additional questions regarding upbringing of the horse, course of training, type of use and previous ownership may also provide valuable clues as to which mistakes or deficits led to the behavior. Knowledge of whether the aberrant or unwanted behavior was acquired through events during juvenile development or later in life is of great importance for therapy and prognosis.

Finally, information about the management system, feeding, daily routine and management as well as the daily use has to be collected. This information serves to evaluate whether the horse-specific needs are currently met or if a deprivation exists or the disturbed or unwanted behavior is caused by frequent frustration or conflict situations. To verify this information objectively, inspection of the barn is important.

It is essential to assess the horse's health status. For this reason, a thorough veterinary examination is probably required in most cases. Pain can additionally be diagnosed by use of appropriate massage techniques (Denoix and Pailloux 2000). Examples will be given in the following section. Data concerning the current vaccination and deworming status should also be collected as they have significance for the establishment of differential diagnoses. For example, excessive tail rubbing can be caused by infection with pinworms (*O. equi*).

Information regarding breed (pedigree), age and gender not only serve identification purposes but also provide valuable information regarding a potential genetic predisposition for the shown behavior. For this reason, the horse's physique should also be evaluated for conformational deficits and the horse assessed according to its character features (p.20).

When evaluating problem behavior, one should never rely solely upon information provided by the owner. It is essential to personally observe the behavioral pattern in question. If the horse does not readily exhibit it, one can attempt to provoke the aberrant behavior with certain triggers. If this is not successful, it is useful to install a video camera in the barn. With its help, the horse can be monitored for a longer period of time without disturbance. The camera should be sufficiently light sensitive and have a quick picture search function.

Problem behavior under saddle or tack is best evaluated by observing the horse in a variety of situations. For example, one can at first analyze its behavior when being turned loose in a run, then during groundwork, when worked by the owner, and finally when worked by an experienced horse expert.

POSTURE AND FACIAL EXPRESSION AS A DIAGNOSTIC AID

Many conspicuous behavioral patterns in horses are attributable to pain, fear and sometimes aggression. For this reason, one should always thoroughly evaluate the horse's posture and facial expression when searching for the cause.

HOW IS PAIN RECOGNIZED?

A general clinical examination by a veterinarian is recommended prior to beginning any behavioral therapy. Some behavioral changes, however, can be used to detect pain for oneself.

Unequivocal signs of acute pain are changes in the horse's movements or body posture. Altered activities such as pawing and kicking against the abdomen indicate visceral pain. Movements of the head and neck towards the body as well as body movements (lying down/getting up, rolling) and restlessness (repeated interruption of feed intake) indicate the degree of acute pain. Favoring of a leg (lameness) indicates painful diseases of the extremities. Further indicators of pain are: insecure stance, stiff gait, reduced willingness to move, increased recumbency time, apathy, unusual posture, and sweating. An introverted facial expression and glazed eyes are additional certain signs of pain (**76**). Depending on the type of disease, some horses show their pain merely by an increased reluctance (e.g. frequent tail lashing). The repertoire of pain-induced refusal behavior extends from a fearful facial expression to increased aggression. In the case of escalating refusal behavior, a painful process or disease generally has to be considered.

Even an alteration in the normal activity rhythm can indicate potential pain. Many horses, for example, will stop eating at the very beginning of colic. Leftover concentrate should therefore always be regarded as a serious alarm signal.

Chronic pain is much more difficult to detect than the acute form. Indicators of chronic pain are: decreased appetite, weight loss, dull hair coat, muscle wasting, apathy, altered facial expression, or gradually altered personality.

76 Acute pain: "pain face" with turned back ears, introverted expression and a tense mouth in a horse with an extremely painful distortion of the knee.

77 Chronic pain: healthy horse. It exhibits a clear and attentive expression and a shiny haircoat.

78 Chronic pain: sick horse, 3 months later (squamous cell carcinoma of the gums). The horse has an introverted look. The haircoat appears dull.

The change from a previously spirited horse (**77**) to an animal that is increasingly unwilling to move, for example, indicates a chronic painful process and has to be taken seriously (**78**).

Unusual muscle tone, commonly known as "tenseness", is a further important indicator of pain in horses. It most often manifests in the form of tense neck and back musculature and the tension can even extend all the way to the tail. Tense movements of the upper and lower jaw along with teeth grinding or chewing movements can also indicate a painful process.

At times, pain can be detected by the so-called "pain face". It is, however, not easily detected by the untrained person, and appears to not always correlate with the degree of pain. A definite sign is a complete lack of ear movements. The ears are usually turned slightly backwards. Horses get "small" eyes and their look appears dull and detached. The nostrils may be narrowed to small slits or curled, and will be twisted with each wave of pain. A tense mouth and clenched teeth can also indicate pain. They are not, however, a certain indicator of pain, as tension is also observed with fear.

Vocalization cannot be used in horses to draw conclusions about pain. The horse does not have a specific cry as the human being, the dog, the rabbit and other warm-blooded animals do. Moaning is not a pain-specific sound, either, but is non-specific and indicates general effort. It can be heard in painful situations, such as with colic, but also with activities such as rolling that are thought of as pleasant. There are, however, numerous reports of horses exhibiting a painful cry in extreme situations. It supposedly sounds untypical for horses and neither resembles whinnying nor moaning. As it is only exhibited in exceptional situations and horses with even the worst case of colic such as a volvulus (twist of the intestine) do not exhibit it, it cannot be regarded as a specific pain cry.

Avoidance reactions of the horse during

manual palpation are a valuable clue to the presence of painful processes. Appropriate techniques can be acquired. A useful example is the Tellington-Touch, which is taught through books and videotapes, and in seminars. The applied pressure should vary because in some regions, firm pressure does not evoke a reaction while light pressure does. Reactions that indicate pain are: throwing the head up, starting, giving way, moving or jumping off to the side, kicking with a leg or lashing the tail and other defensive movements. A decisive factor for the success and interpretability of the examination is that it takes place at a location without distractions. If this is not the case, behavior and treatment cannot be unequivocally related.

Important clues can be obtained from pain-related physiological parameters, although they are not obvious in every case. With pain, heart and respiratory rate as well as body temperature are increased. Furthermore, pain evokes endocrine processes, which are reflected in blood and saliva. These values, however, are only valid indicators of pain in conjunction with other signs.

With acute pain, the sympathoadrenal system is activated. This results in an increase of body temperature, blood pressure, heart and respiratory rate, and in mydriasis as well as increased muscle tone and enhanced sweat production. Furthermore, a number of pain- or stress-induced metabolic reactions including endocrinologic processes are enhanced. Measurable parameters are, among others, ACTH and glucocorticoids, angiotensin II, catecholamines (adrenalin, noradrenalin), vasopressin, endorphin and enkephalins, vasoactive peptide and substance P. In evaluating horses that were assessed clinically to experience moderate to severe pain, Zierz (1993) found a definite relationship between the level of pain and the degree of catecholamine release. Following a point system, he developed a chart for the quantification of acute pain in horses, which includes four physiologic (heart and respiratory rate, body temperature, sweat production) and six ethologic parameters (pawing/unrest, favoring of extremities, painful facial expression, teeth grinding/chewing movements, turning towards the diseased body part, lying down/rising/rolling). These were weighted differently and correlated with the adrenalin and noradrenalin concentration in blood plasma.

In evaluating pain, the situation should be considered. Fear can potentiate pain but can also suppress it completely. Horses probably also show individual differences in pain perception. The breed should also be considered. "Highly bred" horses such as Arabians are particularly communicative. In draft horses and ponies, on the other hand, pain is frequently less easy to recognize from their facial expression alone.

HOW IS FEAR RECOGNIZED?

Extreme fear is easily recognized in horses. Signs are: widened nostrils, rolling of the eyes, nervous movements, sweating, and a tucked under tail. Fear of lesser extent is more difficult to recognize. Often, animals will merely show a stretched out upper lip (out of the context of comfort behavior), a tightly shut "tense" mouth and laid back ears without any ear movement (**79**). Fear of the rider can, among other signs, be recognized in this manner. Care should be taken not to confuse laid back ears due to fear with the ear position shown when the horse is submissive. In the latter case, however, the ears are rather turned to the side while additional indicators of unease such as tense facial expression are absent and the horse moves with the desired degree of relaxation.

79 The lengthened upper lip and the stiffly turned back ears signal fear of the horse trailer.

Signs of pain

- Altered behavior.
- Acute pain: altered motions and body posture.
- Chronic pain: personality change, apathy.
- Disturbances of the overall well-being
- Acute pain: increased heart and respiratory rate and body temperature, sweating.
- Chronic pain: weight loss, dull hair coat.
- Unusual muscle tone (tenseness).
- Avoidance reactions during palpation.
- "Pain face" (ear position, nostrils, eyes).

80 The "threatening face" is characterized by turned back ears, narrowed nostrils and pulled back corners of the mouth (Goldschmidt-Rothschild and Tschanz 1978).

Conspicuous general signs of fear are tense movements all over. They first start at the mouth and neck. A tense horse initially loses the ability to move the upper and lower jaw. Chewing movements are aborted. If tension rises, it spreads from the front to the back. The horse moves more and more stiffly, its gaits are lacking a free forward movement, the tail head is angled and the rear end is tucked under. With overwhelming fear and lack of an escape route, horses become completely unable to move. They virtually freeze. Frequent elimination of unformed manure or urine squirting also indicates fear. While being ridden, high carriage of the horse's head may indicate fear. The animal switches its view to far vision. This means that in the current situation, the rider's dominance does not suffice to give the horse an adequate feeling of security. Some signs of fear are also shown in painful situations. These include tension, lack of ear movements, sweating and increased heart and respiratory rate. This can have a bearing on the differential diagnosis.

HOW IS AGGRESSION RECOGNIZED?
The "threatening face" of horses is obvious: laid-back ears, which are pinned back further the more intensively the horse threatens, narrowed nostrils and drawn back corners of the mouth (**80**).

Aggressive forms of threatening behavior are head swinging, biting threats and actual biting as well as charging and forehand striking with simultaneous threatening grimacing. Defensive forms, which are still very effective, are rear leg threats and rear leg kicks (**81**). Horses mostly threaten humans with this defensive gesture, or they merely show their "threatening face". With pain and fear, defensive threats also prevail.

Aggressive threats directed towards humans are mostly shown by stallions or very highly ranked horses, if the rank order situation is not settled clearly. Other than that, attacks aimed at humans are usually harm-avoiding reactions, which can be attributed to fear or pain. A special case is aggressive behavior shown by horses suffering from misdirected sexual or social imprinting, which has to be considered a severe behavioral aberration.

TYPES OF EXPRESSION SHOWN BY HORSES UNDER A RIDER'S INFLUENCE
The expression of horses mirrors their well-being. For this reason, knowledge and evaluation of the facial expression and body posture play a particularly important role in the evaluation of the influence of a rider. According to its expression, the experienced observer can

81 Aggressive and defensive forms of threatening (Goldschmidt-Rothschild and Tschanz 1978).

1 Threatening swinging: with a threatening expression and a closed mouth but without moving, the horse swings its head towards the threatened horse nearby.

3 Biting threats: the threatening expression is intensified. The mouth is opened, the head is aimed towards the threatened horse (almost horizontally). The teeth may be visible, the neck is swung sideways. Sometimes, a few charging steps are taken towards the threatened horse. During biting, a body part of the attacked horse is gripped with the teeth and bitten while exhibiting the strongest possible threatening expression.

2 Charging: the attacker moves towards another horse with a threatening expression. Neck carriage above the horizontal line, head stretched out forward. Gait: walk, trot or gallop. Charging occurs from a distance of 3–30 m (10–100 ft).

4 Striking: with an aggressive act, the face shows a threatening expression, otherwise it does not (e.g. with ritualized behaviors). The body weight is shifted to one front leg, the other leg is swung forward and is placed back on the ground with the entire sole. In some cases, both front legs are swung forward and stomped down successively, or the horse may rear on its hindlegs and strike with both forelegs.

5 Rear leg kicking threats: the face shows a threatening expression. The attacker's hindlegs are directed towards the threatened horse, the tail is tucked under or is moved wildly back and forth. One or both hindlegs can be lifted and put back down without being stretched out. Kicking threats also occur by backwards or sideways kicking with a threatening expression.

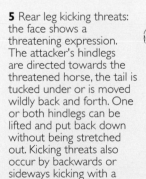

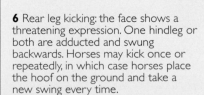

6 Rear leg kicking: the face shows a threatening expression. One hindleg or both are adducted and swung backwards. Horses may kick once or repeatedly, in which case horses place the hoof on the ground and take a new swing every time.

draw conclusions about fear, pain, and aggression (**82**) as opposed to looseness, relaxation, and well-being (Table 10) of the horse. Figure **83** summarizes the most important pertinent behavioral characteristics. The most common refusal movements of horses against the influence of the rider are summarized in Table 11. The more vehemently the horse resists, the more frequently several of these behavioral patterns can be observed simultaneously. For example, pinning back of the ears, tail lashing and going against the bit are frequently observed in combination.

ASSESSING EMOTIONS

Without question, higher developed animals feel fear and pain. This has been proven by neurophysiologic studies and it is evidenced by the objectively noticeable behavioral and expression patterns described above such as specific facial expressions, trembling or an altered body posture. But how should these be assessed? One would not do justice to horses by basing the assessment on one's own or human emotions and transferring them to the horse. The conclusion "I like to sleep in a warm bed, therefore my horse should also be warm at night" would be wrong. Or "I only eat small amounts three times a day, therefore it suffices for my horse to eat little feed, but it has to be the best (most concentrated)". The same goes for fear, pain, and other emotions. We therefore cannot conclude that horses confronted with situations that do not evoke fear in us, will also react calmly. For example, riding past a wild boar enclosure for the first time may not evoke fear in us – we recognize the function of the fence – but may result in a panic-like flight reaction in horses. The same is true for pain. We cannot assess how painful, for example, a broken leg is for a horse. According to our imagination and experience it must be very painful, at least we would not want to move if we had a broken leg. Not infrequently, however, one can observe horses grazing without any particular expression of pain despite a fractured extremity.

It can generally be assumed that horses experience pain, fear, and other emotions, which is called conclusion by analogy (Sambraus 1997b), however, anthropomorphic thinking is the wrong way to assess these.

It is undisputed that horses know negative as well as positive emotions. It would be wrong, however, to interpret these in an anthropomorphic fashion.

Table 10 Features of relaxation and looseness (German Rider's Association 1994; Schnitzer 1996)

- Content facial expression (ear movements, eyes).
- Rhythmically swinging back.
- Closed, busy (chomping) mouth.
- Carried tail, swinging with the body's movement.
- Blowing as a sign of inner relaxation.

Table 11 Defensive movements of horses in response to the rider's influence (Pfeil-Rotermund and Zeeb 1994; Caanitz 1996)

- Ears turned backwards or sideways.
- Tail lashing.
- Head and neck tossing.
- "Going against the bit".
- Visible teeth.
- Opened mouth.
- Violent teeth grinding.

82 A wide open mouth and visible teeth indicate the horse's defensiveness against the rider's painful influence.

83 Expressions of horses under the rider's influence (Waring 1983; Rees 1986; Kiley-Worthington 1989; Zeitler-Feicht 1994).

1 Ears

Ear movement: attentiveness and "willingness to cooperate", auditory orientation, watchfulness
No ear movement: great fear, pain

(a) Turned forward:
"Unison" with the
rider's aids
"Willingness to
cooperate"
Attentiveness
directed forwards

(b) Turned sideways:
Insecurity
Attentiveness directed
sideways

(c) Turned backwards:
Fear and subordination
Discomfort and
defensiveness
Pain, e.g. due to mistakes
in use of the reins ("see-
sawing")
Attentiveness directed
backwards

(d) Laid back flat:
Aggression
Massive defense against
the rider's influence
Great fear

2 Nostrils and mouth region

Slight chewing movements with a closed
mouth: looseness, inner relaxation

(a) Mouth closed with
lengthened nostrils:
Attentiveness
Fear

(b) Mouth tightly closed
with lengthened and
widened nostrils:
Fear

(c) Widened nostrils:
Great effort
Excitement
Fear

(d) Narrowed
nostrils with pulled
back corners of the
nose:
Pain
Discomfort

3 Tail

Violent tail lashing: fear, pain, defence against rider's influence

(a) Raised tail:
Great excitement
Great need for exercise
Signal function for play
(bucking)

(b) Tail carried:
Moderate excitement
Need for exercise
Attentive

(c) Tail hanging:
No excitement
No need for exercise
Pain

(d) Tail tucked
under:
Fear

Basics of handling and learning psychology

A primary prerequisite for prevention and therapy of problem behavior in horses is a way of handling that is adapted to natural horse behavior. For this reason, only those behavioral patterns, movements and performances that the individual horse is provided with naturally can be demanded during training and use. Based on this foundation one can achieve stress-free learning if one understands learning behavior of horses and designs the work accordingly. In doing so, it is only of advantage, and not a mistake as one can sometimes hear, to utilize the natural tendencies and needs of the horse. The following basic rules are valid for all disciplines within the sport of riding and are independent of the training method.

How does a horse learn?

When training horses, it should be kept in mind that they do not have the ability to be scholars in the human sense. Many horse owners do not realize this. Those learning processes that appear easy from a human standpoint often pose insurmountable problems for animals. The first prerequisite for working with horses is to be aware of which learning processes a horse understands and which it does not. Only humans and some of the higher developed primates, such as chimpanzees, are capable of "insightful learning"; other species, such as the dog, are capable of this to a much lesser degree and horses only in exceptional cases. This learning process is based on cognitive processes.

The classical experiment for "insightful learning" in monkeys is carried out as follows: the monkey is confronted with the new situation of a banana hanging from the ceiling. It wants to eat the banana but cannot reach it. It subsequently uses several boxes that are present in the cage, puts them on top of each other and reaches the banana in this manner. For horses, the experiment is modified by placing a full feed bowl behind a long fence in an unfamiliar arena. If it purposefully looked for a passage, it would be capable of cognitive thinking. It does not do this, however, but instead runs up and down the fence excitedly trying to get to the feed. This should not result in horses being called stupid, however, because problem solving in this manner was not necessary in the course of phylogenesis.

Horses learn by habituation, by conditioning (operant and classical conditioning have to be differentiated), by imitation and by imprinting. All learning processes, except for imprinting, are reversible.

HABITUATION

Habituation is one of the simplest forms of learning. With repeated application of the same stimulus, which is associated neither with positive nor with negative effects, the extent of the animal's reaction decreases. This is a useful learning process because it prevents the animal from responding to harmless environmental stimuli by a fearful reaction throughout its entire life (**84**). On the contrary, repeated occurrence of the stimulus results in weakening

84 If foals get used to various objects in a playful manner early on, they are less afraid as adults.

of the reaction over time, or habituation. For the herd-living horse, the reaction of the other group members plays an important role in addition to personal experience. Habituation is not, however, attributable to physical fatigue, but instead to raising of the stimulus threshold. For example, one can take away a horse's fear of motor vehicles by keeping it in a pasture next to a busy road together with companions that are already used to this situation and show no fear reaction whatsoever. Because the other horses' behavior has a calming effect on the horse and the horse has neither positive nor negative experiences with the motor vehicles, habituation will occur. If, on the other hand, one puts a saddle on a horse for the first time and allows it to buck until it stops because it is worn out, this behavior is not attributable to habituation but instead to physical exhaustion. As a general rule, learning by habituation is reversible. Lack of repetition or a one-time bad experience can suffice to evoke the original response again.

OPERANT CONDITIONING

This type of learning is also called "learning by trial and error" or "learning by success". It is based on a behavioral pattern being acquired by satisfaction of a need, or a reward (**85**). For example, a tied horse plays with the rope, the knot suddenly opens and the horse is free. It can go and graze and therefore receives a reward (positive reinforcement). This positive experience increases the likelihood for recurrence of the behavior as soon as the horse is in a similar situation. If attempts to loosen the knot are unsuccessful or if a negative experience is associated with playing with the rope, however, the behavior is less likely to recur. In horse training, operant conditioning is frequently employed. To do so, every step in the right direction is initially rewarded. Later, only those behaviors which come close to the desired exercise, are rewarded.

CLASSICAL CONDITIONING

In the type of learning referred to as classical conditioning, a novel stimulus is incorporated in the evoking mechanism of a certain behavior, and finally evokes the behavior by itself. In this manner, the animal learns to associate a novel signal with a familiar action. An example is the anticipation of food evoked by the rattling of feed buckets. Originally, it is only evoked by the sight of feed buckets, and the rattling is a neutral stimulus. If the horse repeatedly hears bucket rattling prior to feeding, however, an association is made. In the end, rattling of the feed buckets suffices to evoke the anticipation of feed and the desire to eat; the sight of feed is no longer required. Pawing and whinnying prior to feeding are attributable to this learning process, because even the association of an activity with a certain time of day is enough to evoke the behavior. Many behavioral patterns in horses are learned by classical conditioning. The method is also very useful in training or therapy of unwanted behavior. Horses that are afraid, for example, can be "re-tuned" internally and calmed by using a sound that is associated with feed.

Learning by classical conditioning refers to the evoking of reflex-like reactions that are not consciously controlled, and therefore employs subconscious pathways. It is said that by using this method, horses can be made to learn involuntarily. This is, however, limited, because without a certain motivation, a subconscious biological reaction cannot be evoked. With complete satiety, for example, the need to eat is no longer present.

85 Operant conditioning ("learning by success") is the cause if a horse learns to open its stall door.

IMITATION

During learning by imitation or observation, visually or acoustically perceived behavioral patterns of a companion are copied. It may be that the foal learns to eat grass and drink water in this way, by watching its dam (86). Imitation can also be used successfully during training. For example, one can teach a young, inexperienced horse to cross through water by letting an absolutely dependable horse take the lead. The young horse then generally only has to be asked to follow the other one. Imitation must not be confused with social facilitation. With the latter, the behavioral pattern is already known, while the animal acquires a new behavioral pattern when learning by imitation. Social facilitation is present, for example, when horses roll after one another.

IMPRINTING

Imprinting is a special type of learning. It takes place during a species-specific, mostly fixed and phylogenetically preprogrammed time period (sensitive or critical period) and generally results in irreversible behavioral alterations. Processes that are based on imprinting include object imprinting, sexual imprinting, and feed imprinting. With the first type, the foal learns to recognize its dam and therefore its own species by means of olfactory, auditory, and visual sensory impressions. This is indispensable because a newborn foal does not know which species it belongs to or that it is a horse (p.53). Misdirected imprinting occurs when the foal's contact with its dam is disturbed during the critical period and the foal becomes fixated more intensively on another object such as a human being. Until the end of this time period, which in foals can last from about half an hour up to 2 days, imprinting can be redirected to a certain degree.

Factors influencing the willingness to learn

LEARNING TRAINING AND MOTIVATION

The terms learning ability and willingness to learn have to be differentiated. The learning ability of a horse is genetically predetermined. Whether this ability will develop to its full extent depends on the specific training method. An animal with little learning ability but good conditioning can therefore master the same tasks as a more gifted horse without appropriate training. As a general rule, the more animals learn, the easier they learn. This means that the

86 By imitating their dams and other horses, foals learn to discern edible feeds from non-edible ones.

more experiences a horse has in the accomplishment of conditioned reactions, the sooner it will understand the aids and the more refined and lighter those can become. The learning ability should be challenged as early as possible because learning success is greater during youth than with old age.

The learning ability of horses differs individually depending on genetic predisposition. Differences between different breeds and certain stallion lines have been proven. Studies by Erasimus (1988) in Lipizzaner and warmblood stallions, and other studies, showed that no correlation exists between the horse's rank and its learning ability or suitability for riding, although this is often claimed in practice. Learning experiments also did not reveal differences in learning ability between genders.

Stallions are, however, easier to motivate for certain tasks which results in an earlier learning success. The willingness to learn is the decisive factor here. It is determined by the horse's motivation or willingness to act. It describes the inner status of an animal. Aside from the influence of stimuli, it contributes meaningfully to whether a behavior will be carried out or not. Motivation is dependent on several exogenous and endogenous factors. The former include, for example, the sight of feed (treats) or the stimulation by companions. Endogenous stimuli include, among others, hormonal events (heat cycle), dropping of the blood glucose concentration (hunger) and other physiological events.

These influence a horse's cooperation in different ways. A stallion will have difficulty, for example, in walking calmly next to a mare in heat. In this situation he is distracted because of hormonal events and his willingness to act will focus more on the mating act than on dressage lessons. Great fear or panic can even result in a complete learning blockade. In general, excitable and nervous horses are more easily distracted and therefore need more time to learn a task than calmer animals. Their learning ability, however, is not diminished, only their motivation. Curious animals are generally more easily motivated to cooperate. Because learning processes are mainly driven by curiosity, lessons in horse training should be designed to be as interesting and varied as possible. Good learning success and, in parallel, appropriate handling is granted only if it is possible to arouse the horse's motivation for the work demanded. Motivation is most easily raised by rewards.

Other terms for willingness to act or motivation are drive, mood, tendency, and urge.

HOW LONG CAN A HORSE CONCENTRATE?

Directing the horse's motivation towards work leads to concentration. It is a prerequisite for any learning success. This is true not only for people but also for animals. Concentration cannot be extended indefinitely because fatigue sets in after a certain time. How long a horse can concentrate depends on its age, its stage of development, its character and the task it is supposed to perform. Based on experience, younger horses can concentrate maximally for 10 minutes, and older ones for 20 minutes without interruption. Individual variation, especially towards the low end, is possible. This has to be considered!

It is therefore only natural for a horse to react with unwanted behavior if it has been ridden in a dressage-type manner and had to concentrate fully on the rider's aids for an hour, and then is expected to learn a new task at the very end. This does not mean, however, that one should ride a horse for only 20 minutes! It should rather be emphasized that training sequences requiring a high degree of concentration must not last for too long and that a period of intensive work has to be followed by a relaxation period. As American studies have shown, it is sufficient to practice demanding tasks once a week. Learning success will then be significantly higher than with daily repetition.

How does a horse comprehend?

TIME COORDINATION

The horse's thought process differs from that of humans. For us, association of events is part of the normal thought process even if the action and the resulting success or failure occur at different time points. The horse can only form an association if the positive or negative experience occurs in immediate succession to the action. The horse can understand assessment by a person only if praise or punishment is time coordinated, and that means within seconds, with the action. I therefore have to praise my horse for its accomplishment immediately after completion of a well fulfilled task – often a word of praise is enough – and not wait until the dressage lesson is over. It is not unusual, however, to observe riders who will wait until the work is done to pat their horse's neck once and again while they are cooling down. According to human thinking, the horse is rewarded for its performance during the entire hour of dressage work; according to the horse's understanding, however, it is being praised for the activity at that moment. It may, for example, nip at another horse at just this time.

Not only praise, but also punishment needs to follow the action immediately. If one falls off during bucking, for example, it is completely useless to punish the horse once one is up on one's feet again. At this time, the horse has already terminated the activity and cannot relate punishment to it any more. In order to make the horse understand, one has to punish it as soon as it begins to buck or even during bucking.

Also, one should always keep in mind that the horse is incapable of doing anything good or bad on purpose. In the example above, it does not throw the rider off in order to bother him, but because it feels fear or pain or simply has to get rid of its built-up energy.

INCREASING THE LEARNING SUCCESS

Appropriate handling of horses is based on positive reinforcement. This is also the motto of human learning psychology. Motivation and the incentive to repeat a performance can only be increased by praise. Only through praise is the horse able to understand what is good and what is expected. Unfortunately, this elementary fact is often disregarded or forgotten in daily riding and the absence of punishment is often seen as praise. If this is the case, however, the horse cannot assess which type of performance the human regards as good.

A repeated demonstration of the task constellation is most often a prerequisite for a learning success. During the learning period, it is therefore useful to reward every correct reaction (constant reinforcement) (87). During the "can" or maintenance period, the reward does not have to be given regularly. The behavior will even be strengthened by intermittent rewards because they create an attitude of expectation.

Punishment is only useful in exceptional cases, for example in the case of aggression caused by dominance. It is the wrong approach, however, to teach animals by punishment because it lowers their motivation and only results in a negative overall attitude and fear. By punishment, therefore, one can only prevent the horse from doing something, but one cannot motivate it to cooperate. Refusal reactions on the part of the horse are often attributable to a lack of praise and to endless practicing of the same lessons.

Good learning success is based on:

- Lessons that are adapted to the horse's learning ability as well as developmental and training status.
- Correct time coordination of praise and punishment with the action.
- Increasing the horse's motivation for work by rewards and variability of lessons.
- Attention to the horse's maximal ability to concentrate of about 20 minutes.

Tips for correct rewarding

- *Basic principle:* Brief praise is sufficient (one piece of feed has the same effect as 10 pieces). It should however be expressed very clearly.
- *Praising by voice:* This type of positive reinforcement is always usable. It is recommended to train one's voice in order to be able to adequately demonstrate one's satisfaction. Short words such as "good, great, excellent" suffice (in the same manner, one can use the voice very well to demonstrate dissatisfaction, for example with a distinct "no" or a hissing sound such as "ksss").
- *Treats:* Feed is the best understood reward. But careful! It should only be used when the dominance relationship is clearly settled. Used in the wrong way, treats can result in a spoiled and disobedient (biting) horse. With some horses, they can also lead to loss of concentration for the work. Treats are best coordinated with vocal praise. After a certain time they can be left out and the voice by itself can be used (secondary positive reinforcement).

Special types of rewarding with treats

- *Conditioned rewarding:* Feed rewards, which are based on classical conditioning can be used without the problems noted above. The horse learns to associate a rewarding sound (voice signal, "clicker") with the treat, which results in a mood change. In the "can" period, the sound without feed then suffices. This is of great advantage in dangerous situations in which both hands have to be free. For a detailed description of this method see p.128
- *Bribery:* Bribery is given without a conditioned signal. It is offered in advance with the goal that the animal will overcome an aversion and will show the desired reaction. In this manner, for example, one can get a fearful horse to approach. It is wrong, however, to bribe a horse once an undesired reaction has already begun. If an aggressive horse threatens, for example, and one offers a carrot at this very moment – meant as a bribe or to calm the horse – it will perceive this as a reward for the threatening behavior.
- *Mane ruffling:* This is a friendly reward in a horse manner. The horse will interpret patting or clapping of the neck in the same way. In combination with vocal praise, the praising effect is strengthened.
- *Relaxation:* This is a very effective praise during work. "Letting the horse stretch its frame" not only loosens the musculature, but it also helps to decrease psychological tension.

87 Changing the horse's general mood by means of classical conditioning (rewarding sound and feed reward) is a gentle method for decreasing fear, e.g. of the trash can and bags.

Therapy and prevention of problem behavior

Aside from an accurate diagnosis, the horse owner's or trainer's willingness to participate in the treatment is a prerequisite and determining factor for successful behavioral therapy. Frequently, extensive management changes, different handling and riding methods or longer lasting conditioning programs are necessary. These require time and money and most often also require the horse owner or trainer to change his way of thinking. This often long journey will, however, only be completed successfully if the treatment is primarily directed towards fulfilling horse-specific needs in terms of management and handling in the best possible manner. These measures are also the only manner in which to prevent the different behavioral abnormalities from occurring.

In the following section, the basic therapeutic options for behavioral abnormalities and unwanted behavior will be discussed. In order to avoid unnecessary repetition, these will be referred to in the detailed discussion of the individual behavioral abnormalities in Parts D and E.

Therapy and prevention of behavioral aberrations

MANAGEMENT AND FEEDING
Most behavioral aberrations can only be treated by a fundamental improvement of management conditions. The emphasis should be on long eating times, as much exercise as possible by providing additional paddock and pasture access, sufficient contact with barn mates and to the environment, as well as access to varied activities.

As it is difficult to reverse established behavioral aberrations, prevention is of paramount importance. The horses' requirements in terms of environment and their equivalent in

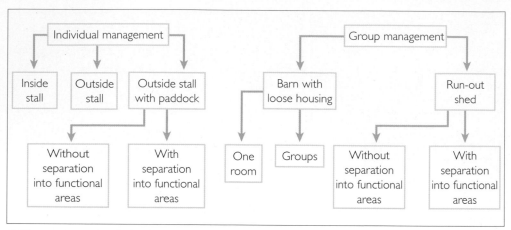

88 Management systems for horses.

practice has already been discussed in detail in Part B. In the following section, several management systems (**88**) and feeding devices will be introduced, which in today's view are largely appropriate for horses in a barn management situation.

Management

Horses' needs are best met in a run-out shed with pasture or, if individual stalls are necessary for certain reasons, in stalls with attached paddocks (**89**). Other management systems can also meet the requirements if deficits are balanced by, for example, several hours of daily access to a paddock or pasture in groups. A special effort should be made to provide access to a variety of activities, because sensory deprivation is the main cause of overexcitement. When horses are stalled all day, for example, the feeding cart is the big event of the day and will become the trigger for many behavioral abnormalities. Management systems, which satisfy the species-specific needs of horses help to minimize these excitement peaks.

Figure **90** shows a stall with attached paddock. It is the most horse-friendly method of individual stall management. It is suitable for horses of all breeds and uses that cannot or are not intended to be kept in groups.

Prerequisites are:

- The paddock must be fully usable in the summer and winter (surface preparation, roof).
- Fencing must allow social contact with the neighboring animal (no electric fence).

Group management, as compared to individual stall management, provides horses with the additional advantages of having unlimited social contact, unrestricted exercise, and the opportunity for social play. These management systems are suitable for horses of all breed and uses except for sale and show barns. If raised accordingly and with knowledgeable management, even adult stallions can be kept in run-out systems, as long as certain requirements are met (p.40).

General requirements for group management are:

- Correct management (group formation, newcomers, and so on).
- Optimal layout (measurements, dividers).
- No bottlenecks or disadvantages with regard to feeding and drinking spaces.

Figure **91** demonstrates group management in a barn with loose housing. It is only suitable for well acquainted horse groups (brood mares, young horses).

Additional requirements are:

- Little or no exchange of horses.
- Good ventilation. Climatic conditions in horse barns are shown in Table 12.

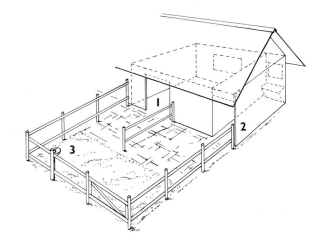

89 A box stall with adjacent paddock and division into different functional areas offers the advantage of promoting exercise.

1 Resting area
2 Feeding area
3 Water source

90 A box stall with adjacent paddock is the best version of individual stall management.

Table 12 Climatic conditions in horse barns (Zeitler-Feicht 1993; BMELF 1995)

Air temperature: outside temperature* (°C)
Air humidity: 60–80%
Speed of air movement in the animal area:
    > 0.1 m/s (0.3 ft/s)
Ammonia content of the air: < 10 ppm
Hydrogen sulfide content of air: 0 ppm
Carbon dioxide content of air: < 0.1 vol. %
Illumination strength in the animal
    area: > 80 Lux

* Barn temperature should generally be similar to the outside temperature throughout the year

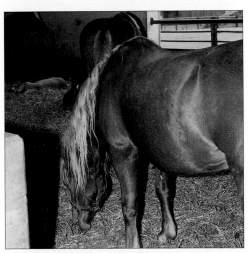

91 Group management in a barn with loose housing is only suitable if horse groups are well acquainted (brood mares, young horses).

In addition to social contact and unrestricted exercise, the run-out shed with pasture (**92–94**) provides, increased stimuli for exploration and the opportunity to choose access to natural climate conditions. Requirements are:

- At least two exits from the barn to the outside or a fully open front.
- Surface preparation in the outside run (covered area, main traffic ways, feeding and watering area).
- Little change in group membership.

All management systems which encourage natural horse behavior and offer varied environ-mental stimuli, such as a run-out shed with pasture, an outside stall, a stall with paddock or access to a run or pasture for several hours daily, are also preferable from a health standpoint. It is now known that horses are among the domestic animals which best tolerate climatic changes, heat and cold as well as snow and rain. Fresh air and sunshine are indispensable for their health and psyche. For this reason, management under outside conditions is by far the best. Healthy horse management, which follows the daily and seasonal changes in temperature and offers as much fresh air and natural sunlight as possible, promotes robustness, and physical and psychological performance.

92 Aside from social contact and unrestricted exercise, the run-out shed offers additional stimuli for exploration and the opportunity to choose different locations under natural climatic conditions.

93 An optimal solution is the run-out system that is divided into different functional areas and thereby further promotes exercise.

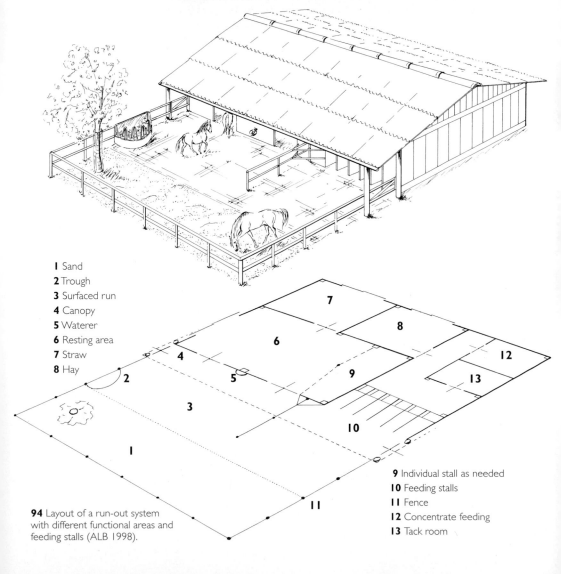

1 Sand
2 Trough
3 Surfaced run
4 Canopy
5 Waterer
6 Resting area
7 Straw
8 Hay

9 Individual stall as needed
10 Feeding stalls
11 Fence
12 Concentrate feeding
13 Tack room

94 Layout of a run-out system with different functional areas and feeding stalls (ALB 1998).

Feeding

Because feeding is a management factor and can be poor even when the rest of the management conditions are at their best, it will be addressed separately. What has to be considered? First of all, appropriate feeding needs to meet not only nutritional requirements but also behavioral needs. This means that feeding practices need to meet the horse-specific requirement for long eating times and intake of large volumes of feed with a low nutrient content. Horses need to be given access to feed for at least 12 hours a day. It is best to offer roughage or straw throughout the entire 24-hour day. Long eating times can be achieved by the following measures:

- Reduction of the concentrate portion in favor of an increased roughage portion or pasture access.
- Partial replacement of energy-rich feed with feed low in energy.
- Installment of economy feeders to increase eating times.
- Appropriate pasture management.

Feeding in this manner not only satisfies inborn eating needs but also keeps horses busy and helps to decrease excitement if abnormalities already exist (p.61).

For concentrate feeding in paddocks, transponder-directed (on call) feeding has proven useful. With its help, concentrate can be divided into small portions (starting at about 100 g (3.5 oz)) and given throughout the day. This has several advantages. Intake of small amounts of concentrate does not result in an excessive loading of the relatively small stomach of horses. Waiting times prior to riding are therefore no longer necessary. In addition, this type of management system provides a constant stimulus for movement and therefore keeps the horse busy. An increase in the level of excitement, as can be observed with concentrate feeding "by hand", is absent or at least significantly reduced. As shown in **95**, the use of automated concentrate feeders instead of traditional feeding leads to a distribution of feed intake throughout the entire day. This corresponds to the natural eating rhythm of horses and, when combined with adequate provision of roughage, allows an adaptation to species-specific feed intake in many respects.

Figure **96** shows a computer-directed feeding device. With this device, each horse has free access to the feeding station. If the horse is entitled to feed, the trough is automatically extended, and is retracted again after the meal is completed. Leaving the feeding station occurs on a voluntary basis or because the horse is pushed out of the way by another horse ("free entry" principle). Requirements for this system are:

- Minimal portion size (one "mouthful").
- Side entrance into the station.
- Sufficient room at the entrance for horses to get out of the way of others.

The layout of a run-out system incorporating automated concentrate feeders is shown in **97**.

Figure **98** shows another variation of the computer-directed feeding system. An access barrier controls the horse's access into the station. It closes when the horse is entitled to feed and the animal can ingest larger amounts of feed without disturbance. Leaving the feeding station is voluntary or is achieved by an electronically directed stimulation device that is

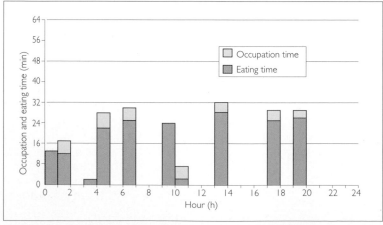

95 Distribution of feed intake throughout a 24-hour day in a computerized feeding system with entry barrier.

96 A computerized automated feeder ("free entry" principle).

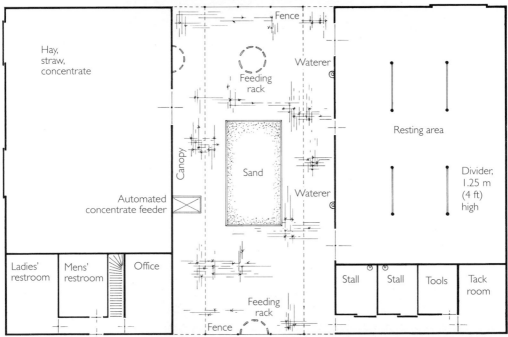

Hay, straw, concentrate

Fence

Waterer

Feeding rack

Canopy

Sand

Automated concentrate feeder

Waterer

Resting area

Divider, 1.25 m (4 ft) high

Ladies' restroom

Mens' restroom

Office

Feeding rack

Fence

Stall

Stall

Tools

Tack room

97 Layout of a run-out system with different functional areas and automated concentrate feeders (ALB 1998).

98 A computerized automated feeder ("entry barrier" principle).

switched on individually ("access barrier" principle). Requirements for this system are:

- Horses that tolerate the stimulation device (electric shock comparable to an electric fence).
- No opportunity for dominant animals to block the entrance.

The stimulation device is controversial in practice. It is often rejected because the use of electricity appears to be incompatible with feeding. It should be noted that an acoustic signal will sound every time before the device is set in motion. Horses learn very quickly to associate the signal with the device. Often, a one-time experience is sufficient to make them leave the feeding stand as soon as they hear the signal. There are, however, horses that despite the acoustic "warning" do not tolerate the use of electricity in the feeding area.

The stimulation device can be turned off for horses that are afraid of it. These animals must not, however, block the station by stopping, which can become a problem with long feeding stand measurements and horses that tend to kick. This is important because a longer block-ade of the feeding stand can lead to redirected aggression (p.64) among the waiting horses. Another important requirement for this type of computer-directed feeding is that blockade of the exit by another horse must not occur. If a dominant animal blocks the exit, the lower-ranked animal in the feeding stand finds itself in a severe conflict situation if the stimulation device is turned on. It is therefore recom-mended to design the exit in such a manner that exiting horses are directed into a different functional area. This can, for example, be achieved by the use of dividers.

With individual stall management, dose dispensers for concentrate can be used to design feeding such that several small portions are offered throughout the day. Synchronized feeders, which simultaneously supply all horses with concentrate, are preferable to asynchronous systems. With the latter, feed is distributed to one horse after the other, which can excessively raise the level of excitement in the waiting horses. A decrease in expectations is also achieved by use of the "Equiball feeder". This is a ball-like object, which is filled with concentrate pellets. It is placed on the stall floor, where the horse can move it around and turn it with its mouth and front feet until concentrate falls out in small portions. This not only increases eating time, but it also keeps the horse

busy and avoids excitement caused by expec-tation of feed. According to Henderson *et al.* (1997), this can reduce the occurrence of stereotypical behavioral abnormalities. The Equiball feeder should, however, only be used in stalls with clean straw bedding or in paddocks with dry ground in order to prevent an accidental intake of larger amounts of bedding that is not suitable for ingestion (shavings, hemp, and so on). Furthermore, the Equiball feeder can be recommended only as a prophy-lactic measure. In horses that already show a manifest behavioral abnormality, one has to differentiate between the types of abnormality. Playing with the feed-releasing ball is, for example, contraindicated in cases of aberrant behavior which occurs during and after feeding such as cribbing (p.137) and tongue playing (p.141). In these cases, the behavioral ab-normality would only be strengthened. A different situation arises with aberrant behavior that occurs due to overexcitement during the expectation period, i.e. prior to feeding. This includes, for example, weaving (p.146) and stall pacing (p.150). In these cases, the Equiball feeder can be a useful measure to decrease the level of excitement and the associated stereo-typical movements. With regard to behavioral abnormalities and attention-seeking behavior, one should refrain from feeding of treats or extra portions of concentrate in the presence of other horses in the barn.

HANDLING

Characteristics of incorrect handling

Asking too much
- Increased fearfulness or tenseness.
- Refusal reactions (e.g. tail lashing).
- Decreasing motivation.
- Backward steps in training.

Asking too little
- Increased inattentiveness.
- Decreasing motivation.
- Refusal reactions (e.g. going "off the bit").

Conflict
- Increased fearfulness or tenseness.
- Substitute behavior (e.g. head tossing).
- Refusal reactions (e.g. pinning back the ears).

The improvement of handling and training techniques is of equal importance to optimization of management as a means of prevention and therapy of aberrant behavior. In particular, one should avoid asking too much, but also too little, of the horse, and creating conflict situations (p.27, p.115). A basic requirement is the consideration of species-specific horse behavior. Many reactions of horses are determined by fear, which is only natural for a flight animal. In order to avoid a hopeless conflict for the horse, therefore, it must not be punished in situations in which it is already afraid. If it is, for example, afraid to pass a pile of wood, lashes with the whip would evoke a conflict situation (fear of the pile of wood and fear of the rider) and only increase the horse's fear. The correct approach in this case is to give the horse a feeling of security by means of trust-building measures, and possibly to let it explore the frightening object first (**99**)(p.91).

In order to prevent problems, special attention should be paid to a sensitive and careful approach to breaking the horse to ride or drive, particularly as the beginning of training is often associated with additional burdens such as a management change or a move to a different barn. A stress-free relationship with the horse is achieved if every exercise that is demanded of the horse is matched to the individual animal, i.e. its level of physical maturity and its behavior. The lessons should be designed in small enough steps to allow the horse to complete each section successfully (see example "rein-backing"). The same approach is applicable for therapy of horses with problem behaviors.

BREEDING

Preventive measures should be given particular attention when breeding horses. As evidence of a genetic disposition for certain behavioral abnormalities such as cribbing or excessive aggressiveness is accumulating in the newer literature, appropriate changes to horse breeding would certainly be of value.

99 In frightening situations, horses should always have the opportunity for sufficient exploration. The horse already shows more curiosity than fear (lengthened upper lip, tense posture) of the wild hogs, the sight of which at first elicited panic.

Appropriate training using the example "rein-backing"

Proceeding in a manner appropriate for horses

During appropriate training, the horse initially learns to back up by doing ground work. For example, the horse can be led into a cul-de-sac and asked to back up by using voice commands such as "back" (**100**). Because the optical and mechanical barrier does not allow the horse to walk forward, but only backward, it will soon understand what it is asked to do. An incorrect response is initially ignored, the correct response is positively reinforced. In the next step, backing up is practiced outside the cul-de-sac with only the voice command. Once the horse masters the exercise in this manner, one can progress to teaching it under saddle by using the now conditioned voice command. Because the horse is not asked too much when using this training method, completion of the separate steps of the exercise can be demanded with consequence and determination. Both of these, paired with positive reinforcement, create respect and trust.

Psychological overburdening

From a psychological standpoint, the horse is asked to do too much if one immediately asks it to rein-back under saddle and uses the reins, legs, and seat as aids without having provided any preparatory exercises (**101**). The same effect occurs if the voice command is insufficiently conditioned.

Therapy and prevention of problem behavior are achieved by:

- Appropriate feeding and management with social contact, sufficient exercise, varied environmental and climatic stimuli as well as opportunities for play while considering the horse's resting, comfort, and sexual behavior.
- Appropriate handling without conflict situations and without excessive or insufficient psychological and physical challenge.
- Exclusion of horses with a genetic predisposition for aberrant behavior from the breeding stock.

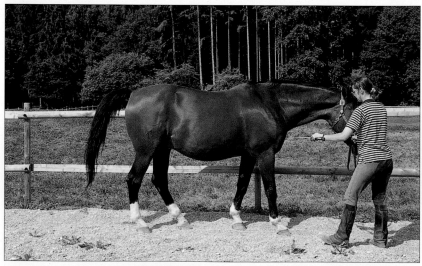

100 Backing up from the ground with the help of vocal commands, whip and lead chain.

101 Rein-backing under saddle without appropriate preparative exercises.

Therapy and prevention of unwanted behavior

Therapeutic measures for unwanted behavior vary depending on the cause, i.e. on whether fear, pain, unclear rank order relationships or incorrect conditioning are the reason for the behavior. This differentiation is not always made when employing the corrective measures commonly used in practice. It is not necessary in every case, either, as many causes such as fear and rank order problems can be closely correlated and can therefore be corrected simultaneously with one particular corrective measure. Despite this fact, therapy should always be matched to the exact causes in order to avoid incorrect treatments and prognoses. For example, use of the exhaustion method as a learning therapy can be completely contra-indicated for a horse that does not stand still on command, if pain instead of "refractoriness", in the sense of a rank order problem, is the cause.

This book will not discuss the different corrective measures commonly used in practice. At this point, therefore, the reader is directed towards the extensive available literature. It will only be said that communication with the horse is possible through voice, touch, weight and leading aids as well as through visual (body language) signs. The mainstay of correction is usually the development of dominance, which in return provides the horse with a sense of security and decreases fears. More and more methods advocate force-free handling of

horses. The TT.E.A.M. method (Tellington-Jones Equine Awareness Method), which, through a combination of the classical art of riding and newer concepts of learning (Feldenkrais), is centered around a force-free education and learning without fear and pressure, has been receiving special attention.

MEDICAL THERAPY AND PAIN MANAGEMENT

For the reasons stated earlier, the first thing to investigate when any type of unwanted behavior occurs is whether an organic disorder or pain exists. If this connection is established, the animal has to be treated accordingly. Aside from classical medicine, alternative methods such as homeopathy, acupuncture, acupressure or physi-cal therapies and different massage methods are equally significant. They are controversial to a certain extent because only a few controlled scientific studies regarding their effectiveness are available. Testimonials out of practice, however, show again and again that they can be very effective. They are of particular significance in the prevention of behavioral aberrations. Increased levels of excitement in timid animals, for example, can be regulated by the appropriate homeopathic constitutional remedy, which can prevent problem behavior from the outset.

Medicinal behavioral therapy with neuro-leptic drugs, tranquilizers, antidepressant drugs, and so on, is generally not required if appro-priate therapeutic measures are employed. Furthermore, most of these preparations are not

Table 13 Methods of behavioral therapy (Kiley-Worthington 1989; Zeitler-Feicht 1994; Lebelt 1998)

Method	Proceedings	Application
Counter-conditioning	Operant/classical conditioning	Fear, learned behavior, rank order problems
Punishment	Conditioning	Rank order problems, learned behavior
Desensitization	Stepwise adaptation with conditioning (positive reinforcement)	Fear, phobias
Sensory overload	Rapid adaptation	Fear
Exhaustion	Rapid adaptation	Rank order problems
Extinction	Consistent avoidance of the trigger situation	Fear, learned behavior, rank order problems

approved for use in horses. If used at all, they must only be used with a strict indication, for a limited period of time and in conjunction with etiologically orientated therapeutic measures.

Understanding and sensitivity are demanded of the owner, if pain-induced refusal behavior is caused by a horse's unfavorable conformation. This deficit can be compensated by an appropriately adjusted riding technique or a different use of the horse. A horse that has difficulties maintaining a posture required for dressage (collection) because of an unfavorable neck base, can, for example, easily become a high-performance trail horse.

Equipment deficits leading to pain can usually be corrected relatively easily. Most often, improved care of the leather parts and blankets is sufficient. In many cases, however, it is necessary to exchange saddles or bits for more appropriate equipment.

LEARNING THERAPIES

The use of learning therapies for treatment of unwanted behaviors that are based on fears, phobias, and rank order issues as well as learned and attention-seeking behavior, is a relatively young area. Generally, methods are used that are based on the natural learning processes in horses (Table 13). The completion of conditioning programs requires intensive work with the horse as well as a patient and consistent approach. The following methods are employed:

Counter-conditioning

In the same manner as a behavior is learned by conditioning, it can again be de-conditioned by counter-conditioning. This correction method is based on systematic establishment of the new, desired behavior, which is incompatible with the unwanted behavior that is to be removed. To achieve this, the desired behavior is rewarded while the unwanted behavior is ignored or, in extreme cases, even punished. Counter-conditioning in the form of operant conditioning is primarily used with causes such as fear, rank order issues (aggression) and learned behavior.

Classical conditioning is especially effective in cases of fear- or pain-induced refusal behavior. With this approach, the horse, while being exposed to the fear-inducing stimulus, is put into a positive general mood by use of a conditioned rewarding sound (voice signal, "clicker"). The goal is for the horse to associate the stimulus with positive instead of negative emotions. Feed rewards, which are based on classical conditioning, are particularly effective. The horse learns at first to associate the rewarding sound with the treat. The treat is only given when it hears the sound, never without it. Pushy horses, that want to eat during the learning period even if no voice signal is given, are corrected in a distinct manner. A sharp "no" or a fast hissing sound such as "ksss" have proven effective. Only when the rewarding sound is conditioned, can it be used to evoke a positive mood. In the conditioned period, the sound by itself suffices and the treat is no longer necessary.

Practical examples of counter-conditioning

Operant conditioning
Problems when lifting the hooves: the desired behavior is achieved by stepwise conditioning. In the beginning, brief lifting of the leg is rewarded; the demands are then systematically raised in the course of conditioning. Pulling away of the hooves or similar reactions are ignored during treatment.

Classical conditioning
Kicking: a horse, which has experienced a painful injury to the hock and has learned to avoid any kind of touching by means of kicking, is touched systematically, beginning at the croup and slowly approaching the hock. This process is accompanied by classical conditioning, i.e. during touching, the conditioned rewarding sound is employed and the horse receives feed. The goal is to achieve a change of mood, which in the horse evokes the sensation that touching does not result in pain or fear but instead represents a positive experience (feed).

Punishment and subordination
Punishment must only be used with massive rank order problems or learned behavior, which cannot be corrected in any other manner. It is contraindicated if fear or pain are the cause of unwanted behavior, and in these cases will only result in worsening of the behavioral pattern. Special care should be taken with horses that are naturally fearful and sensitive (Arabians).

Punishment is only effective if it is administered early enough, i.e. the activity being punished must not yet be completed. A horse which has learned to get rid of the rider by bucking has to receive the lash of the whip the moment it begins to buck. Naturally, this requires good riding skills.

It is better if one is able to recognize the horse's intention in advance. For example, the horse has to lower its head in order to buck and the appropriate countermeasures are taken at precisely this moment. Lashes are in this case no longer necessary. Punishment need not only be equated with use of the whip or spurs: the voice can also be used very effectively as punishment. With sensitive horses, a sharp "no" will abort an unwanted activity at the start.

Generally, the intensity of punishment should fit the extent of unwanted behavior. It definitely has to be harsh enough to be successful. If a person loses in a conflict he or she has provoked, this invariably strengthens the rank position of the horse further.

Wrong use of punishment

Punishment of the wrong action
A herd-bound horse is supposed to be ridden away from the group. In many riding stables it can be observed in these cases that the horse is more or less beaten away by constant use of the legs and whip. It therefore is punished for doing the right thing – going away from the group. The same happens if it stops. The horse is therefore in an insoluble conflict situation (fear of going away, fear of stopping). In addition, it is not able to understand the sense of the exercise if this method of correction is used. The result of the exercise is therefore an increase in fear of leaving the group. The correct approach is to remove the horse from the group in a stepwise manner and under praise (p.192).

Punishment in combination with reward
In order to be effective, punishment must never be administered in combination with a reward, because the latter will make a stronger impression. If a horse "frees its head" to eat grass during riding, it is the wrong moment for punishment if the horse already has gotten a mouthful of grass. The correct approach is to put a stop to the behavior at the start.

Desensitization
Desensitization denotes a learning procedure, which is based on stepwise habituation and counter-conditioning. It is particularly useful for horses with fears and phobias. How does one proceed? One starts by applying the stressful stimulus at a very weakened intensity. It has to be weak enough not to evoke an adverse reaction. Following this, stepwise re-adaptation occurs by gradually increasing the intensity of the stimulus, while ensuring that each step in itself is insufficient to trigger the unwanted behavior. Every step in the right direction is positively enforced and practiced until habituation takes place.

The TT.E.A.M. method for training of young horses is a very useful desensitization method for the correction of fears and phobias.

A practical example of desensitization

Girthiness
The described method should be varied depending on the intensity of the girthiness. At first, the horse is no longer confronted with the saddle and the process of saddling. After a time, one starts by placing a blanket and a girth. The latter has to be of sufficient length and easy to fasten. The horse is then adapted to the girth pressure by running the hand along the girth line.

In the next phase, the horse is lead around with a lightly fastened girth. It is rewarded until it gets used to this. In the next training sequence, the horse, equipped with blanket and girth, is exercised on a lunge line, by performing ground work or by ponying. This is done until the horse perceives the blanket and girth as an everyday occurrence and something entirely normal, and shows no adverse reaction.

In the next training sequence, one can finally place the saddle but it is important to use the same blanket. One proceeds in a similar stepwise manner as initially with the blanket and girth. Only when the saddle is tolerated without any problems, can the rider mount the horse again for the first time. Prior to doing so, the horse, equipped with the saddle, should perform some familiar exercises for about 10 to 15 minutes. It is then taken to a familiar place and held at the head by a helper who distracts it by talking, praise or feeding treats (classical conditioning), and the first mounting can begin. Initially, one remains standing with a foot in the stirrup. If the horse reacts calmly, one is given a leg up to mount without the girth being fastened tightly.

The final fastening of the girth takes place later at a walk after a few turns. The horse is allowed to stride out freely with minimal use of the reins and without any use of the legs.

Sensory overload ("flooding")
In contrast to desensitization, sensory overload is aimed at achieving habituation to the frightening stimulus as fast as possible.

This method was derived from the so-called confrontation therapy in human medicine. The horse is exposed to the frightening stimulus until it shows no further fearful reaction. The treatment must not be removed until fear is completely extinguished. In contrast to humans, however, the horse does not know which therapeutic method is being applied and it can virtually be "overrun" by the sensory overload.

Problems may include the following:

- If the process of sensory overload is terminated prematurely, the result will be a strengthening of the fear reaction instead of its removal.
- Uncontrollable panic reactions can result in injury to the horse, which represents an additional negative experience and may further strengthen the unwanted behavior.
- The method is not useful for very sensitive horses and in cases of phobias.

The method should only be practiced with reservations. Desensitization is preferred as a learning therapy.

Practical examples of sensory overload

Fear of cows
A horse that is afraid of cows is brought into a herd of cows. It remains there until no further fear reactions are observed.

Bagging or sacking out
A horse that is afraid of flapping plastic sheets or cloths is well restrained, then its body is touched with the frightening objects until its resistance and fear subside.

Exhaustion
Similar to sensory overload, exhaustion is aimed at achieving a treatment success as rapidly as possible. The horse's unwanted behavior is provoked until it is exhausted enough to stop by itself and it understands that the behavior results in nothing but its own fatigue. A prerequisite for this therapy is that the unwanted behavior is not caused by pain or fear but is

instead solely attributable to rank order problems.

Problems may include the following:

- If exhaustion therapy is used and pain is causing the unwanted behavior, the method is incompatible with animal protection guidelines.
- The method is not useful for fearful or very sensitive horses or for treatment of phobias.

The method should only be practiced with reservations. Counter-conditioning is preferred as a learning therapy.

Practical examples of exhaustion therapy

Rearing
A horse that has learned to avoid work by rearing up, is provoked to rear until it stops by itself because of exhaustion.

Kicking
A horse that kicks at people is prompted to kick until it gives in because of exhaustion.

Extinction
Extinction is aimed at forgetting of unwanted behaviors. It is achieved by avoiding any situations that originally elicited the behavior. To what extent this results in "forgetting", depends on how ingrained the learned behavior was originally. It is, however, impossible to remove the behavior in question completely from the behavioral repertoire. Ideally, it is reduced to a minimum. For this reason, the term "eradication" or "extinction" is not entirely correct. It would be better to denote this method as weakening.

When using this learning method, one proceeds in different ways depending on the cause. In case of phobias, the animal is not confronted with the situation any more at all. A change of environment may be necessary.

If learned or attention-seeking behavior or rank order problems exist, which are associated with aggression, every situation that may result in repetition of the unwanted behavior must be avoided. If, for example, a horse bites the rider from behind upon mounting, it must not be given this opportunity any more. The rider either mounts facing forward, which provides the opportunity for appropriate correction, or he lets someone hold the horse during mounting. It is important for the extinction of learned behaviors to prevent any encouragement of them. Over time, this will remove the basis for the behavior. A single lapse, however, can be enough to rebuild the full-fledged original behavior.

Practical examples for extinction

Phobias
If a strong phobia is present, it may be useful not to confront the horse with the fear-inducing situation for an extended time. Racehorses with racecourse phobia, for example, are turned out onto pasture for a long period. Afterwards, they are slowly reintroduced to the racecourse (desensitization).

Attention-seeking behavior
With attention-seeking behavior that may be present in cases of pawing and kicking of the stall walls, any type of attention by humans is perceived as a reward. Extinction can be achieved by ignoring. Success is, however, only possible if all people who have contact with the horse work together in the extinction procedure. At the beginning of therapy, an increase in the unwanted behavioral pattern is to be expected. For this reason, it is particularly important to proceed with the therapeutic program during the first few days. One should always consider that any type of attention, including scolding or punishing the horse, will trigger the behavior and therefore has to be avoided consistently. If the treatment is aborted prematurely, the unwanted behavior may be strengthened.

RANK ORDER
If a basis of trust has been established, the horse accepts the human as a type of social partner. The horse will not, however, recognize people as dominant merely because they are human. Neither is one automatically dominant because one can take the horse out of its stall and ride it. Many horse owners are not aware of their rank position until they move around in a group

of horses and no animal pays attention to them let alone makes room (p.43).

Everyone dealing with horses has first to earn his or her dominant rank position. Superiority in rank is based on the following three characteristics:

Personal expression

For people dealing with horses, psychological rank factors are more important than physical ones. The more self-assured and self-confident a person acts around horses, the sooner she will be recognized as the "leading animal". This personality can be attained by accumulating as much knowledge and experience in dealing with horses as possible. Both can be practiced and improved with help of continuing education in courses and riding clinics and with appropriate practical work.

Consistent handling

Consistency and assertiveness in handling horses will establish clear guidelines. This is not only true during work but also particularly so for the daily interaction with the horse. The horse's trust, and along with it the recognition of the person's rank, are lost if one day it is allowed to pinch the person grooming it but the next day it is not. Similarly, the horse must not be allowed to pass the person leading it and reach for some grass on one day, if, the next day, it is not allowed to do these things and is even punished for trying. Inconsistent behavior in this manner makes the horse insecure. Dominant animals will seize the opportunity and get their way. During work, all lessons must generally be designed in small enough steps not to exhaust the horse psychologically or physically. Only under these circumstances can one ask the horse consistently and with determination to complete the exercise. A reward must not be forgotten. Even with rank order problems, it should always follow each successfully completed lesson, because only if superiority in rank is coupled with trust, can a firm relationship between animal and human be established. The horse will cooperate and show true willingness for performance only under these circumstances.

Rank order exercises

Rank order exercises differ with regard to the method of correction (e.g. body language, instrumental aids) but, independent of its make-up, every method is suitable that has the goal of achieving superiority in rank by measures which simultaneously result in a gain of trust. The prerequisite for these exercises is, as mentioned before, a consistent, determined and calm handling procedure combined with positive reinforcement. All exercises have to be practiced in a riding arena or under controlled conditions first, because otherwise concentration could easily be disturbed. Once the horse masters the exercises there, one can also ask it to perform them outside and under distraction.

Many rank order exercises are based on control of the horse's movements by either hindering it from moving or driving it forward. This approach is derived from the observation that dominant horses show a similar behavior towards horses lower in rank. For example, a dominant horse may prevent the subordinate one from moving by "blocking its way" or through "body check". Work on a lunge line or free work in a round pen is geared towards this. To halt on command and remain standing quietly is therefore an important obedience exercise (**102**). The same goes for correct leading, as the dominant animal is the only one that a horse will follow wherever it goes calmly and with a lowered head. Very effective measures are subordination exercises such as backing up or turning in a small circle, which is also called "windmill walking" or "dominance volte". The latter is particularly uncomfortable for horses and can also be used as effective punishment. Backing up during ground work also has a punishing character. Only a subordinate animal will back away from a dominant one. A proven exercise with rank order problems is to drive the horse from the ground, i.e. to lead it from behind with long leads. In this position, one occupies the stallion's position, which exerts a strong dominance effect on the animal (**103**). Aside from these specific rank order exercises, ground work in general is a proven method to get dominance problems under control.

Subordination exercises should, however, not only be practiced during work. It is just as important to make sure that the rules are followed in daily interaction. As a general rule, every activity is initiated by the dominant being. The handler, therefore, decides whether or not the horse is allowed to eat grass while being led on a pasture, the handler decides whether or not the horse is allowed to stretch its frame during riding and so on. Potential obedience exercises during daily handling are: letting the horse side-step or back up on command, for example when cleaning the stall, making it stand still with the door open, and making it come on command.

102 "Halt" on command is an important subordination exercise that may be performed during work or during general daily interaction.

103 Driving from the ground has a strong dominance effect on the horse. In this position, the person takes on the role of the dominant stallion.

A self-assertive and energetic riding technique is also of major importance in the treatment of rank order problems, as long as the rider is well trained and remains sensitive. The basis of correction of unwanted behavior, however, has to be established at a lower level. It begins with the daily interaction with the animal, because rank order problems during handling cannot be solved via dominance in the saddle alone. The obedience exercises described above are, therefore, invaluable during daily handling and groundwork.

If the dominance issue is settled early on by a consistent approach, confrontation rarely occurs because the horse accepts its subordinate position and behaves accordingly. For the herd animal horse, this situation is completely natural and in addition provides a feeling of security. The dominant social partner is, for example, responsible for leading the group in dangerous situations and defending it against threats from the outside. The human being, of course, has to live up to this function.

TRUST-BUILDING MEASURES

The goal of trust-building measures is for the horse to recognize the human as someone it does not have to be afraid of. On the contrary, it is supposed to feel safe and protected in the handler's presence even when confronted with threatening situations. The actual work cannot begin until a basis of trust has been established. A prerequisite is that the human is familiar with the species-specific behavior of horses. Unfamiliar things, for example, will generally evoke an avoidance reaction in horses. It is therefore trust-building to confront the horse with unfamiliar objects slowly and with the help of appropriate aids, and to let it get used to these objects under praise. A loss of trust, on the other hand, occurs if one tries to influence the horse with force in these situations.

Generally speaking, trust-building measures are procedures, which help to establish a positive relationship with the horse. Trust-building measures can be considered both in a narrow and a wider sense. The former include spending time with the horse outside of the usual riding times. Grooming is of particular significance because it gives the human being the opportunity to take on the function of a social partner in mutual hygiene. Special massage and relaxation techniques such as the Tellington Touch are also very useful to intensify the trusting relationship between horse and handler. Scratching of the horse's withers by a person, for example, results in a significant lowering of the heart rate (Mill *et al.* 1996). In this manner, relaxation similar to that during social grooming among horses can be achieved, which can result in a decrease of the heart rate of up to 10%. In order to establish a good, trusting relationship with the horse, it is therefore indispensable to invest more time than just an hour of daily riding and to interact intensively with the horse.

It is trust-building in the wider sense if working with the horse is done in a manner that always results in successful termination with positive reinforcement. This can be achieved theoretically and practically by planning each exercise well in advance such that a successful ending is ensured. The training steps must be kept small and have to be tailored to the individual horse. Physical and, in particular, psychological overexertion would result in a loss of trust.

The basis of a relationship between human and horse is trust, which can be achieved by attention and affection towards the horse, sensitive conduct and a calm and patient but consistent handling method with positive reinforcement (**104**).

MANAGEMENT, HANDLING AND PREVENTION

Incorrect management such as stall confinement for 23 hours a day, concentrate-rich feeding, severely restricted social contact and a lack of environmental stimuli predispose for many unwanted behaviors. In addition, mistakes made during handling and use, such as an improper riding technique and equipment deficits, can result in harm-avoiding reactions. Therapeutically, measures that optimize management and handling have to be taken. These were discussed earlier (p.117). Similarly, preventive measures for unwanted behavior are the same as those described for the prevention of behavioral abnormalities. The emphasis, therefore, is on appropriate management and correct handling from an early age.

Unwanted behavior

Prevention
- Appropriate management and correct handling.
- Consistent training with definite rank distribution and trust-building measures from foal age onward.

Therapy
- Pain: medical treatment, correction of deficits (equipment, riding technique), different use of the horse.
- Fear: trust-building measures, learning therapy.
- Unclear rank order and aggression: subordination exercises, learning therapy.
- Learned and attention-seeking behavior: learning therapy according to cause (fear, rank order problem).
- General: optimization of management and handling.

104 Riding with only a rope halter within a group of people requires the horse's absolute trust in the rider.

Part D: Problem behavior in the barn

In trying to treat problem behavior, one should first assess during the anamnesis whether the problem concerns normal, undesired or aberrant behavior, because treatment methods as well as success rates differ depending on the assigned category. Management- and handling-induced aberrant behaviors, for example, and in particular residual-reactive behaviors, are generally very resistant to therapy, while better chances exist for curing unwanted behaviors. The definitions of these terms are summarized again below:

- Normal behavior: behavioral patterns typically shown by horses in the wild.
- Unwanted behavior: behavioral patterns which largely correspond to the horse's normal behavior but pose problems during management and use.
- Behavioral aberrations: behavioral patterns which, with regard to modality, intensity or frequency, digress considerably and continuously from normal behavior.

The careful diagnostician will notice quickly that several problem behaviors allow an "either–or" classification; some, however, may be exclusively management- and handling-induced behavioral aberrations, for example, cribbing. Most problem behaviors can, depending on their cause, be classified as either abnormal or unwanted behavior.

In addition, behavioral aberrations can be classified according to their etiology as symptomatic, organpathologic, domestication- or deficit-induced, as well as management- and handling-induced. Only the latter represent aberrant behavior in the narrower sense. They reflect past suffering evoked by massive management deficits and mistakes in handling. They are also definitively relevant from an animal welfare standpoint. Behavioral aberrations in this category are frequently irreparable. One should, therefore, be careful in attributing blame. Not uncommonly, the limits of adaptation were crossed long ago and the current management system has no connection whatsoever with the behavior.

In this section, behavioral aberrations that occur mostly within the barn will be discussed with regard to their sequence of events, their causes and health risks as well as the options for therapy and prevention. For didactic reasons, the discussion is structured according to functional areas (p.98). Problem behavior within the barn frequently falls into the category of behavioral aberrations in the narrower sense.

Eating behavior

Cribbing/windsucking

Cribbing is among the best known management- and handling-induced behavioral aberrations of horses. It is relatively common. Studies undertaken in different countries within the past few years have shown that depending on breed, management, and use, between 1% and 8% of all horses crib.

Description. During cribbing, the pharynx is opened through contraction of the upper neck musculature, which results in influx of air into the esophagus. Generally, a burping sound, the so-called cribbing sound is heard. It does, however, not necessarily occur with each swallowing motion. Cribbing is often accompanied by other stereotypical behaviors belonging to the functional area of eating behavior, such as movements of the tongue and lips or licking motions, which, in combination with cribbing, are always exhibited in the same form and pattern. It was formerly assumed that cribbing results in swallowing of air ("windsucking"). Investigations using newer methods, however, showed that this occurs rarely if at all. McGreevy et al. (1995a), for example, showed that only very small amounts of air enter the

105 During cribbing, horses place their incisors on a firm object such as the pasture fence.

stomach while the major portion escapes via the pharynx.

Two forms of cribbing are differentiated: cribbing and windsucking. With the former, the incisors are placed against a firm object such as the rim of a feed trough, the stall wall, or the horse's own front leg, and cribbing takes place (**105**). For windsucking, no object is required. It is exhibited with the head held freely (**106**). Characteristic features are distinct nodding movements of the head against the chest, which are caused by the contractions of neck muscles, followed by an abrupt jerking upwards of the head and, most often, simultaneous lip movement. Windsucking is thought of as the more advanced form and is much less common than cribbing. Some horses are capable of exhibiting both forms.

Predisposition. Management deficits and mistakes made while working the horse, which result in an increasing build-up of emotions, form the foundation for cribbing (Table 14). These insufficiencies appear to be particularly common in the management and training of racing, dressage and eventing horses because a striking number of horses used in these disciplines develop into cribbers. "Highly bred" animals are also affected more often because, when stressed, they tend more towards overexcitement than heavier types. Furthermore, evidence for a genetic disposition exists. Vecchiotti and Galanti (1986) discovered that in Italian thoroughbreds, up to 30% of horses belonging to certain bloodlines were cribbers, while the percentage of cribbers in the entire population of approximately 1,000 animals was only 2.4%.

Table 14 Predisposing factors for cribbing (Vecchiotti and Galanti 1986; Sambraus and Rappold 1991; McGreevy et al. 1995c; Luescher et al. 1996; Zeeb 1997)

Management
- Insufficient roughage and too much concentrate.
- Stalls without straw bedding.
- Foals and young horses kept in box stalls.
- Isolation or severely limited social contact.
- Insufficient environmental stimulation and occupation.
- Suckling deficit in foals raised without a dam.

Type of use
- Race horse training.
- Training of dressage horses.
- Training of eventing horses.

Genetics
- "Highly bred" horses.
- Familial predisposition.

Causes. Causes for the first-time appearance of cribbing are drastic events that result in an extreme emotional upset in the affected horse. Primary causes are premature or incorrect weaning from the dam, an abrupt start into training or sudden preparation for a competition or horse show, excessively harsh training methods, change of the barn for the worse, and isolation of the horse without sufficient exercise due to disease.

Most practitioners agree that cribbing is learned by imitation. Some boarding stables and riding schools will therefore not accept these horses. Scientific evidence to prove this assumption does not exist. On the contrary, many facts indicate that cribbing is not caused by imitation of the neighboring horses, but by insufficient management conditions, which affect these horses to the same extent. In other words, well managed operations do not need to worry, while badly managed ones face an increased risk of predisposed horses developing into cribbers.

Triggers. The most important actual triggers are any events that are associated with an increased level of excitement in the horse. These primarily include events associated with

106 Windsucking is performed with the head held freely. The "detached" facial expression with half-closed eyes is typical.

"pleasure" such as eating of concentrate or grooming. In contrast to weaving horses, cribbers exhibit their behavior primarily after feeding. But cribbing can be observed even during eating. Other activities such as cleaning the stall or grooming and leading away of other horses can also elicit cribbing. Long-standing cribbers, however, do not need these stimuli any more. They crib independently of outside influences for a major portion of the day. One can even watch them doing it when they are turned out into the nicest pasture.

Physiological and health consequences. New knowledge concerning the physiological consequences of cribbing has been gained in recent years. Evidence is accumulating that cribbing decreases excitement in the horse, which is primarily proven by a decrease in the heart rate during the cribbing process. It is by now almost certain that cribbing results in a release of endogenous opioids (endorphins). One piece of evidence for this is the fact that administration of opioid antagonists (e.g. naloxone) significantly decreases the number of cribbing events (Dodman *et al.* 1987, Lebelt 1996). Overall, there is much support for the theory that cribbing has a very positive effect on the horse. It should, therefore, not be assumed that cribbing, once established, indicates compromised well being of the horse.

In the popular and veterinary literature, an increased risk of colic in horses that crib is frequently reported, without offering scientifically understandable evidence. The earlier assumption that swallowed air resulted in an increased accumulation of gas within the gastrointestinal tract has now been clearly refuted. Specialists and equine hospitals further confirm that cribbers, as compared to non-cribbers, do not suffer from an increased risk of colic or from more weight loss problems. The high percentage of thin horses which crib is probably linked to genetic disposition: easily excitable horses are generally slimmer than phlegmatic ones. The cribbing-induced increased dental wear is generally not of medical relevance. Only in advanced stages, can cribbing result in visible dental changes or even premature loss of teeth. Only in rare cases, however, will this interfere with the proper ingestion of feed. Lastly, over time cribbing can lead to a strengthening of the long neck muscles without being of any medical consequence.

Therapy. As cribbing is a residual-reactive behavioral aberration, treatment is successful relatively rarely. Practical experience shows that if management and handling conditions are drastically improved, a certain success can be expected in the early stages, however, cribbing generally persists despite correction of the original deficits. Despite this fact, optimization of management and environment is the only possible treatment in the sense of a cure. It is imperative to decrease the level of agitation. This is achieved through a management system offering lots of variety and by offering enough environmental stimuli and opportunities for activity. The goal is to decrease overexcitement such that the approaching feed wagon or rider no longer represents the one big event of the day. Long eating times have to be emphasized. It is best to supply hay, straw or pasture access *ad libitum*. Feeding roughage before concentrate can also help to decrease the level of excitement. In addition, as much calm exercise as possible and undisturbed contact with companions should be provided. It is wrong to isolate the horse for fear of imitation! While working the horse, relaxation should also be emphasized. Stress can be decreased with long trail rides at a slow pace, moderate endurance training, or trail riding over several days.

The common mechanical and surgical methods such as cribbing collars and cribber operations are not therapeutic but merely an attempt to prevent the occurrence of signs. These treatment methods should not be employed any more because, as studies of recent years show, cribbing is aimed at decreasing stress and therefore is obviously of use to the horse. According to Lebelt (1996), cribber operations in Germany might even represent a breech of Article 6(1) of the German Animal Welfare Act if no medical indication for the procedure exists. Installation of electric fencing in the stall to avoid cribbing also has to be regarded as incompatible with animal protection (Zeitler-Feicht and Grauvogl 1992). By preventing cribbing via installment of Plexiglas shields in stalls and without offering replacement activities, McGreevy and Nicol (1995) could show that prevention of cribbing resulted in an increased cortisol concentration (stress parameter). Apart from this, prevention of one behavioral aberration will invariably result in escape into another.

It is impossible to stop cribbing by learning therapy because it is an aberrant behavior and not an unwanted behavior. It is therefore useless to try to de-condition cribbing; punishment with electric shock, similar to the shock collars used in dogs, is incompatible with animal welfare. The same is true for covering potential cribbing objects in the stall with electric pasture fencing. Furthermore, symptomatic treatment with, for example, cribbing collars without simultaneous optimization of management and use is ineffective, because it does not address the horse's motivation which led to cribbing in the first place. On the contrary, it creates an additional burden for the horse, which could be shown by measuring an increased cortisol concentration. The escape into another behavioral aberration is virtually preprogrammed.

Prevention. Cribbing is aberrant behavior in the narrower sense. It can be prevented by appropriate management, feeding and handling (p.117). These have to be optimized from birth because mistakes made during early development are particularly predisposing for cribbing. At this age it is already important to avoid situations that result in overexcitement, both positive and negative, as much as possible. This also includes, for example, feeding of particularly palatable concentrate feed. It decreases excitement if these types of "treats" are mixed with less palatable feeds. Additional examples (stress-free weaning) can be found on p.57.

Stallions belonging to cribber families should be excluded from breeding. Generally, special attention should be paid to prevention in "highly bred" animals.

Differential diagnosis. Differential diagnoses for cribbing include trough-biting, wood chewing and ingestion, as well as rubbing the teeth against bars or the feed trough, because contraction of the long neck muscles does not occur in these cases. The former, however, can represent an early stage of cribbing, particularly if the surface is licked prior to resting the teeth on it. Similar sounds to those of cribbing, but without contraction of the long neck muscles, can stem from an early embryonic malformation of the pharynx, which occurs rarely. A veterinarian can detect this aberration via endoscopic or radiographic examination.

Based on the "Imperial Decree concerning major defects and liability intervals" of 1899, which according to article 482 of the German Civil Code is still valid, cribbing represents a "guaranteed" defect and the horse can, therefore, be returned within 14 days of purchase if the defect was not disclosed. In Germany, this circumstance results in a depreciation of the sale price for cribbing horses of up to one-third, which represents a considerable economic loss. According to knowledge gained in recent years it is time to re-evaluate the legal situation concerning cribbing horses. Cribbing is also considered an unsoundness in the UK.

Cribbing (similar origin: tongue playing, stereotypical licking of objects)	
Classification	Management- and handling-induced behavioral aberration
Description	Influx of air into the esophagus by opening of the pharynx via contraction of the upper neck musculature
Predisposition	• Inadequate management • Handling inappropriate for horses • Thoroughbreds and refined breeds • Hereditary predisposition (cribber families)
Causes	• Drastic events in the negative sense (emotional build-up and overexcitement due to deprivation, frustration or conflict) • Learned behavior (imitation) is not applicable
Trigger situations	Events that result in increased excitement/agitation • Activities of the affected horse (eating) • Manipulations of the affected horse (grooming, saddling) • Barn activities (cleaning stalls, person traffic)
Consequences	• Lowered heart rate (reduction of excitement) • Potential role for endogenous opioids
Health risks	• Dental changes, tooth loss • Gas accumulation within the gastrointestinal tract is not applicable
Therapy	• Appropriate management and handling according to species-specific and behavioral needs (variety and occupation, goal: decreased excitement) • Appropriate handling and stress free training • Symptomatic therapy (cribbing collars, cribber operations) is not acceptable • Learning therapy is not successful **Incompatible with animal welfare laws**: electric shock, electric fence
Prevention	• Appropriate management and feeding • Appropriate handling

Tongue playing and stereotypical licking of objects

Description. Tongue or licking movements prior to and after drinking or in expectance of food, for example on the way out to pasture, belong to the normal behavioral repertoire of horses. Tongue playing in the barn is a behavioral aberration as is stereotypical licking of objects. With the former, a horse moves and twists its tongue within and outside the mouth, lets it hang out to the side, rolls it upwards, exhibits sucking motions or smacks the tongue against its lips (**107**). Stereotypical licking presents as extensive, monotonous licking movements against walls, bars, doors, and other objects or against the horse's own lips, or as idling licking motions.

107 During tongue playing, a horse moves or twists its tongue within and outside the oral cavity. With this behavioral aberration, the "detached" facial expression is also typical.

Causes and therapy. A similar genesis as that for cribbing is assumed for both types of this aberrant behavior. As with cribbing, they are very resistant to therapy. The only therapeutic approach in the sense of an improvement is the optimization of management and handling (p.117). The horse owner should understand that in general, these aberrations are not harmful to the animal, but instead help to decrease tension and compensate for deficits.

Differential diagnosis. From a differential diagnostic standpoint, tongue playing in the barn has to be separated from bringing the tongue over the bit during riding or driving, which represents an unwanted behavior (p.187). Frequent tongue movements and licking motions are further exhibited with certain diseases of the oral cavity (e.g. tongue lacerations) or dental diseases. In these cases, the aberration has to be classified as symptomatic.

Rubbing the teeth against objects and bar biting

Description. When rubbing their teeth against objects, horses rest their incisors on a firm object such as the rim of the feed trough, and rhythmically wave their heads back and forth (**108**). They may use metal bars in the same manner, rubbing their teeth against them in an up and down motion causing a grinding sound. Health risks include a more or less severe wear of the incisors, inflammation of the gums and premature tooth loss.

108 Rubbing the teeth against the upper door of an outside stall. The door shows obvious rubbing marks.

Causes and triggers. Rubbing the teeth against objects and bar biting do not necessarily represent aberrant behavior, as they can also occur as unwanted behavior or as a combination of both. The former is present if the behavior is exhibited stereotypically, i.e. it is repetitive in terms of the type and sequence of events. Predisposition and causes are probably comparable to those for cribbing. The behavior is predominantly triggered by states of excitement such as impending feeding. If this then occurs, it rewards the behavior and thereby strengthens it. It is also possible for horses to become overly excited if they are kept separately and do not have the opportunity for social interaction with their stall neighbor. The activities are therefore directed against a replacement object. Unwanted behavior is present if rubbing the teeth against objects turns into attention-seeking behavior, where attention provided by a person serves as the reward.

Therapy. Therapeutic measures have to be chosen according to the individual cause, although differentiation is not always easy. Whether or not learned behavior is involved or is exclusively responsible for the behavior, can only be determined by careful observation of the context and the circumstances under which the behavior is exhibited. Treatment of learned, attention-seeking behavior takes place by extinction (p.131). Supportively, counter-conditioning is frequently recommended in the sense that the horse only receives feed when it does not show the unwanted behavior and that feed is removed as soon as the behavior returns. This method, operant conditioning, is very useful in animals kept by themselves such as dogs. For horses, which are usually kept together with companions, it is less useful because synchronous eating represents the normal behavior of this species and the exemption of one animal would only increase its excitement and tension. It is, however, possible to integrate all horses of a group in the corrective measure. It is also often successful to divert the behavior by exercises learned in the form of classical conditioning. Because a combination of attention-seeking behavior and overexcitement is frequently present, management conditions should be changed independent of cause to provide lots of activity and variety. This is especially important in cases of management- and handling-induced aberrant behavior. For treatment, a decrease in excitement should be emphasized. Within the functional area of eating behavior, for example, this can be achieved by extended eating times, less concentrate or, alternatively, less palatable concentrate, or frequent feedings. If a social component exists, moving the horse into a group management system or into a stall with an opportunity for social physical contact can reduce the behavior or eliminate it completely. Even a new stall neighbor can sometimes result in improvement.

Prevention. Rubbing the teeth against objects and bar biting as a behavioral aberration in the narrower sense can be prevented by appropriate management and handling beginning at birth (p.117). This measure is also applicable to attention-seeking behavior, which is frequently triggered by the monotony of a horse's daily routine. Under these circumstances, even being scolded by a person represents a reward for the horse because at least it is being addressed. Attention-seeking behavior can further be prevented by adjusting handling to the learning behavior of horses and avoiding incorrect, albeit unintentional, conditioning processes (p.128). For example, rewards should always be related to desired behavior because horses learn very quickly to associate a feed reward with a certain behavior. In general, procedures that might cause overexcitement in a horse should be executed in a manner that prevents agitation as much as possible.

Differential diagnosis. Rubbing the teeth against objects and bar biting as aberrant or unwanted behavior has to be differentiated from sporadic grinding or rubbing motions exhibited in states of excitement, which may occur as substitute activities in conflict situations (**68**).

Excessive wood chewing

Description. Chewing and gnawing of wood or bark represents normal horse behavior. It is part of the natural behavioral repertoire and to a certain extent obviously has dietary significance. Certain types of wood are avoided while others are preferred. For example, horses like to

---

Rubbing the teeth against objects (similar origin: bar biting)

Classification*	1: Management- and handling-induced behavioral aberration 2: Unwanted behavior
Description	The incisors are rested on a firm object while swinging the head back and forth
Predisposition	Inadequate management Handling inappropriate for horses
Causes	1: Drastic events in the negative sense (emotional build-up and overexcitement due to deprivation, frustration or conflicts) 2: Learned behavior
Trigger situations	1 and 2: Events that result in increased excitement (feeding, social component) 2: Being addressed by people
Consequences	Dental changes, tooth loss
Therapy	1 and 2: • Appropriate management and feeding according to behavioral needs • Variety and occupation (goal: reducing excitement) • Optimization of social contact (regrouping) • Appropriate handling 2: Extinction and classical conditioning
Prevention	Appropriate management and feeding Appropriate handling Consideration of equine learning behavior

*Numbers used for classification correspond to numbers used in the subsequent text (causes, therapy, and so on)

chew on willows whose bark contains salicylic acid, even if they are kept and fed appropriately. This type of wood chewing, however, is only exhibited for short periods of time. Excessive chewing of wooden building parts without eating and digesting the wood, on the other hand, represents an activity without nutritional significance (**109**).

109 Wood chewing as a displacement activity.

Causes and therapy. In order to classify this behavior as aberrant in the narrower sense (management- and handling induced behavioral aberrations), other potential causes first have to be excluded. These include deficits in roughage and minerals, especially trace minerals, insufficient satisfaction of the eating need, and sensory deprivation. Excessive acidification of cecal contents can also be shown in wood-eating horses. Generally, wood chewing can be resolved by appropriate feeding that meets nutritional and behavioral demands. Correction of dietary deficits and optimization of eating times are therefore the mainstay of therapy. It is good practice to offer horses fresh twigs from non-toxic trees on a regular basis to allow some gnawing activity. Leaf-carrying twigs of beech trees, birches, willows and poplars are particularly suitable (**110**). As a general rule, however, these "nibbling treats" should be offered in limited amounts and should never replace adequate feeding of roughage. A horse that was fed shredded pine by-products in its paddock, for example, developed signs of toxicity following excessive intake, in the form of ataxia of the rear end, foaming salivation, inappetence, and a rotten smelling breath.

If excessive wood chewing persists despite correction of the feeding regimen, as can occur in sporadic cases, a management- and handling-induced behavioral aberration exists. In this case, additional measures to optimize management and sufficient exercise should be emphasized during the therapeutic approach.

Differential diagnosis. Ingestion of small amounts of wood is part of the normal eating

110 Offering fresh branches from non-toxic trees on a daily basis is a prophylactic as well as a therapeutic method.

Excessive wood chewing		
Classification*	**1: Behavioral aberration caused by deficiency**	
	2: Management- and handling-induced behavioral aberration	
Description	Excessive gnawing and chewing of wooden building parts	
Causes	1: Nutritional deficits (roughage, minerals, vitamins)	
	1 and 2: Eating need not satisfied	
	2: Sensory deprivation	
Therapy	1 and 2:	
	• Feeding according to nutritional and behavioral needs	
	• Wood for occupation	
	2:	
	• Appropriate management (exercise)	
	• Appropriate handling	
Prevention	Feeding according to nutritional and behavioral needs	
	Appropriate management (occupation)	
	Appropriate handling	

*Numbers used for classification correspond to numbers used in causes and therapy

behavior of horses. Temporary wood chewing in certain stressful situations such as during horse shows can be regarded as a substitute activity and is also normal behavior.

Manure eating and soil eating

Causes, therapy, and prevention. Manure eating is normal in nursing foals up to the 8th week of life and may have dietary significance (p.58). When observed in adult horses, it most frequently represents a deficiency-induced behavioral aberration. Causes generally include either a nutritional deficit or an insufficient satisfaction of the eating need. Manure eating is primarily seen in horses with insufficient access to chewable roughage and therefore insufficient chewing activity. In isolated cases, it can also be associated with an infestation with stomach parasites (*Trichostrongylus axei*). In these cases, however, additional behavioral aberrations such as decreased appetite, diarrhea, weight loss, and performance loss occur.

A similar situation is probable in cases of excessive soil eating, which can also be caused by a salt deficiency. In general, isolated management with a lack of exercise and activity promotes manure eating as well as soil eating. Both aberrations can result in health problems. Manure eating increases the risk of endoparasite infestation and excessive soil eating increases the risk of colic. As is the case for wood chewing, appropriate feeding from a nutritional and

111 In paddocks without feed, sporadically growing grasses are often ripped out with their roots, which can result in ingestion of significant amounts of soil. This increases the risk for colic.

behavioral aspect represents the treatment for both aberrations (p.60).

Differential diagnosis. Excessive soil eating must be differentiated from an involuntarily increased ingestion of soil on overgrazed pastures (**111**).

Polyphagia nervosa (excessive eating)

Excessive eating (overeating) is generally attributable to inadequate feeding, while it only rarely represents a management- and handling-induced behavioral aberration. It finds its expression in the excessive intake of feed, even less palatable feed such as straw, within very short periods of time. Diseases such as a heavy worm burden or dietary deficits need to be excluded as possible causes. Furthermore, the behavior has to be assessed according to "horse measurements" instead of human eating habits (**112**). It is entirely normal for horses to ingest feed for up to 16 hours a day. This limit is also rarely exceeded in cases of polyphagia nervosa. For this reason, therapy must not be aimed towards a limitation of eating time but must instead attempt to provide an appropriate, use-dependent ration while maintaining species-specific eating times. Most often, an excessive need to eat corrects itself over time (months) if animals are consistently provided with free choice access to feed. In order to avoid excessive weight gain, rationing measures should be taken which still allow maintenance of extended eating times. Examples, such as the use of economy feeders, are described on p.61. It is also important to give horses access to additional activities and to

112 Many ponies tend to become fat due to a breed-specific predisposition. Their eating behavior is generally normal.

provide sufficient exercise. If this is not done, eating remains the only activity within the monotonous daily routine.

In rare cases, a management-induced behavioral aberration may exist. As was described on p.59, massive digressions from a normal feeding regimen may result in disturbed regulatory mechanisms of feed intake. If this is the case, therapeutic measures correspond to the previous recommendations.

Locomotion behavior

Weaving

This is one of the most common stereotypical behaviors of horses. Depending on breed, management system and use, between 1% and 9.5% of all horses weave. It generally occurs in stalled horses and here predominantly in horses kept in tie-stalls as compared to those in box stalls. In poorly vegetated corrals, but also in pasture, it can be observed in isolated horses or those suffering from sensory deprivation.

Description. During weaving, the horse stands with slightly spread forelegs and swings the head and neck rhythmically from one side to the other. All four limbs are lifted in turn such that a walk-like movement in one spot results. A combination with other behavioral oddities such as tongue playing, licking of the lips, yawning, aggression against the neighboring

horse, rubbing the teeth against objects, bar biting, rhythmic tail lashing or head shaking as well as whinnying is possible. Head positioning and head movement as well as the range and frequency of deflection differ individually. Variability of weaving is shown in Table 15.

Table 15 Variability of weaving (Radtke 1985)

Weaving periods/day	3–15
Weaving time/day	13–297 min
Deflections/day	400–17,000
Deflection width	80–175 cm (31–69 in)

Predisposition. Similar factors as those described for cribbing are responsible for weaving. These include management deficits such as an insufficient supply of roughage, severely limited opportunity for exercise especially in younger horses, and insufficient social contact. Weaving is often found among racing, dressage, and eventing horses. Stallions are especially predisposed to this behavioral aberration. Evidence of a genetic disposition for weaving exists. Vecchiotti and Galanti (1986) in their examination of Italian thoroughbreds found up to 26% weavers in certain horse families, while the overall percentage in a population of about 1,000 horses was only 2.5%. "Highly bred" horses are also affected particularly often. According to present knowledge, the occurrence of weaving is an exception in draft horses.

Causes. "Initial traumas" for a first-time occurrence of weaving are drastic changes in a horse's life along with an extended psychological burden. In horses studied by Radtke (1985), weaving occurred for the first time after weaning from the dam, at the beginning of training, with active participation in competitions or after a change in ownership and location, and with a sudden drastic reduction of exercise as in the case of stall rest due to disease. As for cribbing, learning of weaving by imitation has not been proven scientifically. However, unintentional conditioning can occur. This is attributable to the fact that in contrast to cribbing, weaving is triggered in the expectation period prior to feeding. Under these circumstances, the horse will perceive the subsequent feeding as a reward for the exhibited behavior. In operations with fixed feeding times, some horses will already begin to weave 1 to 2 hours prior to feeding.

Triggers. Weaving is not triggered by boredom but instead by events that result in an extreme increase of the level of excitement (**113**). Although sensory deprivation is the common cause for both, the emotional state of the horse differs completely. As already mentioned, the most common and most important trigger for weaving is impending feeding. Other activities such as barn work, manipulations involving the neighboring horse, and riding activity can raise the level of excitement to an extent that weaving is triggered in affected horses. In horses that weave excessively, the stereotypical behavior can also occur without a recognizable trigger.

Psychological and health consequences. In recent years new knowledge has also been gained about the physiologic consequences of weaving. In contrast to cribbing, endogenous endorphins appear to be insignificant. Up to this point at least, studies have not shown a beneficial effect of opioid antagonists. It can, however, be assumed that weaving in some way provides an outlet to decrease excitement.

Some evidence exists that serotonergic systems have an influence. In people for example, disturbances of serotonin metabolism lead to depression, and in horses they may result in behavioral aberrations, which will be further discussed later.

The opinion that behavioral aberrations result in decreased performance is widespread. Potential damage to the forelegs as a result of weaving is frequently mentioned in the hippologic literature. This opinion is, however, devoid of a scientific basis. It has been refuted in the veterinary literature for more than 100 years. Newer findings prove that weaving horses do not exhibit an increased frequency of injury to the forelimbs. On the contrary, these horses may perform particularly well (Engelhardt 1990).

113 Weaving in a group on a pasture without vegetation. The behavior was triggered by increased excitement due to the photographer's presence at the pasture gate.

Therapy. Weaving is primarily a residual-reactive behavioral aberration and, accordingly, therapy is difficult. In contrast to cribbing, however, moving the horse to an appropriate management system is often promising. Practical experience shows that horses stop weaving when they are put into a run-out system. If they are moved back to a stall, the stereotypical behavior returns. This provides additional proof for a therapy based on optimization of management and handling. The most important goal in the treatment of weavers should be to decrease the level of agitation because the abnormal behavior is caused by overexcitement. Feeding is of particular importance. Several small concentrate meals evoke less stress for the horse than two large portions. Computer-directed concentrate feeding is particularly useful in a run-out system as long as it is designed properly. For stalled horses, use of the Equiball feeder or automated concentrate feeders are recommended. The latter should synchronize the feed release so that all horses can enjoy their feed simultaneously. Parallel to these measures, roughage should be offered *ad libitum* or pasture access should be available throughout the day.

Aside from an extension of eating times, increased feeding of hay and straw has another potential advantage. Research findings that have been available for several years indicate a role for the neurotransmitter serotonin in the development of behavioral aberrations. In human medicine at least, anti-depressants that selectively inhibit serotonin re-uptake are successfully used in the treatment of obsessive diseases. From their effect, and the fact that administration of serotonin antagonists results in worsening of symptoms, it was concluded that patients with behavioral aberrations have a serotonin deficit (Lebelt 1996). The connection with roughage feeding is based on the fact that this type of feed contains the amino acid tryptophan. It in turn is important for the synthesis of serotonin. Consequently, increased feeding of roughage may increase the available serotonin pool, which may potentially counteract the development of stereotypical behavior. Supplementation of the feed ration with the essential amino acid L-tryptophan (mineral and vitamin supplements with addition of L-tryptophan), from which the organism synthesizes serotonin, could also be of use. According to McDonnell (1998) this measure decreases the occurrence of stereotypical behavioral patterns.

Because of the possibility that weaving can be conditioned, it is recommended that rigid feeding schedules are broken up. These fixed schedules generally increase the level of excitement in horses kept in an environment characterized by sensory deprivation (p.30). Increased opportunity for exercise and unlimited social contact, as can be provided in a run-out system, further decrease excitement. In practice, one can occasionally observe an increased weaving activity in outside stalls with an outside view, although these are considered to be more horse-friendly than inside stalls. This is attributable to the fact that in sensitive, active horses the level of excitement can increase further if they are not given the opportunity to act out their need for exercise. For those horses,

114 The V-shaped top part of the stall door (weaving frame) is supposed to prevent weaving. Most weavers, however, simply take a step backwards and exhibit their abnormal behavior in the stall interior.

outside stimuli, which result in additional agitation, should be reduced as much as possible (p.89).

Mechanical measures to prevent weaving such as tying together of the forelegs, hanging sandbags from the stall ceiling or painting the stall walls with a zebra pattern should be rejected (**114**). They do not represent a treatment of the aberrant behavior because the horse's motivation is not changed. They are merely attempts at suppressing the weaving activity. These measures do nothing but worsen the horse's living conditions and potentially even lay the ground for the development of a new behavioral aberration.

Prevention. In order to prevent weaving, two factors should be considered. The first of these includes all measures which can serve to prevent a behavioral aberration in the narrower sense, including appropriate management, feeding and handling, that take into account species-specific requirements and behavior (p.117). Secondly,

conditioning has to be avoided because it contributes to consolidation of the weaving activity. For this reason, one should plan the daily routine in accordance with the behavior of horses under natural living conditions, which follows certain rules but is never rigid and predictable for the animal (p.30). In doing so, an excessive increase in excitement during the expectation period, for example prior to feeding, can be avoided as long as horses always have access to alternative activities. With "highly bred" horses such as thoroughbreds and refined warmbloods in particular, relaxation of the daily routine in this manner is of great importance. Refusing to breed to stallions from families that contain a striking number of weavers would also be an important preventive measure.

Differential diagnosis. Weaving as a behavioral aberration must be differentiated from sporadic weaving movements in agitated situations, which can occur as displacement activities in conflict situations.

Weaving (similar origin: stall pacing, fence walking, figure eight walking)

Classification	**Management- and handling-induced behavioral aberration**
Description	Rhythmic pendulum movements of head and neck with slightly spread front legs, walking in place; combination with other sterotypies such as lip licking or head tossing possible
Predisposition	• Inadequate management • Handling inappropriate for horses • Thoroughbreds, Arabians and refined breeds • Hereditary predisposition (weaver families)
Causes	• Drastic events in the negative sense (emotional build-up and overexcitement due to deprivation, frustration or conflicts) • Learned behavior a. Imitation is not applicable b. Unintentional conditioning possible
Trigger situations	Events that result in agitation: • Expectation of feed • Social activities (people, horses) • Activities in the barn (bedding, feeding of hay)
Consequences	• Potential influence of serotonergic systems • Contribution of endogenous opioids not proven
Therapy	• Appropriate management and feeding according to behavioral needs (variation and occupation, goal: decrease excitement) • Appropriate handling and stress-free training • Counter-conditioning • Symptomatic therapy (tying up of legs, sand bags on ceiling) is not acceptable
Prevention	• Appropriate management and feeding • Appropriate handling

Stall walking, fence walking and figure eight walking

These three stereotypical movements are seen particularly often in Arabians and, dependent on breed, management system and use, occur with varying frequencies of 1–7% in different populations. They are exhibited predominantly by animals kept by themselves in grassless runs, if neither access to activities nor contact with companions is available.

Description. Stall walking, fence walking and figure eight walking denote stereotypical walking motions (so-called "circus ring movements") that are sometimes exhibited for hours at a time and always show the same pattern (same number of steps, same direction of movement, same turns, and so on). They occur in the stall (stall walking), in paddocks, in larger runs and even in pasture (fence walking and figure eight walking). Figure eight walking or circling can show a smooth transition into weaving. Other odd behaviors such as lip smacking and head twisting can also be shown.

Causes and therapy. The three stereotypical forward movements have a similar etiologic basis to weaving. They also do not generally influence the horse's health and performance negatively. As is the case for weaving, the only treatment option in the sense of an improvement lies within optimization of management and handling. Because stereotypical behavior is primarily triggered by social isolation and by impending feeding, particular emphasis, aside from general measures to decrease agitation, has to be placed on unlimited social contact and behaviorally appropriate feeding with long eating times. Significant improvement can often be seen if the horse is turned out to pasture with companions (p.118).

The opinion that stereotypical movements are caused by boredom is often promoted in practice. However, this is not generally the case. With stall walking, for example, the tracks are most visible in the morning prior to barn maintenance work and feeding. The behavior is not caused by boredom but on the contrary by agitation prior to feeding. It arises because stall confinement without access to other activities limits the horse's needs too much. As a consequence, the level of excitement rises excessively in expectation of impending activities (feeding). Sensory deprivation is therefore the cause; it evokes the stereotypical behavior due to agitation, and not boredom (p.147).

Differential diagnosis. Stall walking, fence walking and figure eight walking are recognizable, as long as the ground is not paved, by clearly marked trails on the ground surface. Short-lived running back and forth in the stall in certain stressful situations, on the other hand, has to be regarded as substitute behavior and represents a normal behavioral pattern and not aberrant behavior. It does, however, indicate that tension between need and satisfaction, in the sense of frustration, exists. If these situations occur frequently, they will over time cause behavioral aberrations (p.28). Special care should therefore be taken to avoid them. Circus ring movements and compulsive movements can also occur in the course of brain diseases such as Borna disease, which is still endemic in certain areas of Germany (Bavaria: 0.02–0.04% of horses) (Grabner 2000) and hepatic encephalopathy.

Excessive pawing

Description and health risks. Pawing represents a normal behavioral pattern. Horses use it for tactile evaluation of the ground, to search for feed, and prior to rolling. Within the natural behavioral repertoire, however, it is only exhibited for brief periods of time. If it is shown excessively, it represents aberrant behavior. Excessive pawing is almost exclusively seen in horses kept by themselves. Extreme forms can lead to heavy wear of unshod hooves, which, if not treated appropriately, can result in abnormal limb positioning and subsequent orthopedic problems.

Causes and triggers. Excessive pawing can occur as a management- and handling-induced behavioral aberration, as learned behavior or both. The former exists if chronic emotional build-up caused the behavior and it is exhibited stereotypically. Similar to weaving, it is triggered by an agitated state such as occurs when barn mates leave or come back, or feeding is expected. In this case as well, subsequent feeding represents a reward and further strengthens the behavioral pattern. Excessive pawing can, however, exclusively represent learned behavior in the form of attention-seeking behavior or begging. Horses can learn the latter of their own accord, but begging is often unintentionally supported by the handler. The behavior is frequently rewarded without the intention to do so by addressing the horse, scolding, or ill-considered feeding.

Therapy. Therapeutic measures depend on the individual cause, which requires careful observation of the context and the circumstances under which the behavior is shown. If unwanted behavior in the form of attention-seeking behavior is present, the therapeutic approach may include extinction and counter-conditioning in the sense of redirection (classical conditioning) (p.128). Deconditioning by operant conditioning is not recommended if the excessive pawing is shown prior to feeding. This was discussed for rubbing of the teeth against objects and bar biting. Because a mixture of learned behavior and overexcitement is frequently present with these types of problem behavior, one should generally aim to achieve relaxation by an overall improvement in the management conditions. This is also true when aberrant behavior is present. Special emphasis should be placed on providing sufficient opportunities for social contact, appropriate calm exercise, and appropriate feeding in line with normal behavior. It is optimal to move horses to a run-out shed with pasture. A further proven method is to cover the stall floor with rubber mats in addition to bedding, as noise stimulation plays a certain causative role in this behavior.

Prevention. Appropriate management, feeding and handling in line with species-specific behavior prevent the occurrence of excessive pawing independent of its genesis. In addition, the specific learning behavior of animals should be considered when interacting with the horse in order to prevent unintentional conditioning.

Differential diagnosis. Intensive pawing is also shown as substitute behavior during excitement. Pawing out of excitement is shown, for example, if horses want to run but are hindered from doing so. In the course of colic, pawing indicates pain. In both instances it is normal behavior and should not be considered to be aberrant or learned.

Kicking against the stall walls

Sporadic, sometimes also more frequent, kicking occurs as an agonistic behavior in the course of social conflict or is a comfort activity to ward off insects (**115**). Constant, stereotypical kicking against the stall walls with the front or rear hooves ("stall-kicking") is only observed in stalled horses. It most often represents attention-seeking behavior but can also be aberrant and can be strengthened by learning processes. Depending on intensity and frequency, it can lead to more or less severe injuries to the fore- and hindlegs. The genesis is similar to that for excessive pawing. Consequently, the same therapeutic measures are recommended.

The behavior may also represent redirected social aggression. The stall neighbor is out of reach and the attacks are directed against the stall walls. Breaking of the individual distance because of insufficient stall size is also possible. The cause can be determined by careful observation of the excessive kicking behavior. If a social component is present, therapy in the sense of moving the horse to a larger stall (individual distance), next to new neighbors (incompatibility), or into a group management system may reduce or eliminate the unwanted behavior.

115 Kicking against stall walls is not a rare occurrence in horses kept in stalls by themselves.

Kicking against stall walls (similar origin: excessive pawing)

Classification*	1. Management- and handling-induced behavioral aberration
	2. Unwanted behavior
Description	Constant, stereotypical kicking against the stall wall with fore- and hindlegs
Predisposition	• Inappropriate management
	• Inappropriate handling
Causes	1: Drastic events in the negative sense (emotional build-up and overexcitement due to deprivation, frustration or conflicts)
	2: Learned behavior: unintentional conditioning
Trigger situations	1 and 2: Events that cause an increase in excitement (feeding, social component)
	2: Being addressed by people
Consequences	Injuries to the fore- and hindlegs
Therapy	1 and 2:
	• Appropriate management and feeding according to behavioral needs
	– Variation and occupation (goal: decrease excitement)
	– Optimization of social contact (reformation of groups, more available space)
	• Appropriate handling
	2: Extinction and classical conditioning
Prevention:	• Appropriate management and feeding
	• Appropriate handling
	• Consideration of equine learning behavior

*Numbers used for classification correspond to numbers used in the subsequent text (causes, therapy, and so on)

Social behavior

Misdirected imprinting

Description. Misdirected social imprinting occurs if the dam–foal relationship, and therefore imprinting on the animal's own species during the critical period, is disturbed by human beings (p.53). This can go as far as the foal recognizing humans instead of horses as its own species. Depending on the severity of the misdirected imprinting, these animals will to varying extents have problems in understanding horse-specific behavior. As a consequence, they will be more or less afraid of their own species. Falsely imprinted horses are difficult or impossible to integrate into groups because they are incapable of reacting appropriately to other horses' threatening gestures. This incorrect behavior increases the risk of conflict and injuries. Another possible consequence is misdirected imprinting with regard to sexual behavior, because the recognition of species-specific sexual partners in horses takes place very early during the ontogeny. Horses that are falsely imprinted in this manner show little or no interest in mares and stallions and instead direct their sexual activities towards humans. This can lead to dangerous situations if, for example, a young stallion attempts to mount the supposed sexual partner, the human. An alternative cause for misdirected sexual behavior is illustrated in 116.

Causes and consequences. Generally, the cause of misdirected imprinting is a disruption of the dam–foal relationship during the critical period. Orphan foals that have to be hand-raised are at a particular risk. Most often their dams have died during birth, although extreme maternal aggression can in rare cases necessitate premature removal of the foal from its dam. Too intensive handling of the foal by humans, however, is not without problems either. The "imprint training" according to Miller (1995) is consciously aimed at imprinting the foal on human beings in order to facilitate handling and training of the horse later on. Although,

116 Attempt of a Haflinger stallion to breed a bull. This behavior was not caused by misdirected imprinting but instead by a build-up of emotions due to long abstinence from breeding.

according to Miller, the dam–foal relationship will not be compromised with appropriate use of the method, it is not without risk. The required manipulations of the foal in particular, which are in part based on the learning method of sensory overload, have to be viewed very critically (p.130). Improper imprinting can result in an increased timidity and socially misdirected development of the foal.

Therapy. Because imprinting is to a large extent an irreversible learning process, treatment of a falsely imprinted animal is extremely difficult. It should, however, be attempted to weaken imprinting on human beings as much as possible, and in parallel to intensify contact with other horses. A particularly careful approach in small steps is required. In the beginning, the problem horse is best placed into a stall with an adjacent paddock. This provides on the one hand the opportunity for retreat into the closed off inner portion, while on the other hand it permits closer but safe social contact across the fence outside. This will help to decrease fears, provided the stall neighbors are calm horses. Subsequently, one can attempt to integrate the animal in question into a group. This should be done using successive integration by first introducing the behaviorally abnormal horse to the lowest-ranked animal of the group, then, when they have gotten used to each other, to the next higher one and so on until it is familiar with the entire group. Distraction from an overly intense social contact can, for example,

be provided by simultaneous pasture access for all horses (p.41). During this time, contact with humans should be reduced to a minimum in order to facilitate the acquaintance with the "new" species members.

Prevention. Socially misdirected imprinting can generally be avoided by appropriate preventive measures. These include avoiding any disturbance of the dam–foal relationship during the critical period. For orphaned foals, one should first of all try to find a surrogate dam. If this is not possible, formation of too close a bond between human and foal has to be avoided. Conversely, the foal must be given the opportunity to communicate with other equine companions (for further recommendations see p.56).

Differential diagnosis. Misdirected imprinting has to be differentiated from maladjustment syndrome. The latter comprises a disease complex, which prevents imprinting of the foal on its dam for medical reasons. Newborn foals may be able to rise but they do not connect with their dam. They walk around the stall aimlessly and try to make contact with strange objects. Aside from this presentation, some foals' vitality is compromised to the point of not being able to rise. Some make barking noises ("barker foals"), others let their tongue hang out to the side. Oxygen deficit and immaturity of the nervous system are the presumed causes. Diagnosis and therapy have to be provided by a veterinarian.

Misdirected imprinting	
Classification	**Management- and handling-induced behavioral aberration**
Description:	The learning process of imprinting on its own species does not take place or is insufficient
Causes	Disruption of the dam–foal imprinting during the critical period by: • Death of the dam • People (Miller method) • Other horses, animals of other species, commotion and so on
Consequences	• Misdirected social imprinting (fear of other horses) • Misdirected sexual imprinting
Therapy	• Successive establishment of contact with other horses • Reduction of human contact at the beginning of therapy
Prevention	• Appropriate raising without disturbance of the mare-foal relationship • With orphan foals, use of a surrogate dam if possible, otherwise raising together with other horses

Self-mutilation (autoaggression)

Self-mutilation and autoaggression represent management- and handling-induced aberrant behaviors, which, according to a Canadian study (Luescher *et al.* 1996), occur in 1.9% of stallions and 0.7% of geldings.

Description. This represents an aggressive behavior directed against the animal's own body. Affected horses most often bite their chest, shoulders or flanks but also all other body parts within their reach. This behavior is often accompanied by whinnying, squealing or kicking. Turning in one spot in connection with flank biting can also be observed. In doing so, the horse appears to "chase" its own body. Aggression may also be directed towards other horses or humans if they approach the horse. Some horses (stallions) only show self-mutilating behavior during the breeding season (**117**), while others exhibit it year-round.

Predisposition. Self-mutilation is almost exclusively shown by stallions, with domestic stallions as well as Przewalski stallions in zoos being equally affected. Sometimes, although rarely, it can be observed in geldings and mares. Geldings most often adopt self-mutilation prior to castration. As in cribbing and weaving, a genetic component appears to be present in this behavioral aberration, as it occurs with striking frequency in some families. Most often, exercise-loving and highly sensitive horses are particularly affected. This may also explain why Arabians show the highest frequency of occurrence of self-mutilating behavior of all breeds.

Health risks. Horses can injure themselves seriously during self-mutilation. The resulting pain will not, however, keep them from continuing the self-destructive behavior. This can also be observed in other species that show self-mutilating behavior. It is therefore assumed that pain is easier to bear for these animals than the ongoing frustration and deprivation.

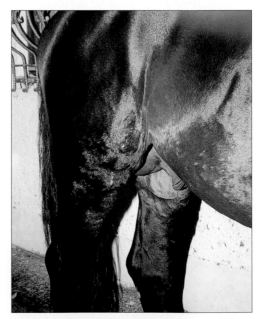

117 Self-mutilation in a breeding stallion. Scars, which are covered with white hairs, are evidence of the behavior, which this horse only exhibits at the breeding station during the breeding season.

Aggression is, however, not only directed against the horse's own body. The risk of injury to humans or other horses also exists. The latter can restrict breeding use of stallions that exhibit the behavior excessively. In extreme situations, a horse may even try to bite its own body when under saddle, which can turn into a dangerous situation for the rider. These horses will also often kick out while biting themselves, which poses an additional risk to people nearby.

Causes. According to current knowledge, self-mutilation exclusively represents a management- and handling-induced behavioral aberration. In contrast to previous presumptions, the actual concentration of male sex hormones is probably less predisposing for the development of the behavior than an inborn heightened potential for aggression. This is without doubt most strongly expressed in stallions but can also be shown by some mares and geldings. If these predisposed horses are kept under inadequate management conditions, frustration and deprivation can result in an emotional build-up, which cannot be compensated for. Because a social partner is lacking, this aggression is then directed against the horse's own body. This also serves to explain the higher occurrence in stallions because, with the beginning of the breeding season, many of them are kept very isolated and without sufficient exercise and sensory stimulation.

Triggers. As is the case for other problems, processes that are associated with a large increase in excitement are of particular importance for self-mutilation. Aside from the expectance of feed these include seeking contact with other horses. In stallions, therefore, the behavior is elicited particularly when mares are led past them, which they are unable to reach.

Therapy. Improvement of the management and handling conditions has to be the first therapeutic measure. It is relatively easy to achieve an improvement in feeding towards a behaviorally appropriate regimen with adequately long feeding times (roughage *ad libitum*), and an increase in exercise, for example with pasture access, use of hot walkers or lungeing, but the requirement for social contact is more difficult to meet. Although the optimal solution would be free contact with other horses, there is a risk of injury to other horses with this type of aberrant behavior. Stall confinement with an adjacent paddock should be tried as an alternative, and closer social contact should be established in small steps. Initially, constant good visual, olfactory and auditory contact with a calm neighbor (for stallions a gelding) is sufficient. Sometimes it is necessary to leave an empty paddock in between the neighboring horses. After a sufficiently long adjustment period and with good compatibility, social contact across the paddock fence can be allowed. Above all with self-mutilating behavior, the daily routine and handling should be designed such that excitement peaks for the horse are reduced. The goal is to normalize the behavior by means of sufficient exercise, environmental variability, and sufficient social contact with a familiar barn neighbor.

Accompanying medical support with psychopharmacologic drugs or hormones (progestins) may be required in extremely self-mutilating horses. If these measures and the fulfillment of horse-specific needs are not sufficient to contain the aggressive behavior, castration should be considered in stallions. Approximately 30% of stallions, however, do not respond to this measure. Because of the potential for a hereditary component, it would further be useful to exclude stallions and mares which exhibit this increased aggressive behavior from breeding. Temporary mechanical prevention of self-mutilating behavior can be useful to avoid further injury and allow wounds to heal. A stiff collar, which prevents biting of the body but allows normal feed intake, may be used. Unsuitable, and from an animal welfare standpoint inappropriate, measures include muzzle placement or tying the horse up short because they further worsen the horse's management conditions and heighten its frustration.

Prevention. Self-mutilating behavior does not occur with appropriate management and feeding. In stallions in particular, sufficient social contact should be provided. Because of a potential genetic disposition, self-mutilating horses should be excluded from breeding.

Differential diagnosis. Increased aggressiveness, heightened excitability and self-mutilation of the front limbs can also occur as a sign of rabies. However, additional clear diagnostic signs such as inappetence, difficulty in swallowing, salivation, lethargy, intestinal stasis, and so on, exist in this disease. Rabies has become uncommon in central Europe but it is still a significant threat to horses in the US and vaccination is generally recommended for horses. In general, out of all reported rabies cases in animals, more than 90% occur in wild

---

Self-mutilation

Classification	Management- and handling-induced behavioral aberration
Description	Biting directed at the horse's own chest, shoulders, flanks and other body parts within reach. Combination with other behaviors such as whinnying, squealing or kicking possible
Predisposition	• Stallions • Hereditary predisposition (aggression potential, sensitivity)
Causes	Drastic events in the negative sense (emotional build-up and overexcitement due to deprivation, frustration or conflicts)
Trigger situation:	Events that result in increased excitement/agitation: • Perception of horses out of reach • Barn activities (feeding, people)
Consequences:	• Injury to the self-mutilating horse • Injury to other horses and people
Therapy:	• Appropriate management and feeding according to behavioral needs – Opportunity for lots of exercise – Variation and occupation (goal: decrease excitement) – Optimization of social contact (successive establishment of contact with other horses) • Castration of stallions Incompatible with animal welfare laws: muzzling, tying up short
Prevention:	• Appropriate management and feeding • Appropriate handling and stress free training

---

animals. In 1998, the highest number of rabies cases in horses since 1981 occurred, with 82 reported cases. According to an estimate by the Cooperative Extension Service of the University of Kentucky, College of Agriculture, approximately 40 cases of rabies in horses occur every year in the US. In 2000, 49 states, D.C. and Puerto Rico reported 7,369 total cases of rabies in animals, of which 93% occurred in wild animals and 6.9% in domestic animals (information from the National Center for Infectious Diseases website).

Heightened aggressiveness

HEIGHTENED AGGRESSIVENESS WITHIN A GROUP
Description. Dominance-induced aggressiveness is a normal part of the behavioral repertoire of horses. It is used to establish a rank order or to ascertain an already existing hierarchy. The range of behaviors shown in this context includes everything from a slight laying back of the ears to massive attacks including well aimed use of the hooves and teeth. This normal behavior is particularly evident when a new horse is integrated into an already existing group (**118**). In this case,

conflicts are more or less severe and last for varying periods of time, depending on the newcomer's rank status and tendency to fight, but they will eventually subside. In a well integrated group, laying back of the ears, rear leg and bite threats or an occasional pinching will then suffice to document rank position. Persistent aggressiveness in a group, which repeatedly results in injury, does not correspond to normal horse behavior and has to be evaluated as to its causes.

Causes. Generally, normal behavior of horses is present (see differential diagnosis). Rarely, socially disturbed horses are responsible for heightened aggressiveness within a group; however, a single animal can suffice to increase the risk of injury for all. This aberrant behavior is most often based on social deprivation during foal development or on bad experiences. The result is heightened aggressiveness out of fear of one's own species. Less common is a disposition for heightened aggressiveness. Such an inborn behavioral defect will manifest particularly intensely in the presence of management and handling deficits. As a general rule, learning processes can further increase heightened intraspecies aggressiveness.

118 Massive rank conflicts are normal if a new horse is integrated into a group without special precautions.

Heightened aggressiveness within a group	
Classification	**Management- and handling-induced behavioral aberration of one horse or several horses**
Differential diagnosis	Normal behavior (cause: management deficits)
Description	Ongoing heightened aggressiveness within a group with repeated occurrence of severe injuries
Cause	Fear due to social deprivation (one or several horses)
Consequences	• Injury to the aggressive horse
	• Injury to other horses and people
	• Discrimination, stress and increased unrest
Therapy	Gradual establishment of contact with other horses or removal from the group (stall with paddock)
Prevention	• Raising of young horses in groups
	• Exclusion from breeding of horses with inborn heightened aggressiveness
	• Correct design of group management systems and expert management

Therapy and prevention. If fear of other horses is the cause, the affected horse should initially be removed from the group in order to re-integrate it gradually at a later time. The best approach would at first be to keep the horse in an adjacent paddock. From there, the socially disturbed horse can make contact with its previous group. At the same time, however, a safe retreat into the inside of the stall needs to be available. Only when the horse does not show any more fear of the other horses in this safe environment, can it be brought back together with the other group members one at a time. Depending on the severity of the aberration, this can require a varying amount of time. For most socially disturbed horses, management in a small group (two to four animals) or in an individual stall with paddock is the better alternative. Horses with an inborn heightened aggressiveness should definitely be moved to such an individual system. If deficits in management and handling are present, their origins need to be explored and appropriate improvements need to be made. Suggestions for this approach can be found on p.37.

Differential diagnosis. Most often, frequent conflicts and repeatedly occurring major injuries in a group management are attributable to deficits in the group concept and management. These include insufficient space, lack of opportunities to escape for lower-ranked animals, or an ill planned group structure. Under these circumstances, management is responsible for the heightened aggressiveness among horses and the animals' reaction has to be regarded as normal (p.31).

SEXUAL AGGRESSIVENESS IN STALLIONS
Description. Excessive aggressiveness of breeding stallions towards mares is not uncommon in traditional management systems, i.e. management in individual stalls. Without proper precautions, use of these stallions for breeding would result in

serious injury of the breeding partner. But mares are not the only ones at risk. Aggression can also be directed against humans and against the stallion's own body. The latter would represent the starting point for the previously described self-mutilating behavior (p.154).

Causes. The cause of excessive aggressiveness towards mares is most often a lack of experience in the natural breeding process, because most breeding stallions never get to know the normal events of breeding. In addition, misdirected conditioning for the breeding process is present. When servicing mares in-hand, breeding stallions get used to the mare not showing any resistance because her readiness to mate was previously tested with the help of a teasing stallion. Furthermore, the mare is most often prevented from kicking by hobbles. Breeding without risk, however, virtually conditions the stallion to associate each sexual arousal with a rapid and successful ejaculation. It is even further removed from the natural situation and less problematic for the stallion to mount a phantom for semen collection and subsequent artificial insemination. Stallions used exclusively in this manner cannot

Sexual aggressiveness in stallions	
Classification*	1: Unwanted behavior 2: Management- and handling-induced behavioral aberration of one horse or several horses
Description	Biting and kicking the mare during the breeding act
Predisposition	Hereditary predisposition (heightened aggressiveness) Inadequate management Inappropriate handling
Causes	1: Lack of experience, learned behavior (misdirected/false conditioning) 2: Drastic events in the negative sense (emotional build-up and over excitement due to deprivation, frustration or conflicts)
Consequences	Injuries to other horses and people Starting point for self-mutilation
Therapy	1 and 2: Appropriate management and feeding according to behavioral needs 1: • Opportunity for lots of exercise • Counter-conditioning 2: • Variation and occupation (goal: reducing excitement) • Expert, calm, consequent handling
Prevention:	• Appropriate management and feeding • Appropriate handling • Raising of young horses in groups • Exclusion of stallions with heightened aggressiveness from breeding

*Numbers used for classification correspond to numbers used in causes and therapy

be used for free breeding in a herd without preparation because they are unfamiliar with the defense reactions of a mare that is not ready to breed. Massive aggression is just as preprogrammed in these situations as is complete unwillingness to breed. In individual cases, an inborn tendency towards heightened aggressiveness can exist. Horses predisposed in this manner will react especially sensitively to mistakes made in management and handling.

Therapy and prevention. A definite therapeutic must in cases of heightened aggression is an improvement in the management conditions. The more exercise and occupation provided for the stallion on a daily basis, the easier it will be to decrease overexcitement and to manage aggressive behavior (**119**). In this manner, the stallion will learn that not every opening of the stall door implies an impending breeding act. Satisfaction of the species-specific needs and physical balance will further contribute to psychological calming, which must be a primary concern. For this reason, handling also has to occur in a calm and consistent manner. This requires a large amount of authority, expertise

119 The Spanish walk is an exercise to reduce aggression.

and sensitivity on part of the handler and carer. Daily rank order exercises with positive reinforcement are recommended to establish dominance of the handler. Deconditioning of the learned behavior can be attempted after improvements in management and handling have been made. Lessons based on classical conditioning or those associated with a calming sound and feed can be successful. Depending on the extent of the stallion's libido, redirection or at least a certain distraction can be achieved.

Last but not least, gentleness of stallions should be considered when choosing them for breeding because a certain hereditary predisposition for aggressive behavior exists. This, in connection with optimization of management and handling conditions, also represents the most important preventive measure. Further information can be found on p.51.

MATERNAL AGGRESSIVENESS

During the critical period, a more aggressive behavior than usual of the mare towards members of other species as well as other horses represents normal behavior and serves to ensure an undisturbed imprinting process (p.53). Even beyond this period, a heightened aggression potential of the mare is a normal reaction because in the wild, her willingness to defend the foal is a prerequisite for its survival.

At times, however, the mare's aggressiveness is also directed towards her own foal. In individual cases this can go as far as the newborn not obtaining colostrum, starving to death, being seriously hurt, or even being killed by the mare. Many factors may be involved as causes for this misdirected behavior. Varying therapeutic approaches, therefore, have to be taken depending on the individual cause.

Disturbance of the dam–foal relationship
Causes. First of all, external influences during and after birth can evoke aggressive reactions in the mare. These include, for example, disturbance by other horses or dogs but also by humans (p.152). This can result in the dam not becoming sufficiently fixated on her newborn foal. The potential consequence is a lasting rejection of the foal in combination with massive attacks when it attempts to suckle. In individual cases, disturbances during and after birth can also result in a stress-induced misdirected defense reaction, i.e. one that is directed not towards the intruder but against the mare's own foal. Under these circumstances, the foal can also be seriously hurt.

Therapy and prevention. If the foal cannot remain with its dam, it needs to be moved to a surrogate dam as soon as possible. Raising the foal by hand should only be used as the last resort. To avoid too strong a bond to humans, the foal must have close social contact with other horses and should not be fed with a bottle but instead with a bucket with a drink nipple. As a preventive measure, a quiet and shielded place should be provided for birth and the period immediately following birth. The necessary requirements for an undisturbed bonding between dam and foal have already been described on p.56.

Lack of experience

Causes and differential diagnosis. Maternal aggressiveness of the mare towards her foal is most often observed in mares giving birth for the first time. In these cases, fear or pain or both are the cause. This behavior is generally attributable to a lack of experience. In some mares, even the unfamiliar sight of a resting foal can elicit aggressive reactions; in others, the first suckling attempts at the firmly filled udder lead to massive rejection. As differential diagnoses, painful diseases of the udder (e.g. mastitis) have to be ruled out and treated appropriately.

Therapy and prevention. If fear or pain causes the aggression, one should helpfully intervene. The mare must not be punished for her behavior but must learn under praise to associate the foal with a positive experience. In most cases it will be sufficient to restrain the mare temporarily and allow the foal to suckle for the first time. As a positive reinforcement and to distract the mare, she is fed during this time and is calmed by speaking to her. The first nursing will result in a positive experience for the mare because the painful pressure within the udder subsides. In addition, several hormones are released, including oxytocin, which are thought to evoke a feeling of well-being. Most often, the problem will subside after a few repetitions and the mare will accept her foal. As a preventive measure it is recommended to keep maiden mares in herds together with foals. The inexperienced animal will then learn to become used to the sight of resting, suckling, and playing foals. Further recommendations can be found on p.55.

Inborn behavior

A genetic component for maternal aggressiveness cannot be excluded. According to Houpt (1995), mares of Arabian origin, and in particular certain blood lines, tend towards aggression against their own foals with a significantly higher frequency than other horse breeds. In affected horses, the behavior is usually exhibited immediately after birth and is not attributable to external influences. It is further shown not only with the first-born but also with subsequent foals. No effective therapy exists in these cases; however, restraint or treatment of the mare with tranquilizers such as acepromazine can be successful in milder cases. A drug named sulpuride may also be of use, but the drug is currently not licensed in the US. In most cases, it is recommended to separate the foal from its dam because this form of aggression cannot be easily controlled. As a consequence, it is recommended that these mares are excluded from breeding.

Maternal aggressiveness	
Classification	1: Unwanted behavior
	2: Management- and handling-induced behavioral aberration of one horse or several horses
Description	Aggression of the mare against her foal
Causes*	1: Peri- and postnatal disturbances (people, horses, other animals)
	2: Pain and fear (lack of experience)
	3: Hereditary heightened aggressiveness
Consequences	• No dam-foal bonding
	• Risk of injury to the foal
Therapy	1: None (foals: surrogate dam or raising by hand)
	2: Counter-conditioning
	3: None (foals: surrogate dam or raising by hand)
Prevention	• Raising of young horses in groups
	• Appropriate management of dams (herd)
	• No disturbance during the imprinting period
	• Exclusion of mares with heightened aggressiveness from breeding
*Numbers used for causes correspond to numbers used in the therapy section	

Comfort behavior

Tail rubbing

Description and health risks. Sporadic tail rubbing is normal horse behavior in the context of solitary grooming. It is shown with increased frequency during shedding. In contrast, longer lasting or stereotypical tail rubbing against objects has to be regarded as aberrant behavior. Excessive tail rubbing results in loss of tail hair and carries the serious risk of ascending infection.

Causes. In most cases, a symptomatic behavioral aberration is present, which is attributable to dermatological or parasitic diseases (**120**). Causes include:

- Endoparasites such as pinworms (*O. equi*), whose females cause significant itching when migrating to the anus in order to lay their eggs.
- Ectoparasites such as mites and lice, which find particularly good living conditions under the tail head of sweating horses, can cause increased itching.
- Allergic and fungal skin diseases can also cause more frequent tail rubbing.
- Constant rubbing and scratching of the tail is a sign of the cauda equina syndrome (polyneuritis equi), a widespread clinical syndrome of as yet unknown cause (Grabner 2000).

Although uncommon, constant rubbing against objects can also represent a management- and handling-induced behavioral aberration. As in cribbing and weaving, management deficits and mistakes in handling that repeatedly result in social and psychological frustration as well as chronic conflict situations, are predisposing.

Therapy and prevention. The therapeutic approach to excessive tail rubbing has first of all to include determination of whether a disease is present or proper care of the horse has been neglected. Appropriate therapeutic measures (e.g. deworming) have to be taken. Mares in heat may exhibit increased tail rubbing and can simply be equipped with a tail wrap for this period. If a management- and handling-induced behavioral aberration is present, environmental conditions must be improved. If tail rubbing is elicited by certain activities or by overexcitement, tension should be decreased through a

behaviorally appropriate feeding regimen as well as sufficient social contact, environmental stimulation and exercise (group management, pasture access) (p.117). Prevention primarily should include regular grooming of the horse as well as preventive health measures. With regard to aberrant behavior, the general recommendation is to design management and handling of the horse from birth onwards in such a manner that species-specific needs are met and physical as well as psychological overburdening is avoided.

Differential diagnosis. Increased tail rubbing during shedding must be differentiated from other causes. It represents normal behavior and can be maintained for extended periods in insufficiently groomed and underfed horses. In addition, some mares show increased tail rubbing when they are in heat, which is also normal and usually not of pathological origin.

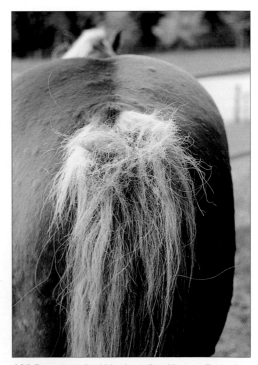

120 Excessive tail rubbing is attributable to a disease in almost all cases. In this horse, the cause was urticaria resulting in extreme pruritus (itching).

Tail rubbing (similar origin: excessive solitary grooming)

Classification*	**1: Symptomatic behavioral aberration**
	2: Management- and handling-induced behavioral aberration
Description	Excessive rubbing of the tail against objects and loss of tail hair
Causes	1: Parasitic or dermatologic diseases (endo- and ectoparasites, mites, fungus, allergy)
	2: Drastic events in the negative sense (emotional build-up and overexcitement due to deprivation, frustration or conflicts)
Consequences	Infection and inflammation
Therapy	1: Medical treatment
	2:
	• Appropriate management and feeding according to behavioral needs
	• Appropriate handling
Prevention	1: Regular grooming and preventive health measures
	2:
	• Appropriate management and feeding according to behavioral needs
	• Appropriate handling

*Numbers used for classification correspond to numbers used in causes, therapy, and so on

Excessive grooming

Causes and triggers for excessive gnawing at the horse's own body are largely similar to those described above for excessive tail rubbing (p.161). Therapeutic measures are therefore analogous. Similarly, social grooming or excessive mane and tail biting can be exhibited in an exaggerated manner. This frequently occurs if social grooming was prevented for a long time (**121**). With unlimited social contact, therefore, the behavior can be expected to normalize over time. In addition, management conditions should be designed to provide variety. Evaluation of the feed ration for potential deficits should also be considered. Aside from mineral and vitamin deficiency, lack of structured forage can result in excessive grooming as a type of substitute activity.

121 Social grooming is a natural need of horses.

> ## Excessive grooming (similar origin: excessive solitary grooming)
>
> | | |
> |---|---|
> | Classification* | 1: Behavioral aberration caused by deficiencies (hair eating)
2: Symptomatic behavioral aberration
3: Management- and handling-induced behavioral aberration |
> | Causes | 1a: Nutritional deficits (roughage, minerals, vitamins)
1b: Social deficiencies
2: Parasitic or dermatologic diseases
3: Drastic events in the negative sense (emotional build-up and overexcitement due to deprivation, frustration or conflicts) |
> | Therapy | 1a: Correction of the nutritional, roughage, mineral or vitamin deficit
1b: Appropriate management (social contact, occupation)
2: Medical treatment
3:
• Appropriate management and feeding according to behavioral needs
• Appropriate handling |
>
> *Numbers used for classification correspond to numbers used in causes and therapy

Head tossing, headshaking

Description. Under various circumstances, horses exhibit a variety of head movements as normal behavior. Shaking of the head is usually shown in the context of insect repulsion or due to inflammatory processes in the head and ear region. Nodding movements or horizontal back and forth movement of the head occur with agonistic behavior such as threatening and herding. Head nodding further supports accurate focusing of the eyes on objects. Rotary and swinging head movements occur as substitute activities in conflict situations or more generally in states of overexcitement. All these types of head movements, however, have a relatively short duration. Intensive shaking of the head, on the other hand, represents aberrant behavior of a completely different origin. The syndrome has been termed "headshaking". It describes a behavior during which the horse exhibits violent, rhythmic head movements in a vertical or, less commonly, a horizontal direction without a detectable external stimulus.

Causes for headshaking are very variable. They therefore have to be evaluated carefully by medical examination and thorough anamnesis. Appropriate therapeutic measures can only be employed if an exact diagnosis has been made. They will differ considerably depending on the cause.

Disease
Causes. In about 10% of cases, a symptomatic behavioral aberration is present, which may have one of the following causes:

• Guttural pouch mycosis.
• Sinusitis with fluid accumulation in the sinuses.
• Dental diseases.
• Diseases of the eyes and ears including the inner ear and equilibrium.
• Painful aberrations of the neck musculature and spine.
• Allergic and central nervous diseases.

Therapy. First of all, it has to be determined whether a symptomatic behavioral aberration is present. To achieve a diagnosis, extensive clinical, endoscopic, hematologic, and radiographic examination may be necessary. If a cause can be detected, therapy will be directed at treatment of the specific underlying disease.

Photosensitivity
Causes. According to current knowledge, the most common cause of headshaking is photosensitivity. Recent studies from the US, Germany, and Switzerland showed that a large proportion of headshaking is light dependent. The presumed cause is a hypersensitivity of the infraorbital branch of the trigeminal nerve, which is amplified by light-dependent irritation of the optical nerve.

It has not been determined, however, how this hypersensitivity develops. A seasonal occurrence can be observed. Horses exhibit the abnormal behavior mostly during the spring and summer and much less or not at all during the fall and winter. In the barn or a dark riding arena, head-shaking is observed rarely or not at all, and is much less intense. It recurs immediately, however, when horses are brought into bright sunlight. In general, clinical signs become more overt during work, which may indicate a psychological component. Headshaking is mostly seen at a trot and less often at a walk or canter. It can occur to an extent that makes the horse unrideable. Excessive pawing, rubbing of the nose against the ground or against objects (**122**), and sneezing occur as accompanying features.

Therapy. If photosensitive headshaking is diagnosed, chances of a cure are not good. In general, avoidance of light exposure during work in the spring and summer is recommended. The riding technique should be particularly sensitive and should be adjusted to the individual horse. Symptomatic therapy, the success of which varies, is the only other available option at this point. It includes the use of dark nylon nets or eye masks with dark lenses, which lessen the incidence of light to the eye, as well as additional nets around the nostrils. In some horses, these measures result in a significant reduction of photosensitive headshaking (**123**). Another option is drug therapy with cyproheptadine, which requires long-term treatment and can be associated with side effects (colic). Successful treatment in the sense of an improvement occurs in about 70–80% of cases (Madigan 1996, Feige and Wehrli 1998). Cyproheptadine, however, does not cure the disease but merely suppresses the clinical signs of headshaking. Alternative treatment methods (homeopathy, nosodes) work very successfully in some horses. Administration of melatonin and neurectomy of the infraorbital branch of the trigeminal nerve are less successful and not without risk and therefore should be rejected (Mair and Lane 1990, Madigan 1996).

Management- and handling-induced behavioral aberration

Cause. If stereotypical headshaking is shown in the barn and independent of season, a management- and handling-induced behavioral aberration may be present. Systematic studies of this occurrence are, however, lacking at this time. In general, a similar genesis as that of weaving and cribbing is assumed. First-time occurrence is thought to be particularly associated with abrupt management changes (move to a different barn) and social isolation. Sometimes, the behavior shown in the barn can become worse when working the horse. According to Lebelt (1998), this may be attributable to stress-induced activation of neuroendocrinologic systems (increase in cortisol and endorphin levels during physical stress), which is generally associated with worsening of stereotypical behavioral patterns.

Therapy. As with other abnormal behavioral patterns, management and handling should be adjusted to meet horse-specific needs as much as possible if a management- and handling-induced behavioral aberration is present (p.117). Emphasis should be placed on sufficient social contact, for example, by means of pasture access together with other horses. Feeding regimens should be changed to allow longer eating times by offering more roughage and less concentrate.

Unwanted behavior

Cause. Headshaking can also be caused by pain or fear due to equipment deficits or improper influence of the rider. In this case, it does not represent a behavioral aberration but rather an unwanted behavior. As this form of headshaking is primarily seen during use of the horse, it will be further discussed on p.190.

Therapy. Headshaking as an unwanted behavior should be treated according to the underlying cause by eliminating deficits (e.g. improvement of equipment and riding technique) or by implementing trust-building measures. In many cases it represents an avoidance reaction against the hard hand of a rider or an ill fitting or harsh bit. In these cases, improvement may be seen with a change to a different bit or a bitless headpiece and with a lighter use of the reins. The use of harsh bits, side reins that limit movement and other means to prevent head-shaking have to be rejected for animal welfare reasons. The same is true for equivalent measures within the stall (p.190).

Health risks. If a primary disease is not present, health risks for horses due to headshaking are not recognized at present. It remains to be determined how painful the potential hypersensitivity of the trigeminal nerve is. The occurrence of sudden, jerking head movements "as if due to electric shock" suggests sudden jolts of severe pain. Excessive headshaking can severely limit a horse's use as a riding or carriage horse and can also potentially endanger the rider.

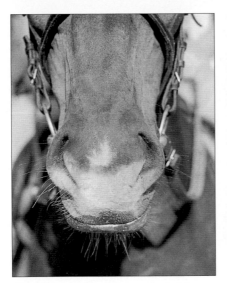

122 Intense rubbing of the nose against the ground or objects in headshakers indicates a photosensitive event.

123 Mechanical devices against headshaking such as eye masks and nose protectors can result in complete resolution of clinical signs in some horses.

Head tossing, headshaking

Classification*	**1: Symptomatic behavioral aberration** **a: Disease** **b: Photosensitivity** **2: Management- and handling-induced behavioral aberration** **3: Unwanted behavior**
Description	Violent, rhythmic movements of the head in vertical or horizontal direction without a recognizable external stimulus
Causes	1a: Disease 1b: Photosensitivity 2: Drastic events in the negative sense (emotional build-up and overexcitement due to deprivation, frustration or conflicts) 3: Pain (fear), learned behavior
Therapy	1a: Medical treatment 1b: • Mechanical protective measures ("sunglasses", nylon nets) • Medical treatment 2: • Appropriate management and feeding according to behavioral needs • Appropriate handling 3: • Removal of the cause for pain • Counter-conditioning Not acceptable for animal welfare reasons: mechanical suppression of headshaking
Prevention:	• Regular health checks • Appropriate management and feeding according to behavioral needs • Appropriate handling and stress free utilization of the horse

*Numbers used for classification correspond to numbers used in causes and therapy

Resting behavior

Failure to lie down

Description. As classical flight animals, horses mainly rest in a standing position. It is therefore natural if a horse spends a very short time per day lying down and that it only occupies about 10% of the 24-hour day. Adult horses only spend about 20 minutes per day or less in lateral recumbency. It is also natural for adult horses to lie down only if their need for security is satisfied. Aberrant behavior, on the other hand, exists if a horse does not lie down at all for an extended period.

Causes. Generally, a failure to lie down represents normal equine behavior (see differential diagnosis). In some cases pain can be the cause if horses fail to lie down, because lying down and, in particular, getting back up are strenuous movements for horses and place great strain on their joints. For this reason, horses with arthrosis, acute arthritis, back problems or old horses with varying signs of wear are reluctant to lie down (**124**).

Health risks. According to current knowledge, and in contrast to the still widespread belief that horses can sleep standing, horses need to go into sternal and particularly lateral recumbency to feel refreshed physically and psychologically. If horses fail to lie down over extended periods of time, the body's ability to regenerate, and with it the horse's performance as well as its psychological well-being, will be compromised (p.70).

Therapy. Therapy is generally successful if the particular cause can be removed by an improvement of management conditions or by medical treatment. Older horses will lie down despite having "stiff" joints if they are provided with soft and dry ground with especially good traction, and if they have sufficient room. In a group management situation, personal experience through studies has shown that a seemingly large enough space by itself is not sufficient to allow all horses to rest in sternal and lateral recumbency equally. Even if the resting area is large enough, lower-ranked horses will be disturbed disproportionately more often during resting. Under these circumstances it is recommended to improve resting opportunities for lower-ranked horses by providing additional installations (e.g. dividers) or by taking certain management measures (e.g. a resting area free of "feed", i.e. straw). This issue was discussed in detail on p.71.

Differential diagnosis. Most often, a feeling of insecurity is the cause of a failure to lie down. For example, the unfamiliar environment after a move to a new barn, a very isolated environment, or a group management situation without sufficient opportunity for retreat or with an improperly composed group can prompt horses to exhibit this behavior. Additionally, management deficits can make it difficult or impossible to lie down. These include insufficient space to allow the required movements, an insufficiently long rope or chain in tie stalls, a ground surface without traction, or wet bedding. Under all these circumstances, management is responsible for the horse's failure to lie down and the horse's reaction has to be regarded as normal.

Failure to lie down

Classification	**Symptomatic behavioral aberration**
Differential diagnosis	Normal behavior (cause: management deficits)
Description	Failure to rest in sternal or lateral recumbency over an extended period of time
Causes	Disease (arthritis, degenerative joint disease, back problems)
Consequences	Insufficient physical and psychological regeneration
Therapy	• Medical therapy
	• Appropriate barn/stall design for horse
	• Regular health checks
Prevention	• Careful use of the horse
	• Appropriate management

124 Lying down and particularly getting up are strenuous movements for older horses. For this reason, horses with varying musculoskeletal diseases will often avoid lying down.

Part E: Problem behavior during handling and under saddle or tack

Problem behavior during handling or during riding and driving is generally not considered aberrant behavior but represents unwanted behavior. An exception would be the presence of a phobia, in which case the behavior has to be called aberrant. The term phobia is used if the fear reactions exhibited diverge significantly from the norm. They often have their origin in a traumatic experience. In these cases, there is often no clear-cut difference between unwanted behavior and a behavioral aberration, and classification may be difficult. One can, however, assume that a phobia is present if, despite a sensibly dosed progressive desensitization, the horse's defense reactions remain the same or become even more violent as soon as the horse is confronted with the stimulus.

Unwanted behavior, to a large extent, represents normal, species-specific equine behavior. It is, however, uncomfortable or even dangerous for human beings. These behavioral patterns are, therefore, also referred to as vices or disobedient behavior. Both terms however favor a one-sided thought process: the misleading verbal connotation associated with the word "vice" was discussed on p.93. If a horse has a vice or is disobedient, the thought automatically comes to mind that it is not behaving well, that its actions go against the rider's wishes or, as is often said, that the "stubborn old jade" does

not want to go. With this attitude, the therapeutic approach is evident. The horse has to learn to obey, if necessary under pressure.

However, the main cause of problem behavior in these cases is pain or fear or both. Zeeb (1997) describes the behavior as "harm-avoiding reaction". In this case, the approach to correction will be entirely different. This is not meant to sound as if unwanted behavior is not associated with rank order problems; nor is it disputed that an assertive and energetic riding technique, provided the rider is good and remains sensitive, may be required in the treatment of problem horses. The spectrum of causes of unwanted behavior, however, includes far more than simple disobedience. An extensive diagnostic work-up, which takes all possibilities into account, is therefore indispensable for successful therapy with regard to the human and the horse.

In the following section, the most common unwanted behaviors will be discussed with regard to their causes, therapy, and prevention. The examples were chosen to be representative of other similar behaviors, such that problems not specifically mentioned in this context can be treated accordingly. In contrast to most management- and handling-induced behavioral aberrations, unwanted behaviors carry a greater chance of success with treatment.

Unwanted behavior during handling

Problems during handling of horses are not rare. Many horse owners, however, put up with the unwanted behavior, especially if the horse works well under saddle or in front of a carriage. Problem behavior during handling is, at first sight at least, often independent and is not necessarily associated with problems during use of the horse. Could there be a connection with

the opinion that it is sufficient to dominate a horse under saddle in order to be recognized as higher in rank? Is the rider then really the dominant one or does the horse only obey out of fear? Only during handling will it become evident whether the rank order between human and horse is settled and whether they truly have a trusting relationship.

Unwillingness to be caught

Description. In the literature, individual stalls are often described as having the advantage of making the horse "easily available", while for group management systems, the disadvantage of a "decreased availability" is stressed. The problem of horses that are unwilling to be caught once they are in a paddock or pasture must therefore be widespread. The problem ranges from a temporary inability to catch the horse to the necessity of bringing the entire group into the barn in order to catch one horse.

Causes. If a horse is free and removed from the immediate human influence, it will primarily act according to its own needs. These are in turn dependent on the current motivation. If, for example, the horse wants to eat grass or be with its companions when a person approaches to catch it, and if it is higher in rank than the person, it will see no need to follow the person's wishes. The cause in this case is a rank order problem.

Fear is associated with this behavior with equal frequency (**125**). This can be attributed to different triggers. In most cases the horse has had bad experiences in the past or it is afraid of the approaching person or of people in general. Lack of trust or lack of a bond with the person approaching or with people in general can also cause the behavior. In these cases, a combination of fear and unsettled rank order frequently exists.

Sometimes, particularly in young horses that love to run, unwillingness to be caught is associated with an invitation to play. This behavior can be recognized by characteristic posture such as a raised tail head and forward ears. The behavior is not necessarily associated with a rank order problem. Some horses will be easy to catch after a few rounds of galloping and bucking.

Therapy. Independent of cause, unwillingness to be caught is best corrected by counter-conditioning in the form of classical conditioning. In the beginning, the horse should not be worked hard but should only be caught to groom it or do other pleasant things. It is useful to perform the behavioral therapy in a small paddock (without grass), at first with the horse by itself and then together with another, very people-friendly horse. Spacious pastures are unsuitable because large areas tempt horses to run, and

---

Catching of horses

What should not be done
- Chasing after the horse.
- Cornering it.
- Approaching it from behind or from the front.
- Punishing it after catching (yanking the lead rope!)

How it is done correctly
- Approaching slowly, using conditioned call.
- Giving space.
- Approaching from the side (shoulder height).
- Rewarding after catching (praise, petting, treats).

Hint: even escaped horses have to be rewarded
Horses that repeatedly escape from the barn or the pasture are easier to catch if one does not immediately walk back to the barn once they are haltered. The horse would perceive this as punishment. The horse makes a positive association on the other hand if it is caught and then allowed to continue to graze. If the walk home is begun a few minutes later, the horse will not associate this with being caught any more. Being approached by a person will therefore not leave a negative association.

---

grass will distract from the exercise. Counter-conditioning should further not be attempted in the midst of many horses because the program is best associated with the offering of treats. In this case, therapy would be destined to fail from the start because feeding of only one horse would result in a massive conflict within the group.

If counter-conditioning is the method of choice, the horse first learns to associate the approaching person with a positive experience.

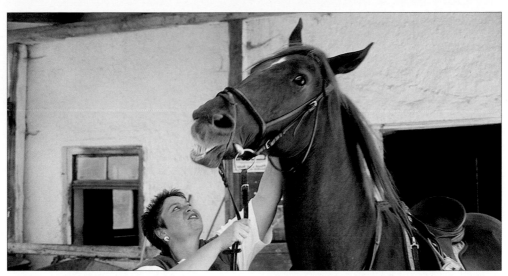

125 Pain and fear, and also rank order problems, can cause avoidance behavior during bridle placement.

In the beginning, one should therefore always bring some feed for the horse. It is important to always use the same call when approaching the horse, for example a soft "come, come" or "hoho" (Rai 1996). As soon as the horse has learned the association "call = treat", which usually takes place very rapidly, one approaches the horse while using the conditioned call and waits to offer feed until it takes at least one or two steps in one's direction (p.128). This is repeated until it has become natural for the horse to come towards the person as soon as it hears the call. If this is achieved, treats are no longer, or at least not always, required. This is the final goal; it must, however, also be reached under different conditions! One therefore continues by practicing in the pasture. If the motivation to eat grass is too great, one can make oneself more interesting. Many horses will, for example, become curious and draw near if the approaching person becomes smaller and smaller in front of them, squats down and remains in this position. The conditioned call has to be used at all times, however, because otherwise the horse may become scared and run off.

Very fearful horses should not be haltered at first during the conditioning program. It is important for them to learn to approach the person and to be touched by that person out of trust and their own will. In these cases, a treat is not necessary each time as long as the call has been conditioned. Talking to the horse in a friendly manner, patting and ruffling the mane are sufficient. The halter should only be placed once the horse has lost its fear and is able to remain relaxed next to the person. The halter is best placed while using the conditioned call and simultaneously giving a treat. Chewing and eating will distract the horse from its fear and will evoke a positive mood. The Tellington-Touch, which has proven to be a useful trust-building measure in fearful horses, has the same relaxing effect.

Classical conditioning is promising as a technique for dealing with rank order problems. Under no circumstances must the horse be punished after it is caught because, once the halter is placed, it has shown the desired behavior. It must be praised for this! Under these circumstances, rank order exercises are necessary and should be performed daily with determination and consistency: 20 minutes are needed at first, later on 5 minutes will suffice. Examples of these exercises are described on p.132.

Prevention. Unwillingness to be caught is best prevented by teaching the horse from the beginning that being approached by a person is associated with a positive experience. With classical conditioning as described above, even foals can be taught to approach people voluntarily. Once a trusting relationship has been established, halter placement becomes a minor consideration. It is important to visit horses sporadically in their paddock or in pasture without taking them to work every time. This is particularly true for young horses that are frequently left to themselves and are only removed from pasture to have their feet trimmed, to be vaccinated or be dewormed. One should make it a rule not only to catch young horses for uncomfortable manipulations, but also for subsequent positive experiences. These may, for example, represent a move to a different pasture or a walk to explore the area. If the horse is treated in this manner in its youth, catching it will not be a problem later on. The

conditioned call has proven useful and it should always be used when the horse is approached, be it to groom it, to leave it in the pasture or to ride it. It should be remembered that horses do not respond to calls as fast as dogs do, but instead often need a few minutes of "consideration" before they start to move. It is a very common bad habit to herd horses off a pasture or to even chase them with a whip. Any horse can be taught to come when called. In larger groups, it suffices when the leading animals are conditioned to the call. If they come when called, the others will follow and will, if a positive experience (e.g. feed) results repeatedly, react to the call themselves within a short time.

Unwillingness to be caught

Classification	**Unwanted behavior**
Description	Avoidance behavior when being caught
Causes	• Lack of an established rank order
	• Fear
	• Learned behavior
	• Play
Therapy	• Counter-conditioning (classical conditioning)
	• Rank order exercises
	• Trust-building measures
Prevention	• Positive conditioning and habituation starting at foal age
	• Positive experiences associated with catching and thereafter

---

With or without halter?

Should horses that are hard to catch be turned out to pasture with or without a halter?

What are the advantages?
In favor of a halter, no lengthy manipulations are necessary to catch the horse. If necessary, a short rope, with a knot tied at the end, of about 10–20 cm (4–8 in) length, can be left on the halter. It is important that the halter fits well so that the horse cannot get caught, for example when scratching with the rear foot or rubbing against objects. Leather halters are preferable because they break more easily than nylon halters. Without sufficient trust, however, even a halter will not help to catch a horse!

What are the disadvantages?
The disadvantage of a halter is that it can only be used safely if it is sufficiently tight. Fatal accidents of horses due to loose halters are not rare, and most halters seen in practice are too loose (**126**).

Conclusion
In general, halters represent an additional risk for the horse and are in the end not helpful in catching the horse if trust in the person is lacking. It is better to get the horse to come voluntarily by means of positive conditioning paired with rank order exercises. Horses that have established a trusting relationship with people and respect their superiority in rank will not run away from them.

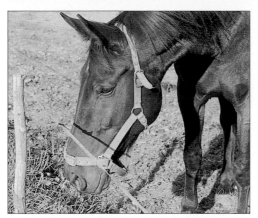

126 Loose halters are dangerous. They should at least be manufactured to tear or open in response to a strong pull in order to prevent potential accidents when the halter is caught.

Unwillingness to be led

Description. Generally, horse owners do not perceive difficulties when leading the horse as problem behavior. On the contrary, a prancing horse is thought to improve one's image more than one walking calmly behind its handler. The latter, however, represents normal horse behavior. Under natural conditions, horses complete any change in location on trails, where they walk like "ducks in a row". The dominant mare takes the lead, which provides the necessary security to the following animals. Horses that walk calmly behind one another therefore feel safe and trust their leader. This means that severe problems in the relationship between human and horse can be present if a horse is unwilling to be led.

Causes. Unwillingness to be led is unwanted behavior, which is attributable to the horse not having learned to follow a person or to be led. The behavior is also frequently associated with rank order problems, i.e. the horse does not recognize the person walking in front of or beside it as dominant. Insufficient basic training is often responsible for this behavior because special leading exercises are rarely part of a horse's schooling program. Later on in training and when riding is first started, correct leading is generally not emphasized either. It is also not uncommon for fear to be the reason for this unwanted behavior. It can be attributable to bad experiences or to general fear of people, but it can also be evoked by environmental influences. The latter may be the case, for example, if a stalled horse that has exclusively been ridden in a covered arena encounters tractors, cows, and so on, for the first time when being led out to pasture. If protection and trust in people are lacking in this situation, the horse will refuse to be led out of fear. Therefore, a combination of fear and lack of dominance of the handler is present.

Therapy. Correcting unwillingness to be led is at the same time an obedience exercise, which serves to clarify the rank order. Counter-conditioning in the form of operant conditioning has proven to be a useful method. It can be done as instrumental conditioning by use of aids such as lead chains and whips, or by means of body language with positive reinforcement and, if necessary, punishment. At first, exercises are performed in an enclosed, quiet area such as a riding arena. Once the leading exercise is performed correctly in this environment, the next level of difficulty, i.e. leading outside or in the presence of other horses can be approached. The goal is to have the horse follow in the desired position and on a loose lead line under all circumstances and to have it adjust to the person's speed. It is only allowed to eat if it has been given clear permission to do so.

When instrumental conditioning is used, the lead chain, provided it is fastened correctly (**127**), allows variable pressure to be applied to the nasal bone, which serves as punishment. The whip is used primarily to limit the available space and not to hit the horse. The horse is encouraged to

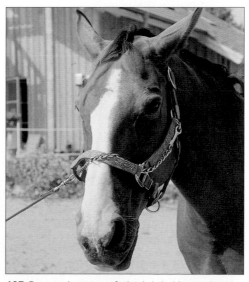

127 Correct placement of a lead chain. Horses should learn to be led from the left as well as the right side to prevent one-sidedness.

follow by command; the same one should be used every time. If the horse wants to rush past the handler, the boundary line is indicated with the whip. Simultaneously, one briefly and, if necessary, firmly tugs on the lead chain and lets go again immediately. A constant pull would be wrong. The tug on the lead chain is accompanied by a sharp "no". In this manner, and without having to use force, the horse learns to recognize its space and to follow a person. It is always useful to use a lead chain with this correction method. Simply tugging on a lead rope impresses few horses in this situation. If they are then punished because they are disobedient, confusion and fear are the only result.

When using body language for correction, the horse is taught to follow or stop by using certain body movements, which imitate horse behavior to a certain extent. If this method is mastered, horses can be taught to follow without the need for force or corporal punishment.

If a horse refuses to go forward, it has to be determined whether fear or stubbornness is the cause. If the former is present, the gentlest method is to work with the conditioned call as described earlier (p.171). Additional trust-building measures such as touching the horse all over its body are also helpful (p.134). The same goes for horses that alternate, out of fear, between storming forward and stopping. In these extremely fearful animals it is further recommended to combine leading exercises with ground work. This represents a good combination of trust-building measures and obedience exercises. The latter are particularly important for fearful animals because they serve to reinforce the human being's position as the "protective leader". If rank order problems, laziness, or stubbornness are the exclusive cause of the unwillingness to follow, the horse should be encouraged to move forward by a helper with a whip, who, positioned off to its side, walks behind the horse. In this case, vocal reinforcement by means of an energetic command supports the intention. In addition, ground work is necessary, during which the person can reinforce his dominance by means of obedience exercises such as stopping and backing up.

As is true for all unwanted behaviors and also for leading, appropriate management with sufficient exercise is the only way to ensure a balanced temperament in the horse. If this is not provided, the built-up need for exercise itself can result in an unwillingness to be led. When dealing with very hot-tempered horses, it is therefore reasonable not to start leading exercises until they have had sufficient exercise.

Prevention. Because the horse, as was already discussed in the section on social behavior (p.31), regards humans as a type of social partner, it should learn as early as possible to follow them. Leading exercises should therefore be a fixed item in the basic training of young horses (**128**). In good breeding operations, special leading exercises are usually performed because the foal has already had to be shown in halter at breeding shows. Amateur breeders, on the other hand, tend to neglect this training step or do not consistently complete it. Even large breeding operations often neglect this important exercise due to lack of time. Imported horses often have not had any leading training at all. Even well trained horses begin to "forget" when the exercises are neglected because conditioning and habituation are reversible learning processes. If, for example, the handler does not care whether the horse follows him or her calmly or reaches for grass, the road to problem behavior is very short.

Horses should learn early on to tolerate being led. Once taught, proper leading must be practiced consistently in order to maintain it.

128 Leading exercises should be a fixed element during basic training of young horses.

Unwillingness to be led	
Classification	Unwanted behavior
Description	Avoidance behavior or aggression when being led
Causes	• Lack of training of the correct behavior
	• Unclear rank order
	• Fear
Therapy	• Instrumental counter-conditioning (aids such as lead chain and whip or body language)
	• Rank order exercises
	• Trust-building measures
Prevention	• Positive conditioning and adaptation starting at foal age
	• Positive experiences associated with the process and thereafter

Problems during loading

Description. Transportation of horses is a common necessity today because few horses spend their entire life in one place. Participation in sports events, sales, and trips require a horse that is easy to load. This is even more important if emergency situations arise and the horse has to be taken to a clinic. Difficulties when loading horses are, however, a common occurrence in practice. The decisive factor is that horses first need to learn this process because voluntary entry into a horse trailer without prior practice cannot be expected from any horse. It is, after all, natural protective behavior of the former animal of the plains not to enter voluntarily a dark and narrow "cave" without any opportunity for escape (**129**).

Different types of problems in loading horses exist. The most common is a more or less violent refusal of the horse to step onto the ramp or into the trailer. Other horses, however, will enter the trailer without problems and only show restlessness at the beginning and during the journey. This can range from occasional kicking and banging against the sides to virtual panic. Yet other horses enter the trailer without problems and remain calm during the journey. They do, however, become restless once the vehicle stops or refuse to leave it.

Such behavior is stressful for both the handler and the horse and represents a physical as well as psychological burden for both. In addition, violent defense reactions are not without danger for both human and animal in this situation. Aside from this, horses that are transported under stress are less able to perform. Furthermore, they cannot be used in competitions if they are under the influence of tranquilizers. The avoidance behavior can have critical or even fatal consequences in cases of acute disease such as colic, where transport to a clinic has to occur as quickly as possible.

129 The horse's refusal to enter a "dark cave" is normal behavior if no previous training has taken place.

Predisposition. In general, problems with loading are more commonly seen in horses that tend towards overexcitement or are very fearful than in less sensitive breeds.

Causes. The main cause of the problem is fear. Depending on the type of problem during loading, it is attributable to different triggers. In most cases, it is the instinctive fear of a dark "cave" that causes horses to refuse to enter a trailer. It will be increased further by coercive measures on the part of the human. Frequently, the behavior is attributable to insufficient basic training. If a horse of 3 or 4 years of age, and without any prior practice, is more or less forcibly loaded onto a trailer because, for example, it has been sold, the negative association with this event is preprogrammed. It will recall the situation the next time someone attempts to load it and will try to resist even more violently. In contrast, horses that have learned as foals to be loaded together with a dam that is familiar with the loading process, rarely have problems later loading into a trailer.

Fear of driving is the cause if a horse walks into the trailer without problems but starts to struggle violently as soon as the engine is started. This may have been triggered by the engine noise or a negative experience while driving. The driving style is certainly responsible as well. Inconsiderate driving makes it difficult for the horse to balance and increases stress. Common mistakes are sudden use of the brakes, taking bends too fast or too sharply, or accelerating immediately after a curve while the trailer is still within the bend. A loading phobia can develop if a horse is involved in a traffic accident, falls down in the trailer or, even worse, falls with the trailer and is injured.

Restlessness that develops in the course of the journey or when the trailer stops can be attributable to fear of the destination with which negative experiences are associated. This may develop, for example, if a horse is afraid of competitions and is only transported to participate in them.

Therapy. A prerequisite for successful therapy is a sufficiently large vehicle with regard to length, height, and width. Heidemann (1985) showed in her studies that the size of the vehicle influences loading behavior of horses significantly. Claustrophobia and injuries can be avoided if the measurements are appropriate for the horse's size. A minimum width of the standing area of 80 cm (31.5 in) is generally recommended. The length of the standing area depends on the horse's breed and should be about 2.05–2.2 m (6.7–7.2 ft) for warmbloods.

Requirements for horse trailers

- Sufficient size (length, height, width).
- Well-lit inside area with electric lighting.
- Shallow (at most a 20 degree angle between ground and ramp) loading ramp with non-slip, sound-absorbing covering (rubber mat) or a vehicle that can be lowered hydraulically.
- Sound-absorbing, non-slip covering of the inside (rubber covering, bedding).
- Padded chest and rear bars that can be adjusted in height and length.
- Padded dividers.
- Padded side walls at least 2 m (6.6 ft) in height.
- Closable ventilation system above the horse's head.
- Rounded corners and edges.
- Good road holding and built-in shock absorbers.

As with all fear-induced unwanted behaviors, the recommended therapy for loading problems consists of a combination of systematic desensitization and counter-conditioning. Prior to starting treatment, however, it is necessary to practice leading and to reinforce rank order through obedience exercises. Once the horse has learned to follow a person trustingly, behavioral therapy as such can begin. For horses that rapidly tend to become overexcited, a long ride prior to the loading training may be helpful as it relaxes the horse and also makes it tired.

Sufficient time, patience, and consistency are the prerequisite for success with this stepwise habituation. To carry out the behavioral therapy, the trailer is brought into a paddock or a pasture where it may be useful to dig it into the ground or alternatively fill the sides of the ramp with soil if the horse has free access. The interior should be as bright as possible (**130**), which can be achieved by opening the top, if it is possible to do so, or at least opening the front door. To get the horse to approach the trailer voluntarily, it is fed concentrate only in proximity to the trailer. Feed is brought closer and closer to the trailer each day until the ramp is reached. At this point, it is particularly important to proceed slowly in order not to jeopardize the success. In small steps of about 20–30 cm (8–12 in), the feed bucket is placed higher and higher up the ramp each day until it is placed inside the trailer. Often, a horse will more easily overcome its fear if its front feet are

130 A light colored interior makes the trailer more "horse-friendly".

131 Tarps can be used in many ways during training to reduce fears (e.g. of the trailer roof).

placed onto the ramp by hand.

Once the horse walks into the trailer without hesitation and can be fed there, which sometimes takes several weeks to achieve, the first trips can be undertaken. These should be short and ideally end with a pleasant event such that the horse will associate positive experiences with getting off the trailer. One may, for example, let it graze in a particularly good spot or meet up with other riders and go on a relaxing trail ride.

If excessive fear of the trailer or a phobia is present, it may be useful to divide the loading process into small individual steps. These are practiced independently of each other, so that the horse does not initially make a connection to the loading process as such. Each completed exercise sequence is positively reinforced upon success and ignored upon failure, after which the exercise is repeated at a lower level. The following exercise steps, which can be performed in combination, are examples of how to proceed:

Stepping onto a wooden ramp. Initially, the horse learns to walk trustingly across boards or a wooden bridge. The goal is to get the horse used to the dull sound of its hooves on wood and to practice walking forwards and backwards, respectively, up and down an incline. The surface always has to be stable and non-slippery and provide good traction. Finally, the exercise is practiced on the trailer ramp as described above.

Stepping into a dark room. Through leading exercises, the horse learns to follow a person trustingly even if the location appears suspicious. The goal is to get it used to dark, narrow rooms. Barns, overpasses, and garages can be used for practice. Feeding stalls with high walls are also very suitable, because just like the trailer, they contain feed. During training, one should consider that the equine eye adapts more slowly to sudden changes in brightness than the human eye. For this reason, horses are more skittish with regard to sudden light/dark changes than people and are also blinded more severely by spotlights and lamps. Initial trailer exercises should therefore be performed in daylight. In general, horses see better with diffuse lighting than with a point source of strong light. For fearful horses and in the dark, it is therefore better to place the trailer into a better-lit area than to illuminate the interior.

Walking beneath a roof. Through leading exercises, the horse learns to lower its head and not jerk it upwards when walking beneath a roof. A tarp is very useful for this exercise. First, the horse is acquainted with the tarp (**131**). In the next step it is held above the horse, at first rolled up, and then spread out like a roof.

Practicing steadiness. The horse learns to walk on unsteady ground. For this exercise, a seesaw or solid boards placed onto tires are useful. The goal is to get the horse used to balancing its body and thereby prepare it for the swaying of the trailer floor during a ride.

Tips for problem-free loading

- Horse trailer that meets the requirements.
- Calm, consistent approach.
- Feed in the trailer (treats and hay for occupation).
- Odor (manure) from the horse's own stall in the trailer.
- Second horse already on the trailer.
- Entering towards the barn.
- Placing hooves on the ramp.
- Allowing time to look (light–dark change) and smell.
- First trip together with another horse (must be safe to load and drive).
- Short first trips with pleasant ending (allow to graze).

Once these exercises have been completed successfully, the stepwise loading training is begun as described previously. If the horse still shows fear of the trailer, entry is facilitated by positioning the trailer in such a manner that it is entered towards the barn, and an optical barrier (e.g. a wall) exists on one side. If the horse still refuses, the lunge line or crossed-arm method remains another option. For this method, the horse is pushed lightly from behind and is simultaneously praised and encouraged, but never yelled at. For very fearful animals, it is useful to combine the loading process with classical conditioning exercises. The calming sound with feed reward, for example, is useful because it distracts the horse and therefore diminishes its fear (p.128). Once it has entered the trailer, it is fed and calmed down under praise. The horse must not be tied before the rear bar has been fastened.

"Forcible" loading of horses may be necessary in emergency situations, but should be avoided whenever possible. It merely leads to further worsening of fear because from this moment on, the horse will make negative associations with the loading process. Except in emergency situations, short-term sedation of the horse, which is sometimes requested by horse owners, is strongly warned against, because it impairs the horse's balance and can result in falling with subsequent panic and severe injury. Furthermore, it is not always possible to interrupt the rising level of excitement, which increases the risk of a fall even more.

Fear during the ride is more difficult to treat than fear of entering the trailer. Correction would be easier if people were allowed to ride in the horse trailer. In Germany and most other countries, however, this is illegal. The emphasis of treatment therefore has to be on making the ride as pleasant as possible for the horse in order to avoid stress situations. First and foremost, this requires a good driving style and a vehicle with good road holding and sufficient room (**132**). In addition, exercises to practice steadiness such as walking on a seesaw are recommended. It is further helpful to position the horse facing backwards in the trailer. Smith *et al.* (1994) found that horses prefer this position and that fewer balance problems occur than if the horse is positioned facing forward. Treatment is supported by use of a trailer-safe companion horse and sufficient hay to eat.

If phobia-like fear and panic of engine noise exist, systematic desensitization is the treatment method of choice. Initially, the horse is brought into the trailer without being driven anywhere, which allows calming and positive conditioning of the horse as the vehicle is standing, and is made familiar with the engine sound. Once the horse accepts this process without problems, the demands are increased in a stepwise manner (slow driving and stopping, short trips on a straight road, and so on) as described on p.128.

How horses should not be loaded

- In a rush (worsening of fear).
- With beating and yelling (worsening of fear).
- By pulling on the halter (pull evokes counter-pull).
- Under the influence of tranquilizers (impairment of steadiness and reactions).

In some cases refusal to load is attributable to rank order problems. This situation can be differentiated from refusal out of fear by observing the horse's expression. Fear is recognized by the horse's movements (tension) and by rolling eyes, trembling, sweating, an elongated upper lip, or a tucked under tail (p.108). In contrast, a horse that "does not want to" shows no such signs but instead takes on a sawhorse stance or simply just stands there. In this case, the lunge line method with two lines should be used to show the horse that the human is stronger. In addition, repeated obedience exercises during daily interactions are

132 Trailers with diagonal positioning provide a pleasant view during waiting periods but fewer balance problems occur if horses travel facing the rear of the trailer.

Loading methods

Lunge line method
When using one lunge line, it is fastened on one side of the trailer entrance (tie ring), placed around the horse's rear end slightly below its tail head and held and/or tightened by a person on the other side. If two lunge lines are used, they are fastened on each side of the trailer, are crossed behind the horse and are held and/or tightened by one helper each on the right and the left side.

Crossing arms
For this method, two people, who either hold each other's hand or cross their arms behind the horse, try to apply pressure below the tail head and thereby cause the horse to bend its hindlegs and go forward.

recommended, which serve to establish and reinforce the rank order.

Prevention. Loading problems are best prevented if the horse learns early on to walk into the trailer. It is easiest to lead the foal and its safe-to-load dam into the trailer. Due to the natural inclination of young horses to follow their dam, this approach generally does not pose any problems. Once in the trailer, dam and foal should be rewarded with some feed in order to create a positive association for the young

animal from the beginning. The young animal is then led off the trailer and it is best to practice backing up early on. If the youngster is allowed to turn inside the trailer and exit forward, it will continue to attempt this as an adult. Then, however, turning around inside the trailer can become dangerous because as soon as the horse gets stuck or hurts itself, the once easy to load horse may turn into a problem horse. Leading exercises into the standing trailer are repeated for several days until the young animal is completely comfortable with the process. One can also vary the procedure by loading the foal together with another familiar horse, and alternating the order in which the older or the younger horse walk onto the trailer. In the next training step, the young animal practices by itself. A prerequisite for loading exercises is a sufficiently bright trailer with a shallow and non-slippery ramp.

Once leading exercises into the trailer have been completed, the first trip can be undertaken. It should be short and occur in the company of the dam or another familiar horse. In addition, a particularly careful driving style is required to avoid negative experiences during transport. When a young horse is transported by itself for the first time, at least the trailer and its odor should be familiar. The destination of the trip should also be carefully considered and should be associated with a positive experience for the horse. It is, for example, helpful to drive to a new pasture or to combine the first trip alone with a pick-up of another horse. If horses get used to entering the trailer and riding in it in the described manner, difficulties are generally not encountered later on.

Problems during loading

Classification*	1: Unwanted behavior
	2: Handling-induced behavioral aberration (phobia)
Description	Violent refusal of the horse to enter or leave the trailer or panic during the trip
Predisposition	Fearful, easily excitable horses
Causes	1: Fear
	2: Unclear rank order
Therapy	1:
	• Systematic desensitization and counter-conditioning (classical conditioning)
	• Trust-building measures
	2:
	• Rank order exercises
	• Counter-conditioning (lunge line method)
Prevention	Positive conditioning and habituation starting at foal age

*Numbers used for classification correspond to numbers used in causes and therapy

---

Problems during hoof trimming and shoeing

Description. In the course of evolution, the horses' legs and their ability to run fast were their only weapon and survival aid during actual or perceived danger. Standing still, lifting, and holding up the hooves, therefore, is a sign of trust towards the human and represents a behavior that has to be learned.

Under management conditions, it is necessary that every horse, whether it is ridden, driven or lives in pasture, be presented regularly to the farrier for hoof trimming. Problems, especially during shoeing, occur commonly. The range of avoidance behavior extends from jerking the feet from the handler's hand, kicking and rearing up to panic-like attempts to avoid the procedure at all cost. This behavior is not without danger for the involved persons as well as the horse.

Causes. The main cause is fear, which is most commonly attributable to lack of basic training. Getting young horses used to regular hoof care is generally neglected. This is supported by the findings of Schmid (1994) and Ulbricht (1994) in the course of their scientific studies regarding hoof health. The first mistakes are made with foals. Most youngsters are not taught to be caught or to be led, and definitely not to lift their hooves. But without these preparative measures, problems during the first visit to the farrier are virtually preprogrammed. With many young animals, therefore, forcible measures are used for the first time at this point. A vicious circle begins and the horse becomes more and more afraid of the treatment each time. The fear is increased even more if the horse has to be shod, which is associated with a burning smell and hissing noises. Horses are sensitive to these kinds of impressions, especially if they associate them with a negative experience. Not only its own fear, however, but also that of the owner can influence the horse. Many owners are afraid of their horse's reaction and of the potential danger of getting hurt when nails and hot irons are handled (**133**).

Avoidance reactions during trimming and shoeing can also occur without the horse having had bad experiences during hoof correction. The cause of the behavior in this case is a lack of respect for the person holding up the hooves. For these horses, it is sometimes simply uncomfortable to hold up a leg for an extended time, especially if it is standing awkwardly or the leg is angled too much. Some horses simply have not learned the necessity of standing thus consistently enough.

Generally, correct hoof trimming and shoeing are not associated with pain for the horse. This is, however, only true for sound horses. If they suffer from diseases of the musculoskeletal apparatus such as spavin, pain can also be the cause of unwanted behavior.

Therapy. Initially, it has to be determined whether fear or even pain causes the unwanted behavior or whether a rank order problem is present. Only in the latter case must the following exercises be pursued more vigorously. However, forcible measures are not appropriate even in these cases. It is preferable to emphasize one's dominance by means of appropriate obedience exercises (ground work). Generally, horses will be willing to hold up their hooves if they respect and trust the person who handles them during a visit to the farrier. This should also be considered when choosing a farrier.

With fearful horses, dominance exercises also help because these animals need a particularly strong sense of protection and security when confronted with intimidating situations. Trust-building measures are helpful supportive techniques in the treatment of fear.

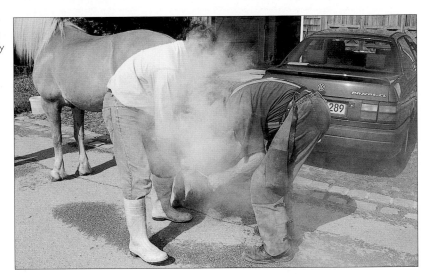

133 Placement of the red-hot iron is frightening not only for the horse.

How should correct hoof care be performed?

Type of hoof care	Correct hoof care	How it is done in practice*
Hoof correction		
Shoeing and trimming	Every 6–8 weeks	Every 6–8 weeks: 35% of horses Every 9–12 weeks or less: 65% of horses
Procedure:	Expert (ensures balanced weight distribution; prevents often irreparable future damage)	By an expert: 70% of horses Sporadic or regular trimming by the owner without training: 30% of horses Generally: Particular negligence towards young horses, breeding animals as well as ponies and small horses (trimming or shoeing intervals of 12 weeks and more: 62% of ponies, 87% of Haflingers)
Hoof care		
Washing	Two to three times a week if kept on dry soil	Hoof care is often inconsistent, sporadic or absent
Cleaning	Daily or before and after use	With grooming: 62% Prior to riding: 43% After riding: 57%
Greasing	After washing (to protect the absorbed moisture)	After washing (to protect the absorbed moisture): only recognized by 50% of horse owners

*According to Schmid (1994) and Ulbricht (1994)

Because generally, lack of basic training has to be made up for, the horse needs to re-learn the process of lifting its hooves and being shod from the beginning. This is achieved by adaptation in combination with operant and classical conditioning. One may proceed in the following manner.

At first, standing still is practiced because it may be required for an hour or more during shoeing. To do this, the horse is simply tied up repeatedly for short periods of time. Next, lifting of the hooves is optimized with the goal being that the horse lifts its feet on command (always use the same one) or light touch. If the horse kicks and fear is the cause, it will learn this exercise faster if it is distracted by the conditioned calming sound and feed (p.128). It is important to stand off to the horse's side in order not to get kicked. If the horse refuses to lift its feet out of unwillingness (rank order), the leg can be pulled up with help of a cloth or by tightly grasping the hair around the ergot. The voice is used to emphasize one's intent. The duration of lifting the hoof should be short at first, even with rank order problems, and is lengthened successively so that the horse can learn to balance on three legs for longer periods of time. Positive reinforcement has to occur while the leg is lifted, because if one waits to reward the horse until it sets its foot down, it will associate the two. Once the horse has learned to lift its hooves, one begins to prepare it for future manipulations of the hoof. One can, for example, tap the foot with a metal object or simply wash the hooves thoroughly and grease them afterwards. As a general rule, the person and not the horse should always determine when the hoof is set down again.

With very fearful animals, one should use every opportunity to get them used to the farrier atmosphere, the smell and the noise, without them being affected by it themselves. Together with another calm, farrier-proof horse, the fearful horse can, for example, learn that the shoeing process is associated with neither negative nor positive experiences. General training to prevent shying from strange odors (burning smell at fireplaces, and so on) and noises (hammering, drilling, hissing) can also be very helpful.

With difficult, spirited horses, it has generally proven useful to take them on a long ride prior to the shoeing appointment. Superfluous loco-motory energy should definitely not be the cause for problems during shoeing. Many horses will also be calmer when a familiar horse stands next to them. Nibbling on hay can also help to decrease fears.

Helpful hints for problem free shoeing

- Familiar person at the horse's head.
- Occupation or distraction of the horse.
- Conditioned rewarding sound.
- Hay feeding.
- Talking to and petting the horse.
- Calming effect of a second horse.
- Correct lifting of the hooves (not too high or crooked).
- Setting the hoof down in between (especially horses with arthritis or degenerative joint disease).
- Check: is the horse balanced?
- Calm, relaxed atmosphere (patience, calmness).
- Understanding, well trained farrier.
- Sufficient exercise prior to shoeing.

Prevention. Unwanted behavior at the farrier is best prevented by beginning to teach the horse to lift its hooves as a foal. To do so, the foal must tolerate the halter as well as leading and holding trustfully. One begins by lifting the forelegs. One hand is run slowly down the leg from top to bottom. When the cannon bone is touched, most foals will tend to bend the carpal joint and lift the hoof voluntarily. This exercise is repeated several times for both front legs without holding the hoof up for long. During the next step, the leg is held up for a period of time to practice balancing because the horse has to learn to keep its balance on three legs. Subsequently, one begins to lift the hindlegs by running a hand from the croup downward to below the hock. If the foal kicks during the first touches, this should initially be ignored because it does not yet understand the point of the exercise. After a while, most foals voluntarily lift their leg and pull it forward underneath the abdomen. The leg is then held in this position for an initially short, then longer time. Once the foal can balance its weight, the hoof is carefully pulled backward. This position is practiced as well while taking care to hold the leg straight without tilting it, and not too high: this is true for each of the exercises. If one proceeds consistently in this manner and rewards each step, one will soon have a horse whose hooves can be lifted and worked on without problems. It is generally recommended to make the horse familiar with the shoeing process as a foal. The sooner it gets to know the smell and noises at the farrier shop, the less fear it will show when its turn comes to be shod. It is best to let the foal accompany its dam to the farrier. If she is not shod, which is often the case in brood mares, dam and foal can accompany another horse. The exercise is, however, only useful if the horses that are shod are safe to work on themselves and if the atmosphere at the farrier shop is calm and relaxed (**134**). Treats will further ensure the success of this prophylactic exercise.

Trimming and shoeing problems

Classification	Unwanted behavior Handling-induced behavioral aberration (phobia)
Description	Avoidance reactions or aggression during hoof trimming
Predisposition	Fearful, easily excitable horses
Causes	• Fear • Unclear rank order • Pain
Therapy	• Habituation and counter-conditioning (operant or classical conditioning) • Trust-building measures • Rank order exercises • Considerate approach (pain)
Prevention	Positive conditioning and adaptation starting with foals

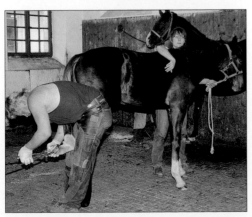

134 A sensitive approach eliminates a foal's fear of the still unfamiliar hoof trimming.

Aggressiveness during handling (biting and kicking)

Description. Biting and kicking are normal components of a horse's behavioral repertoire. They serve to establish and document rank order and as a defense. Biting is classified as an aggressive threatening gesture, while hindleg kicking is mostly used for defense (p.109). While heightened aggressiveness towards other horses is primarily regarded as a management- and handling-induced behavioral aberration, aggressive actions towards humans generally represent unwanted behavior. Depending on the extent, this behavior can become dangerous for the person and the risk of injury is great.

Predisposition. To a certain extent, a heritable predisposition for heightened aggressiveness exists. It has been proven definitively that aggressive offspring occurs more frequently in certain stallion lines. This primarily includes horses that are bred for specific performance features such as enhanced jumping ability. In addition, animals of higher rank in a herd are predisposed to aggressive behaviors.

A gender-specific disposition for either biting or kicking exists. Stallions tend more towards biting than mares and geldings. Mares, on the other hand, are, in the author's experience, more liable to kick.

Causes. Possible causes include rank order problems, fear, and pain. In rare cases, inborn heightened aggressiveness or misdirected imprinting can also be present (p.152). The unwanted behavior is further deepened and strengthened by learning processes.

Rank order problems arise when the human has neglected to attain, or is incapable of maintaining, the dominant position. As has been mentioned repeatedly, the horse regards the human as a type of social partner. Consequently, it has the inborn need to clarify its social rank in relation to the human. If the horse is in the dominant position, aggression is normal behavior and merely expresses superiority in rank. If the horse is higher in rank, it will therefore also not accept it when the human does things he is not entitled to as a subordinate partner. For example, a higher ranked animal always has first pick at feed. The horse will alert the human to this fact by threatening and if necessary biting, as soon as he or she, appears with feed. Similar situations can arise if the human crosses the individual distance "without permission" or tries to make the horse back up or step aside. Typical behaviors associated with rank order problems are biting upon entering the stall or snapping at people walking past in the barn aisle.

Aggressiveness caused by fear has a completely different motivation. It represents aggressive behavior as a defense (**135**). Animals that are low in rank, fearful, or very sensitive tend towards this behavior particularly often. In Arabians and horses with Arabian influence, for example, biting and kicking directed against people often represents a fear-induced defensive behavior. Fearful animals generally show agonistic behaviors with the goal of defending themselves, such as hindleg threatening and hindleg kicking. This is also the case if a rank order problem in combination with fear-induced aggressiveness is present. Fear generally results from a lack of trust in people or from negative experiences. Harsh training methods as well as physical and psychological overburdening can result in the horse losing trust in the "social partner" human and regarding him or her as a frightening enemy.

Pain as a cause of aggressive reactions should not be disregarded. This can be evoked by, for example, disease processes such as back problems. Equipment (e.g. an ill-fitting saddle) can also cause pain. In these cases, aggression is often simply defensive behavior because the horse's goal is to be left alone.

Aggression due to dominance, as well as fear- and pain-induced aggression, can be deepened by learning processes. A learning process should be suspected if the horse has had the experience of evading human influence by means of aggressive behavior. If the horse is successful in, for example, getting the human to abandon hoof cleaning or saddling, it will perceive this as a reward. Consequently, the aggressive behavior will become strengthened more and more. By giving in, one therefore trains the horse involuntarily to exhibit unwanted behavior. If pain is the cause, the learning process begins when the horse can directly relate a person's action to the occurrence of pain. This is the case, for example, if the rider causes pain by mounting and riding a horse with back problems.

Aggression is further dependent on the environment and the psychological balance of the horse. As was discussed on p.28, frustration begets aggression. A horse whose species-specific needs are not satisfied will therefore tend to bite or kick more than a horse kept under appropriate management conditions.

Therapy. Treatment methods vary dependent on cause. Thorough anamnesis and careful observation of the exhibited aggressiveness are therefore paramount for treatment success.

With dominance-induced aggressiveness, the behavior has to be approached by counter-conditioning. Punishment may be required as an exception. Correction has to be well thought through from the beginning. Any situation, in which the horse shows aggressive behavior and could gain advantage over the human, must be strictly avoided. If, for example, a horse bites the rider during groom-

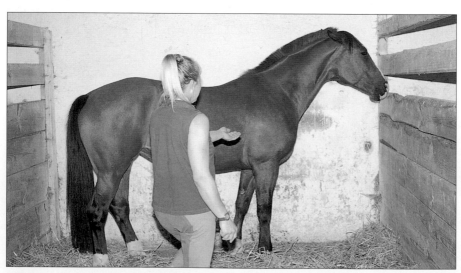

135 Refusal to be caught is often caused by fear, which leads to defensive behavior.

ing as soon as he turns his back, it has to be tied well enough to not allow this to happen. If the person is prepared for the attack, punishment must occur during or, at the latest, immediately following the attempt to bite or kick. It must be sufficiently strong to make the horse back away or show other gestures of subordination. As a general rule, any conflict must be settled to the advantage of the human because defeat after confrontation would further strengthen the horse's position.

With dominance-induced aggression, another therapeutic emphasis has to be on the performance of obedience exercises, with the aim of making the horse accept its indisputably subordinate position towards the human. An inexperienced horse owner should acquire sufficient theoretical and practical knowledge through courses and clinics before attempting therapy in such a horse. Although a horse showing dominance-induced aggressiveness can be given to a trainer for treatment, this does not change the fact that the owner must establish a leadership position towards the horse. Only under these circumstances will safe handling of the horse be possible in the long run. Aside from treatment, sufficient exercise and social contact should be ensured and the concentrate portion of the feed should be reduced in favor of the roughage portion.

Counter-conditioning is also indicated for treatment of fear-aggressive animals. In contrast to dominance-aggressive horses, however, these animals must never be punished. This would only strengthen aggressive behavior because the fear of the person increases further and, in addition, the animal feels reinforced in its behavior. If possible, the behavior can also be addressed by extinction. In order to do this, all situations in which the behavior is shown must be avoided, which requires good planning. With a consistent approach, weakening of the aggression and forgetting may be achieved over time.

In general, trust-building measures should be employed with fear-aggressive animals. To this end, it is indispensable for the person to spend not only 1 hour a day riding the horse but to invest additional time to interact intensively with the animal. The goal of treatment is to change the horse's perception of the person from "enemy" to "friend". Simultaneously, rank order exercises, best performed during ground work, should be implemented as a supportive measure. Positive reinforcement should be emphasized in order to re-establish confidence in the human. Definitive assignment of rank is important for fearful animals because they are

in particular need of protection from the dominant partner.

Painful processes should be diagnosed and treated accordingly by a veterinarian. Equipment deficits that cause pain must be corrected. If the aggressive behavior persists despite correction of these causes, a learning process is present. In other words, the horse has learned to avoid painful manipulations by means of aggression. Depending on whether the learned behavior is shown out of fear or dominance, the correction methods mentioned earlier should be used.

In choosing a stallion for breeding, it is advisable to consider not only his performance, pedigree, and beauty, but also his character features. Animals with heightened aggressiveness should be excluded from breeding. Alternatively, treatment methods described for dominance-induced aggressiveness should be employed. If this approach is unsuccessful, sale of the horse should be considered because it may become quite usable in the hands of an expert. Drastic methods based on the idea of letting the horse experience "helplessness", from which only the human being can rescue it, have to be viewed very critically. The goal of this method is rapid submission based on physical inferiority, which ranges from tying up individual extremities to casting the entire horse. If used inappropriately, for example in horses with fear- or pain-induced aggression or in sensitive horses, this "breaking" can result in complete uselessness of the horse and is not compatible with appropriate handling from an animal welfare standpoint.

Prevention. The basis for aggressive behavior is often established in the young horse during its early development. In many cases, negligence in the schooling of young horses and unrestricted feeding of treats, drive horses to bite. For example, one is tempted not to take the playful nibbling and pinching of foals seriously. It is tolerated or at best punished with mild scolding. In no time at all, playful behavior can then turn into painful biting or even result in serious injuries.

At this point, one has already lost one's dominant rank position. For this reason, the importance of consistent training of foals cannot be emphasized enough. One should orient oneself to the educational methods used in horse groups. Even the youngest foal will learn always to yield to the dominant animals, and will understand that it cannot pinch or jump on adult animals without being punished for it. Young horses must therefore learn early on to tolerate manipulations by people (p.86). Suckling foals should already learn to wear a halter, to be led and groomed, and to lift their hooves. This first training should always be friendly, can be playful, but must be absolutely consistent. Minor obedience exercises such as yielding to the wheelbarrow, yielding during stall cleaning, and so on, should become daily routine. Definitive dominance-aggressive behavior starts at an age of 2–3 years when the horse begins to establish its rank position in the group. If this behavior is also directed towards people, an immediate reaction is necessary. Often, a sharp "no" and a raised hand to block the way will suffice. The situation is resolved when the youngster backs away or shows another gesture of subordination. If rank order is established and consequently maintained early on in this manner, confrontation will occur only in rare cases because the horse will accept its subordinate position and behave accordingly.

Adult horses can be driven to aggressive behavior by spoiling them and showing excessive tolerance. For example, unrestricted feeding of treats virtually provokes biting. If a carrot or apple is used as a bribe in the sense of "I'll give you something, if in return you do me no harm", the path towards an aggressive demanding of a reward is very short. To avoid this, anyone buying a horse of their own or working with horses in general, should become familiar with horses' behavioral patterns and correct handling. One has to be aware of the fact that horses have a strong sense of rank order and that the human cannot escape this if he wants to communicate with the horse (p.131). Handling horses in a manner that respects species-specific behavior is, therefore, the best prevention against the development of such problem behavior. In this context, it shall be re-emphasized that treats must not be fed indiscriminately but instead must only be given if the horse has accomplished a task satisfactorily or if it is connected to a learning process, as was described on p.116.

Aggressiveness (biting, kicking) during handling

Classification	Unwanted behavior
Description	Defensive or aggressive threatening behavior towards humans
Predisposition	• Hereditary predisposition
	• Gender-specific predisposition
	– Stallions: primarily aggressive forms of threatening
	– Mares: primarily defensive forms of threatening
	– Geldings: primarily defensive forms of threatening
Causes*	1: Unclear rank order
	2: Fear
	3: Pain
Therapy	1:
	• Extinction
	• Counter-conditioning and punishment
	• Rank order exercises
	2:
	• Extinction
	• Counter-conditioning and punishment
	• Trust-building measures
	3:
	• Medical treatment
	• Removal of the cause (equipment deficits, riding mistakes, and so on)
Prevention	• Rank order exercises during early training of young horses
	• Trust-building measures during early training of young horses
	• Regular health checks
	• Appropriate equipment including its proper care, good riding technique
	• Exclusion from breeding of horses with hereditary predisposition

*Numbers used for causes correspond to numbers used in the therapy section

Unwanted behavior under saddle or tack

Bringing the tongue over the bit

Description. When bringing the tongue over the bit (or "putting the tongue out"), which can occur during riding or driving, a horse temporarily or constantly sticks its tongue out of its mouth and often leaves it hanging to the side. In doing so, most horses actually leave their tongues underneath the bit. Some, however, place them above the bit, thereby trying to evade the influence of the reins. The behavior is therefore not merely a blemish, but can also increase the risk of an accident for the rider or driver. Once the horse has learned to bring its tongue over the bit, chances of correcting this behavior are slim. At this stage, a horse will even stick its tongue out when a bitless bridle is used. In the beginning, however, this unwanted behavior can usually be treated successfully.

Predisposition. Placement of the tongue over the bit is favored by a "shallow" mouth (short distance between the front of the lips and the corner of the mouth). Horses that tend to become rapidly overexcited are also affected more frequently. According to practical experience, a horse with a weak rear end that pushes more than it carries the horse, is also disposed to this behavior. This is attributable to the fact that these horses tend to rush forward, which weak riders correct by merely pulling on the reins.

Causes. Bringing the tongue over the bit under saddle and in front of a carriage is exclusively caused by pain (**136**). It is primarily attributable to an ill fitting, oversized, or overly harsh bit and to hand mistakes of the rider or driver. The riding technique, for example the forced "collection" of a horse by means of auxiliary reins, or mistakes made in turning and flexing exercises, as well as problems with the horse's neck and back can be causative factors. Ultimately, however, it is always pain caused by inappropriate influence. The horse attempts to avoid this by moving the tongue off to the side. It is also possible that it uses its tongue as a cushion to avoid painful jaw pressure.

Therapy. A horse will never spontaneously bring its tongue over the bit but instead develops the behavior gradually. The very first signs should be taken seriously because once established, the behavior is virtually irreversible.

The goal of therapy is to eliminate the painful influence. In the early stages it is often sufficient to change the riding technique or to be particularly sensitive with the reins. The choice of a bit is also very important. Oversized, ill fitting and overly "harsh" bits have to be exchanged for more horse-friendly ones. If the horse's training level allows it, it is often beneficial to switch initially to a bitless bridle. Sometimes, the behavior can also be curbed by increasingly occupying the horse's mouth. This can be achieved by using a bit equipped with additional small joints or with a "playing chain". In many cases, a bridle that lifts the bit and therefore decreases or eliminates bit pressure on the tongue is helpful. This can be achieved, for example, by means of rubber disks that are connected across the back of the nasal bone, or by fastening the noseband upwards across the nose. One should, however, always consider that any type of bridle is only as good as the rider's hand. Bits can never make up for a rider's mistakes.

Many mechanical devices such as the tongue controller bit or the spoon bit are offered as classical therapies. They are meant to prevent the horse from laying its tongue on top of the bit. These methods should be viewed critically from an animal welfare standpoint because their effect is often based on additional creation of pain. Tying or taping the tongue to the lower jaw, which is not uncommonly practiced in standardbred racing, should be rejected

136 Bringing the tongue over the bit during use is exclusively caused by pain. At an advanced stage, it is almost impossible to treat.

completely. Some riders also use this type of "correction". In competitions, however, according to the regulations of the German Riding Association (FN), the tongue must not be tied. The FN can give permission in cases where a legitimate reason for tongue-tying exists. This virtually never happens (oral communication by the FN). In German standardbred racing, tongue-tying was not "mitigated" until it received negative press for animal welfare reasons. In Switzerland, tongue-tying has been illegal since 1997 (**137**). In the US, tongue-tying is allowed in both thoroughbred and standardbred racing. It is forbidden in dressage competitions and reining competitions (information from the *USA Equestrian Rulebook 2002*). The rulebooks for the different types of competitions should be consulted to find out about the legality of tongue-tying for the different breeds and competitions.

It is the wrong approach to try to correct a horse, for example a bolting horse, by using a harsher bit. This only creates pain. The consequence is fear and further strengthening of the unwanted behavior.

Prevention. Because placement of the tongue over the bit is exclusively attributable to painful influences during riding or driving, the best prevention is a good riding technique and a sensitive hand from the beginning of training. It is essential to familiarize the horse thoroughly with voice commands, which can then support the other aids during riding. For driving, voice commands are a basic requirement. The best

137 For animal welfare reasons, tongue-tying is prohibited in standardbred racing in Switzerland.

approach is by appropriate ground work. The choice of a suitable bit is of equal importance. In conventional riding stables, knowledge in this regard is often imparted insufficiently or not at all. It is therefore each individual's responsibility to learn about the mechanism of action of different bits within the horse's mouth. Good riding equipment stores and specialized literature can be used as resources. When breaking young horses to ride, special attention should be paid to a well fitting, appropriately fastened bridle. The bit must neither be too thin, which is known to make it harsher, nor too wide. The bridle must be fastened such that the corners of the mouth are not or only minimally pulled upwards. The bit must, however, not be too loose either because it will then tempt the horse to play with it, or it may hit against the wolf teeth. With a loose bridle the horse may learn to avoid the "nuisance" by placing its tongue over the bit.

Conclusion. Placement of the tongue over the bit can be avoided by a well fitting, appropriately fastened bit, a sensitive hand and a good riding technique.

For years, Preuschoft *et al.* have been investigating the question of how much weight a person places on a horse's mouth. Their pulling strength measurements (Preuschoft 1999) show that the "harshness" of the reins' influence is ultimately dependent on the strength with which the rider pulls. This strength is generally underestimated by riders and trainers as well as in educational books about riding. The measurements showed average pulling strengths per rein of 5–75 Newton (0.5–7.5 kg), with peak measurements around 150 Newton (15 kg). They varied depending on the rhythm of the gait and the rider's influence. The greatest pulling strengths on the horse's mouth were measured at a trot. At this gait, they exceeded the lowest values five- to nine-fold, while at a canter the excess was four- to six-fold and at a walk it was two- to four-fold (**138**). Although differences between single and double reins (double bridle) could not be detected, each type of bit showed a characteristic mechanism of action, which further increased the pulling strength within the horse's mouth: this increase was two- to 3.5-fold for simple snaffles and eight-fold for double bridles. Consequently, a horse at a trot is exposed to pulling strengths on its mouth of 24–128 kg (53–282 lb)!

Auxiliary reins have to be regarded very critically because they further increase the pulling strength significantly. The draw rein has to be discussed first. It works according to the principle of a pulley and doubles pulling strengths. The Koehler or

Bringing the tongue over the bit under saddle or tack

Classification	Unwanted behavior
Differential diagnosis	1: Management- and handling-induced behavioral aberration (tongue playing) 2: Symptomatic behavioral aberration
Description	Horses constantly or temporarily let their tongue hang out of the mouth during riding or driving
Predisposition	• Shallow mouth • Easily excitable horses, horses that "rush forward"
Causes	Pain
Therapy	• Sensitive, "soft" hand • Good riding and driving technique • Bitless bridle • Lifting up of the bit **Not acceptable for animal welfare reasons:** • Tying of the tongue • Tongue corrector bit, spoon bit, and others
Prevention	From the beginning of training: • Good riding and driving technique • Well fitting, "gentle" bit

Thiedemann rein can have a similar effect. The neck-stretcher carries its name without justification because its effect is the exact opposite. It virtually punishes the horse for extending its neck downwards by increasing pressure against the corners of the mouth. The horse can only avoid this by an upwards curling of the neck. The "rear end activator" has to be judged negatively from an animal welfare standpoint because it results in pulling strengths in the mouth of several 100 kg.

Differential diagnosis. The differential diagnosis for this unwanted behavior is tongue playing, which belongs in the category of management- and handling-induced behavioral aberrations. Tongue playing is shown in the absence of rein influence and mostly occurs in the barn. Although it is also characterized by tongue movements, a completely different origin is present. Therapeutic measures therefore also have to be different. Tongue playing is discussed on p.141.

Unusually frequent tongue and licking movements are also observed in the course of different diseases of the oral cavity (e.g. tongue laceration) or the teeth. Letting the tongue hang out of the mouth, or decreased tongue tone can be caused by nerve paralysis (cranial nerve XII = hypoglossal nerve). Brain and guttural pouch diseases can also be associated with tongue paralysis. In these cases, the behaviors have to be classified as symptomatic behavioral aberrations.

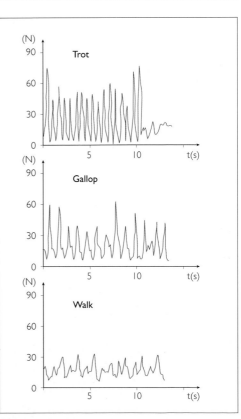

138 Graphs showing the force exerted by the reins on the horse's mouth in Newtons (N, 1 N = 0.1 kg) (Preuschoft 1993).

Head tossing, headshaking under saddle or tack

Description and differential diagnosis. This behavioral aberration is characterized by repeated, involuntary tossing upwards of the head or exaggerated nodding movements (**139**). As was discussed on p.163, for head tossing and headshaking in the barn, it represents a syndrome with many different causes.

Differential diagnostic considerations include:

- A symptomatic behavioral aberration caused by disease.
- A symptomatic behavioral aberration caused by increased photosensitivity.
- A management- and handling-induced behavioral aberration caused by deprivation, frustration and conflicts (emotional build-up).

If all types of aberrant behavior can be excluded, unwanted behavior may be present. This is likely the case if the horse headshakes exclusively under saddle or tack but rarely or never in the barn or on pasture, and if additional features such as a more frequent occurrence with sunshine, nose rubbing, and sneezing are absent.

139 Headshaking can greatly impair use for riding and driving.

Causes. Pain resulting in fear is generally the cause of this type of unwanted behavior. Most often, it represents a reaction to a rider's overly harsh hand, because the horse can communicate pain in no other manner. Incorrect posture of the rider or an ill fitting bit (too high, too low, hitting against the wolf teeth) can also evoke this behavior. An ill fitting, painful saddle or bridle should also be considered. For example, a tight browband, a pressure-exerting neck strap, or a noseband that is fastened too low or too tightly can cause intensive head tossing and headshaking. Finally, it can also represent learned behavior. This is the case if the horse maintains the behavior despite correction of all deficits. Most often, the process begins with headshaking due to pain and fear. If the rider subsequently gives in with the reins or even terminates the work, this is perceived as a reward for the shown behavior. The likelihood of repetition once a similar situation occurs is therefore high.

Therapy. Therapy has first of all to include elimination of all deficits causing pain and fear (riding technique, equipment). Painful processes such as tenseness of the neck musculature have to be eliminated. Learned behavior can be treated by counter-conditioning. If the behavior is based on fear, operant conditioning with positive reinforcement should be employed in combination with trust-building measures (p.134). In individual cases, learned behavior can be related to rank order problems. In these cases, corrective measures during riding that put a stop to the behavior from the beginning, such as shouting (a loud voice is often successful) or a lash with the whip, can be useful (operant conditioning with punishment). Success will only be achieved, however, if obedience exercises that serve to clarify the rank order are performed prior to correction (p.132).

For animal welfare reasons, a mechanical restriction of head movements by use of different auxiliary reins such as martingales and side reins has to be rejected. They only increase the force acting on the horse's mouth and do not change the cause of the problem at all (p.188).

Prevention. As was described on p.188, the best way to prevent headshaking under saddle or tack caused by pain and fear is a well fitting saddle and bridle, a sensitive hand, and a good riding technique from the onset of training.

Head tossing, headshaking under saddle or tack

Classification	Unwanted behavior
Differential diagnosis	Symptomatic behavioral aberration (disease, photosensitivity)
	Management- and handling-induced behavioral aberration
Description	Violent head movements in horizontal or vertical direction when working the horse
Causes*	1: Pain (fear)
	2: Rank order problems
Therapy	1:
	• Medical treatment
	• Improvement of riding and driving technique
	• Elimination of equipment deficits
	1 and 2: Counter-conditioning
	Not acceptable for animal welfare reasons:
	Mechanical restrictions (auxiliary reins)
Prevention	• Sensitive, good riding and driving technique
	• Well fitting equipment from the onset of training

*Numbers used for causes correspond to numbers used in the therapy section

Herd-boundness

Description. The need to be with companions of the same species is part of the species-specific behavior of horses. It developed over millions of years because in the course of evolution, the individual animal's only chance to survive was in the company of other horses. This need, generally denoted as herd instinct, is still unchanged today. It therefore represents a proof of trust if the horse follows the rider's demands and walks away from its companions.

With herd-boundness the horse tries to remain with the other horses and often refuses to be led or ridden away from them. Unwillingness to follow, when attempting to lead the horse out of the barn, and unwillingness to enter the jumping arena also fall within this category.

Predisposition. A certain breed disposition for herd-boundness exists. Ponies and horses with draft horse influence tend to show this behavior more often. Stressful situations during the horse's youth also have a predisposing effect. These are often associated with mistakes made during weaning from the dam or separation from other horses with which a close bond had been formed. Horses undergoing a relatively short upbringing period, sudden barn change, and abrupt start of training especially tend towards herd-boundness. It is, therefore, particularly common among racehorses as well as among animals that are kept in individual stalls and have not been raised in a herd.

Causes. In general, herd-boundness is considered unwanted behavior. It is primarily attributable to fear. If it diverges significantly from the norm, however, a phobia exists, which must be considered as aberrant behavior. Phobias are often attributable to severe traumatic experiences. Weaning from the dam at an age of 3 or 4 months, for example, can evoke separation phobias in foals. Most often, however, herd-boundness merely represents fear of being left alone because during basic training separation from the mother and other horses was not practiced. Fear of expected uncomfortable events may also be the cause. This occurs if separation from companions or the familiar barn is frequently associated with negative events. For example, unwillingness to enter the arena is attributable to this fear because the horse associates this process with a negative experience.

It is not uncommon for herd-boundness to represent a rank order problem. In the case of herd-boundness, this is closely related to fear because the horse trusts its equine companions more than the human. In any case, the rider's rank does not suffice to provide the horse with the feeling of security it needs to move away from the protection of its companions. This situation is often encountered in riding schools. The ongoing changes in riders, and the inability of beginners to provide the horse with security by exerting dominance, result in the horse feeling safer with its equine companions. In some cases, the rider may be afraid and transmits this feeling to the horse, which results in the unwanted behavior. In addition, overuse and inconsistent aids can confuse and unnerve the horse enough to make it react by herd-boundness. Last but not least, the behavior may be learned. This is the case whenever the rider abandons his or her attempts to ride away from the group. The reward for the horse in this case is that is remains with the group.

It should also be mentioned that herd-boundness can be shown as a natural behavior in the form of a protective instinct. This is encountered particularly in stallions and geldings with pronounced stallion-like behavior that were kept with a mare, or brood mares that were kept with their foal for long periods of time, and have established an extreme bond. These horses usually only show the behavior when they encounter strange horses, for example during horse shows. In their normal environment or with spatial separation, these animals will generally behave entirely normally.

Therapy. Therapeutic measures are similar independent of whether unwanted behavior or, in the case of a phobia, aberrant behavior is present. In the latter case, however, treatment is much more extensive and is not always entirely successful. Although after completion of therapy, animals with phobia-like fears will be able to be ridden by themselves in a familiar environment and will remain in their familiar barn without companions, they are at risk of relapsing when exposed to unfamiliar, unnerving situations.

The therapeutic approach should include systematic desensitization in combination with counter-conditioning (p.128). An extensive trusting relationship between horse and handler is an indispensable requirement for successful completion of such behavioral therapy. It may therefore be necessary for the rider to perform rank order exercises and trust-building exercises with the horse prior to commencement of the conditioning program as such (p.132). Once the rider has gained dominance over the horse and is able to provide a sufficient feeling of security, the actual "anti-herd-boundness exercises" can begin.

Therapy of herd-boundness by desensitization requires that the demands are decreased and separation is practiced in small steps. Each practice sequence must place so little demand on the horse that it evokes no or only a mild fear reaction. In addition, counter-conditioning is used to positively reinforce the desired behavior, in this case separation or being alone, every time. The reward supports the desired behavior and helps to decrease fear. The following approach has proven useful in practice.

During a trail ride in a group, one initially practices riding at the end of the group, in the middle, as well as in front. The next step is to ride in front of the group and to increase the distance to the group by a few meters. To do this, the horse is best ridden at a trot and collected. With progression of training, the distance is increased more and more. Finally, one can separate from the group for a short while and join it again at an arranged meeting point. This exercise is repeated in different locations. In this manner, the horse learns in small steps to accept that separation is not a problem and that it will always return to its companions. It also learns to associate separation with a positive experience because it is rewarded when it moves away from the group.

Another variation of this exercise is to begin the trail ride as a large group, and to perform exercise sequences during which the group is successively divided into smaller groups of two or three horses until finally each rider works alone with his horse. Visual contact with the other horses is initially maintained for the herd-bound horse. Once it has gotten used to the distance from the others, it is ridden out of sight of the others for a brief period of time. This exercise is also repeated in different locations. Large riding parks with natural obstacles or large stubble fields, in which round bales can serve as temporary visual barriers, are well suited for this type of "anti-herd-boundness training".

Herd-boundness in association with a pronounced protective instinct is virtually impossible to correct. It can be avoided by appropriate prophylactic measures, which are described in the following paragraph.

How should a herd-bound horse be corrected?
This is how it should not be done…
It is frequently observed but entirely wrong to "beat a horse away from the group". With this very questionable treatment, the horse is inevitably put in a conflict situation. On the one hand, it is punished for doing the right thing, moving away from the group; on the other hand, it is beaten if it tries to remain with the group. No matter what it does, it is beaten. For some people, this approach may be somewhat logical, however, horses are incapable of such powers of deduction. They can only associate their actions "moving away" or "remaining with the group" with the respective positive reinforcement or punishment. Statements such as "the horse knows what it is doing wrong" only indicate that the rider knows little about a horse's learning ability.

140 Separation exercises from the dam and herd are an important element of the basic training of young horses.

This is how it is done correctly...
As an instructor is always present when riding in a group, he or she should initially lead the herd-bound horse away from the group. With frequent repetition combined with praise, the horse will learn over time that walking away from the group is not associated with negative consequences. The student should practice further, by riding the horse in different positions within the group, finally taking the lead, and separating from the group, as was described for the "anti-herd-boundness training".

Prevention. Foals raised in operations with natural management conditions will frequently not be herd-bound at all. Over time, they continue to separate from their dams and in parallel establish bonds with other horses. This also proves the importance of stress-free weaning. The best preventive measure against herd-boundness is therefore raising foals in a group, which ideally consists of horses of different ages. At the earliest, the first separation should occur at an age of 2 months, when the foal has already become very familiar with the other members of the group (**140**). It is best to leave the foal with the group and take away its dam, while successively increasing the time of separation. Additional helpful hints for stress-free weaning were given on p.63.

For further training, which can begin once the foal has learned to be led by a halter, the foal is temporarily led away from the other horses carefully and without force. Initially, a few meters are enough. Positive reinforcement in the form of a reward must not be neglected. It promotes the establishment of a positive association with such undertakings and helps them to be performed successfully and without evoking fear. These separation exercises will not only increase the foal's self-confidence but will also strengthen the handlers rank position and the foal's trust in people. The exercises should be continuously extended during early training. The young animal may be taken along on walks or may learn to walk across obstacles in a riding arena. For a horse that has been prepared in this manner and that is allowed to remain in its familiar environment, it is then only a small step towards being able to stay on its own without people or other horses.

Even as an adult, however, horses can develop into herd-bound horses. It is very likely for two horses that are integrated into a new group together to form an especially strong bond. Horses in these situations are particularly prone to herd-boundness. One should be prepared for this occurrence and should practice separation in due course, for example by going on long trail rides with other horses or alone. This measure is of general value if a horse is noticed to establish an excessively strong bond with another horse.

Herd-boundness (similar origin: unwillingness to follow, unwillingness to enter the arena)

Classification	**Unwanted behavior** **Management – and handling-induced behavioral aberration (phobia)**
Description	Violent avoidance behavior when trying to separate the horse from its companions
Predisposition	• Draft horses, ponies • Inadequate management • Inadequate handling
Causes	• Fear • Unclear rank order • Protective instinct
Therapy	• Desensitization with counter-conditioning • Trust-building measures • Rank order exercises
Prevention	• Raising in groups • Stress-free weaning • Separation exercises

Shying

Description. Shying is the typical reaction of a flight animal such as the horse, when its sensory organs signal a dangerous situation. Sporadic shying in the form of startling, for example with the sudden appearance of a deer or dog, is entirely normal and typical for the species. It occurs even with experienced, calm horses with good riders. In these cases, however, the rider will be able to control the horse without major problems and in a relatively short period of time. Shying is a problem if it occurs frequently or is violent enough to represent a danger for both horse and rider. The range of shying reactions extends from brief jumping to the side up to panic-like bolting (**141**). In extreme cases, shying horses break through fences and barriers and in their panic run across roads or across impassable terrain.

141 The range of shying reactions reaches from jumping off to the side and panic-like bolting to "going down on the knees" and falling.

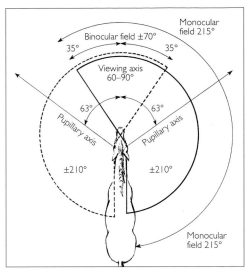

142 Graphical representation of the hearing range of human and horse (Heffner and Heffner 1983).

143 The horse's binocular and monocular field of vision (Brückner 1995).

Predisposition. Horses react to visual, auditory and olfactory stimuli more rapidly and sensitively than humans (**142**, **143** and Table 16). "Highly bred" horses are generally sensitive but some draft horses and ponies may also show increased skittishness from birth onwards. It represents an individual characteristic, as described by Wolff and Hausberger (1994) (p.53). The current and previous management conditions also play a role. Because of sensory deprivation, horses kept in a dark stall throughout the day tend to shy significantly more easily than horses in a run-out system, which are exposed to different en-vironmental stimuli such as passing tractors, playing children, and barking dogs on a daily basis. In general, shying is favored by management systems in which horses lack exercise, stimulation, and occupation. It is not uncommon for horses kept under these conditions virtually to seek out reasons to react with such explosions of temperament.

Table 16 Characteristics of the horse's sensory organs and perception as compared to humans

Vision
- The total field of vision at approximately 330° is larger than in humans.
- The field of three-dimensional vision at approximately 60°–70° is smaller than in humans.
- Three-dimensional and accurate distance vision are less developed than in humans.
- Near adaptation (accommodation) is less developed than in humans.
- Vision in dim light is significantly better than in humans.
- Adaptation to rapid changes in brightness (speed of adaptation) is slower than in humans.
- Range of adaptation to very bright light and deep darkness is broader than in humans.
- Color vision is developed to a lesser extent than in humans. (Color vision in horses is similar to that in red–green color-blind people.)
- Accuracy of motion vision is significantly better than in humans.
- Special characteristic: completely motionless objects, e.g. people standing still cannot be identified as such by horses (Brückner 1995).

Hearing
- Reception capacity of sound waves is larger than in humans.
- Horses are better at hearing high frequencies but worse at hearing low frequencies than humans.
- Most sounds are heard as well by horses as by humans.

Smell
- The sense of smell of horses is significantly better developed than that of humans (microsmatics), but not as well developed as that of dogs (macrosmatics).

Causes. Initially, it is important to determine whether an organic reason for the behavior exists. Eye diseases, for example, which are associated with a decreased visual field, can lead to increased jumpiness in response to unfamiliar auditory stimuli.

The major cause of this behavior, however, is fear. It in turn can have different reasons. Lack of experience, for example, which is often due to insufficient or insufficiently variable training and management, can cause the behavior. Flight from a threatening object or an unfamiliar noise is then the normal inborn reaction. It is also possible that a previous negative experience causes the unwanted behavior. The memory of the respective object or a similar situation will then cause the horse to shy over and over again. Fear can also be induced by the rider's influence. An overly hard, ungiving hand, an overly harsh bit or suppression of visual perception can evoke shying reactions. As was already discussed in the section on investigative behavior, shying is virtually provoked if the horse is not given an opportunity to observe the "dangerous" object for a sufficient period of time and to investigate it by olfactory examination (p.91).

Finally, the rider's fear can also be transmitted to the horse. If the rider is afraid of every passing truck when riding outside, the horse will also tend to expect a wild animal behind every bush. The riding technique should be considered as well. A "dreaming" horse on a long rein will be startled more easily than an actively ridden, collected horse; this goes for the rider as well.

As with other unwanted behaviors, rank order problems are closely linked to fear in this case. Repeatedly shying or panicking horses often lack confidence in the higher ranked "species member", the human. They will then react on their own behalf. As a general rule, a rider of low rank will not be able to provide the horse with the necessary protection and security in a frightening situation to prevent the species-specific flight behavior from occurring.

Learned behavior can also be present. Horses with fearful riders, for example, will be conditioned to shy from any frightening object. The reward is provided if the rider returns home or discontinues riding. In many cases, however, the cause lies in the different manner of thinking and different perception of human and horse. While the rider regards an object as harmless and tries to ride past it by use of strong aids, such as whip and spurs, the horse only experiences more fear. It therefore learns to regard such objects or situations as particularly dangerous and its shying reactions will become more and more violent each time.

Therapy. If the horse shies out of fear, its origin needs first to be investigated. If lack of experience or a previous bad experience is the cause for the behavior, desensitization is the preferred method. The horse is allowed to get used to the frightening object in small steps. It is best to combine this procedure with classical conditioning, where the horse's general attitude, as soon as it shows fear, is changed by a calming sound and simultaneous offering of feed, as described on p.128. It is almost impossible for a horse to be afraid and chew at the same time!

In detail, desensitization could be approached as follows. A horse that is afraid of bicycles (they are particularly unpleasant because they approach almost silently from behind) is first led near a standing bicycle and is brought as close to it as possible without showing any, or only a very weak, fear reaction. The horse is rewarded during the approach (classical conditioning) and immediately afterwards (operant conditioning). The goal is counter-conditioning by which the animal learns to associate a positive event with the originally frightening object. The distance to the bike is now decreased, but again only as much as is possible without evoking a panic reaction. In the next step, the horse is allowed to sniff at the bike until it tolerates it without any problems. Once this is the case, a helper can sit on the bike. At first, he should only move around within the horse's field of vision. Once the horse has got used to the situation, one can practice with the bike

---

Tips for passing frightening obstacles

- Give fearful horses enough freedom of the head and sufficient time for visual and olfactory investigation.
- Changing the horse's overall mood by classical conditioning (calming sound with or without feed) helps to decrease fear. This should be used while approaching.
- After passing a frightening object, leave at a slow pace. Galloping away would be associated with flight. This would ruin all previous efforts.

approaching from behind. At first, the approaching bike rider verbally warns the horse; later on, he can approach silently. Finally, the situation is practiced in varying locations and under varying conditions (with and without talking, using the bicycle horn, and so on). Depending on the degree of fear, desensitization in the example case of a bicycle can require hours, or even days and weeks. If the relationship between human and horse lacks trust, trust-building measures should be employed prior to desensitization (p.134).

With shying reactions, rank order problems almost always exist. Exercises that establish the rider's dominance are, therefore, an indispensable prerequisite (p.132). A very useful exercise during the "anti-shying training" is teaching the horse to follow willingly when being led. It is recommended that fearful riders first improve their personal charisma and their skills. A riding clinic may be required. Correction of riding skills or equipment is also necessary if shying is caused by pain due to the wrong or excessively harsh influence of the rider.

Learned shying, which is originally based on fear, can also be treated by desensitization and counter-conditioning. "Old" mistakes such as forcing the horse past the frightening object must be avoided under all circumstances. On the contrary, it may be useful to dismount and allow the horse to approach slowly. This procedure does not entail a loss in rank, as many riders believe. It is also calming to support the approach to the frightening object by classical conditioning (calming sound and feed). In many cases it will suffice to let an experienced horse go in front. One should not forget that generally, a horse will not accept an object as harmless until it has had an opportunity for olfactory investigation.

If an organic disease is present, it should be treated and, in case of any permanent damage, the riding technique should be adapted. If the field of vision is impaired, ground work exercises can be helpful to get the horse used to certain situations; these should take place in a familiar environment.

The importance of the horse's management situation should not be underestimated. Outside stalls, paddocks, pasture access, and run-out systems provide sensory input and at the same time have a relaxing effect because the horses are able to observe their environment, which corresponds to their natural behavior. According to experiences of seasoned horse experts, "straw eaters" are particularly calm animals. This observation may not least be attributable to the fact that these horses are sufficiently occupied by chewing all day long, which, aside from sufficient exercise, is an important prerequisite for content and level-headed horses. If a horse shies despite all efforts and if fear or pain can be excluded, an exclusive rank order problem or resulting learned behavior is present. In this situation, it is useful if the good rider makes the horse leg-yield to pass the object. But even in this situation, the horse should be given the opportunity to stand quietly in front of the object for some time and so realize that nothing happens to it. Praise must not be withheld. With notoriously shying horses, whose motivation is based on "unwillingness" due to a rank order problem, one should prevail energetically. In this case, the rider should attempt to remain in a forward motion and to pass the obstacle without stopping, if necessary by counter-bending the horse.

It is also important to try to regard the situation from the horse's point of view. Objects that appear harmless to us, or invisible occurrences such as the odor of a pigsty, can represent the exact opposite for a horse. If one can recognize these situations in advance, one can transmit one's energy and will to prevail on the horse and in this manner pass obstacles without major shying reactions.

Prevention. Prevention is better than correction. This is also true for shying. One should, therefore, start getting horses used to many different impressions at a very young age, which is easiest to accomplish at the side of an unafraid dam. The goal is to alter the inborn flight reflex by positive experiences in order to make it controllable. In parallel, trust in the dominance of people has to be established, and must never be disappointed. To achieve this, aids must always be clear and the rider has to insist on the horse following his or her commands in every situation.

An "anti-shying training" should be designed to be playful and variable. This is achieved by confronting young horses with ever changing situations and thereby challenging their natural curiosity. At this age, they show a particular interest in all new objects such as balls, plastic tarps, bicycles, bells, horns, and so on. The basic mood underlying curiosity is positive and should be preserved. One should, therefore, always have a reward handy when approaching new objects or investigating them more closely. If one practices in this manner during early development, one will obtain a horse that does not react with panic-like flight to unfamiliar situations as an adult, but instead shows a controlled reaction (**84**).

	Shying
Classification	**Unwanted behavior**
	Management- and handling-induced behavioral aberration (phobia)
Description	Violent flight reaction elicited by visual, olfactory or auditory stimuli
Causes*	1: Organic disease, pain
	2: Fear
	3: Unclear rank order
	4: High spirits (need for exercise)
Therapy	1:
	• Medical treatment
	• Appropriate equipment
	2:
	• Desensitization
	• Counter-conditioning (classical, operant)
	• Trust-building measures
	3:
	• Counter-conditioning
	• Rank order exercises
	1–4:
	• Appropriate management and feeding according to species-specific requirements
	• Good riding skills
Prevention	• Stepwise habituation to unfamiliar objects, smells and situations with positive reinforcement
	• Rank order exercises
	• Appropriate management with sufficient exercise
	• Regular health checks

*Numbers used for causes correspond to numbers used in the therapy section

This type of training is also recommended as prevention or therapy for the adult horse. Under controlled conditions, such as in a riding arena, the horse is confronted with a variety of frightening objects such as paper and plastic bags flapping in the wind, umbrellas that are opened, strollers that are rolling past, and so on.

It should also be considered that even an optimally trained horse will, at times, encounter situations in which it shies. This is normal. The same occurs if the animal has not been confronted with a certain frightening situation for a long time. This is attributable to the fact that adaptation is a reversible learning process and that the learned subject has to be refreshed periodically by practice. It is therefore entirely normal if a horse that has learned by conditioning not to be afraid of cows, shies away from them at the first encounter after the long winter break. Rehabituation will, however, take place much faster than the initial learning period.

Rearing

Description. Rearing is a coordinated sequence of movements, which is shown primarily in the context of social conflict and during play fights. It is shown mainly by stallions, but mares also master the movement. As an unwanted behavior under saddle or in front of a carriage, rearing can become dangerous for the human as well as the horse because of the risk of flipping over backwards. This is attributable to the labile state of balance during uncontrolled rearing. In contrast, the dressage horse learns to balance when entering the levade or the passage.

Predisposition. A distinct gender distribution exists. Stallions by nature tend more towards rearing. In cryptorchids or late-castrated geldings or geldings with stallion-like behavior, the unwanted behavior is also encountered more frequently. Easily excitable animals are especially predisposed. The type of use is also important.

144 Rearing is not "refusal to work" but instead occurs mostly due to pain or fear.

Rearers are in particular found among dressage and gaited horses, which are ridden with a high degree of collection.

Causes. In practice, rearing is often denoted as "refusal to work". This interpretation is too one-sided and, moreover, misleading, as it implies that the horse tries to evade use, more or less because it is lazy. Even though rearing can be associated with rank order problems, the "upwards unloading" is generally an expression of hopelessness. In many cases, fear, which is often based on pain, is the main reason for this problem behavior (**144**). For example, rearing is primarily caused by an excessively hard hand or by incorrect influence of the rider such as hitting hard on the horse's back or forcing the horse to go forward while holding it back at the same time. An excessively tight bridle, an ill fitting, pressure-exerting saddle, or a premature or excessively harsh use of advanced bits such as a bar bit or a curb bit can also cause the avoidance behavior. Thus, a rearing horse almost always finds itself in an insoluble conflict situation. In the example of forcing the horse forward, the conflict arises from the fact that

going forward, and therefore obeying, causes pain or fear; but stopping does as well because the horse will generally be punished for doing so. Aside from fear and pain that are caused by incorrect influence of the rider or by equipment deficits, pain resulting from organic damage such as diseases of the spine can also be responsible for the unwanted behavior.

However, a horse can also rear because of fear unassociated with pain. This will, for example, be the case if an easily excitable or already very excited horse is overwhelmed. Inconclusive aids resulting in confusion, overly difficult tasks, or decreasing concentration ability of the horse can be the cause. Many horses will also rear during rein-backing if one attempts to teach them under saddle (p.126).

If the rider is incapable of preventing the unwanted behavior by appropriate measures, horses learn rapidly to use it for their own purpose. This learned behavior always arises if the horse learns that the avoidance behavior is associated with success. If the rider, for example, terminates the exercise prematurely because he or she is afraid of the horse rearing, the horse will perceive this as a reward. Rearers can learn to use their "trick" in a calculated manner if they do not recognize the rider's dominance or if the rider is not capable of communicating with the horse by means of clear commands. If the rider is thrown during rearing, however, it would be wrong to punish the horse after getting back up. By this time, the horse has already forgotten about its action and is no longer able to associate punishment with the event of rearing. Frequently however, fear of people will result from incorrectly exercised punishment, independent of whether a rank order problem, fear or pain, or learned behavior was the cause of the problem behavior. In some horses, incorrectly exercised punishment can also result in aggression.

Therapy. Pain as a cause has to be excluded first. Consulting a veterinarian as well as examining equipment and riding technique and improving them as necessary are recommended. Harsh bits should be exchanged for simple or double-broken snaffle bits or bitless bridles, but not for mechanical hackamores.

Only if pain as a cause has been excluded, can correction of the behavior under saddle begin. Counter-conditioning in the sense of operant or classical conditioning is the best suited method of behavioral therapy. Therapy is not entirely without danger. It requires especially good riding skills and very sensitive perception of the horse's behavior under saddle. For this reason, rank order exercises should initially be conducted in the form of groundwork in order to establish clear dominance from the beginning. An additional important accompanying measure is the horse's management in a system that offers many opportunities for occupation and exercise. Several hours of exercise per day in a group, and a reduction in the amount of concentrate in exchange for an increased amount of roughage, can often work magic.

Correction will vary depending on the cause. If fear is or was (with learned behavior) a factor, the goal of therapy should be to establish a trusting relationship between human and horse by means of praise and a good riding technique. In order to achieve this, the demands placed on the horse need to be decreased first. Simple exercises, which should, however, contain a lot of bends and turns, are sufficient. Emphasis should be placed on a relaxed but animated forward motion. The latter is particularly important, as the horse has to stop in order to be able to rear. If its intention to stop becomes evident, one can distract the horse by moving forward energetically and riding into a turn (volte, circle). These measures under saddle can be supported by the appropriate learning therapy. If operant conditioning is chosen, the horse is praised at the very moment that it accepts the rider's cues and does not rear. While riding, praise is best exerted by voice. If the horse rears, however, one should try to passively sit it out by leaning forward and loosening the reins. A sharp "no" or shouting at the beginning or during the event can be used as punishment, or the horse can be made to complete an obedience exercise such as the "windmill" immediately after coming down (**150**). Under no circumstances should a frightened animal be punished. Classical conditioning, which can result in redirection, is very useful for therapy of rearing out of fear. Here, the horse is energetically ridden forward as soon as tension or a shortened stride indicate its inclination to rear, and simultaneously, its motivation is redirected by use of a conditioned calming sound or another exercise based on classical conditioning. Freddy Knie, the famous trainer of free dressage, treats stallions that have become aggressive during the rearing training for circus acts in this manner. He distracts them by making them "kneel" and simultaneously puts them into a position from which an attack is impossible (**145**).

Punishment is only useful if fear and pain can be excluded and if rearing is attributable to rank order problems. Punishment must, however, be exercised during rearing or immediately after coming down. Another method, which is not without risk however, is exhaustion therapy (p.130). Here, the horse is provoked to rear until it stops due to exhaustion, because the event requires a lot of strength. If, however, pain was the initial cause and went undetected, such treatment must be regarded as cruel. Many a horse has been lame for months because of an incorrectly employed exhaustion therapy. Drastic methods of force such as the "Russian punishment method", during which the horse is thrown to the ground during rearing, is held there and beaten in order to evoke a feeling of helplessness, have to be viewed very critically from an animal welfare standpoint. This method is absolutely contraindicated if pain or fear is the cause of the behavior, or if the horse is very sensitive and subordinate. As a general prerequisite, such methods should only be employed by responsible persons with sufficient experience.

Independent of cause, training of rearers has to be approached in very small steps. Praise should be offered immediately after every accomplishment in order to re-establish the horse's pleasure in work. Rewards can therefore be generous when working on correcting a rearer.

Prevention. Appropriate management with lots of opportunity for exercise and occupation, as well as appropriate feeding according to nutritional and behavioral requirements, in combination with appropriate handling, effectively prevents rearing. Training methods based on trust and dominance prevent the occurrence of problem behavior. At the same time, the riding technique must be sensitive and the equipment must be animal friendly and suitable for the horse's level of training. Rearing is particularly common in horses whose gaits are shortened with the help of bar bits or curb bits and training aids, and are therefore "collected" inappropriately. The general rule for dressage work is that relaxation has to come before collection. For this reason, young horses that have not been conditioned sufficiently need to be ridden onto the bit carefully instead of being forced into a presumably ideal position with the help of training aids. It is also recommended to train young horses first with the help of groundwork. Once they can be controlled and directed in hand with voice commands, work under saddle can follow. As was mentioned previously, the tendency to rear is often promoted by teaching the horse to rein-back under saddle without any previous groundwork. The trigger for rearing in this case, which is commonly described as "refusal to work", is fear because the horse fails to understand the exercise and is overwhelmed. Appropriate exercises for rein-backing were described in the section on "stress-free handling" (p.126).

In his basics of conditioning riding horses, Schnitzer (1996) pointed out that the contradiction between the classical riding technique and that which is practiced to the highest level of performance in many riding stables, is particularly striking today. Instead of riding "from behind forwards" and to regard relaxation as the essential prerequisite for any further work with the horse, this rule is virtually turned around. With strong hand use, horses are ridden "from the front backwards", which is often further supported by training aids. The horse's opportunity to move loosely and then become collected is therefore impaired. With this riding technique, horses cannot develop their moving potential freely and fully. In addition, it can lead to muscle tension or even an excessively painful pushing together of the dorsal spinous processes of the vertebrae of the back, and other problems. Problem behavior such as rearing, bucking, and bolting are therefore preprogrammed with this riding technique.

The only way to allow the natural moving potential to develop without physical or psychological damage is to master and employ a riding technique that conforms to the horse's physiology. Admittedly, training of a horse according to the rules of classical riding takes a long time and is completed by few to the highest level (**146**). This should not scare off the conventional rider, however. The end of the scale does not necessarily need to be reached; the more basic exercises are sufficient for the recreational rider. By taking to heart the general rule that relaxation and forward-downward riding are the basis for appropriate riding (**147**), and by excluding practices such as "bringing the horse's forehead behind a vertical line" (**148**), aimed at "pulling the horse loose", and the use of various training aids aimed at increasing the force placed on the horse's mouth, one is already taking a step in the right direction. It is then possible for both horse and rider to enjoy their work.

145 Trust and subordination are required for the exercise "compliment".

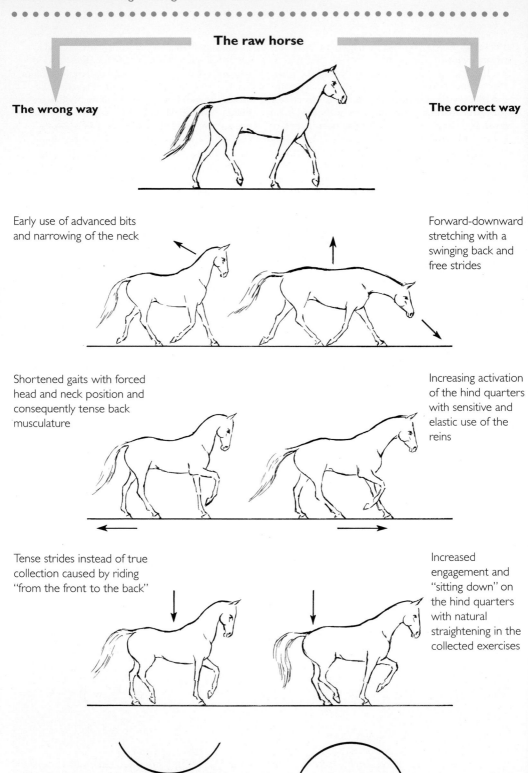

The raw horse

The wrong way

The correct way

Early use of advanced bits and narrowing of the neck

Forward-downward stretching with a swinging back and free strides

Shortened gaits with forced head and neck position and consequently tense back musculature

Increasing activation of the hind quarters with sensitive and elastic use of the reins

Tense strides instead of true collection caused by riding "from the front to the back"

Increased engagement and "sitting down" on the hind quarters with natural straightening in the collected exercises

146 Training of dressage horses (Schnitzer 1996).

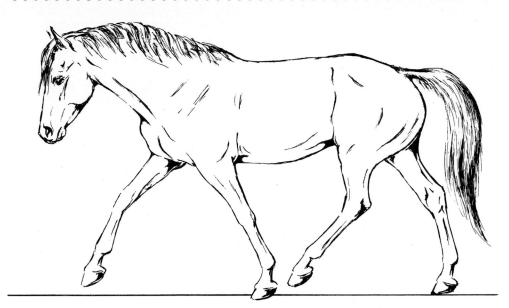

147 Even the recreational rider should be able to make the horse carry itself within an extended frame and accept the bridle (Schnitzer 1996).

148 Riding "with the forehead behind a vertical line" is often the cause for painful tension. Unwanted behaviors such as rearing, headshaking, and bucking can result.

Rearing	
Classification	**Unwanted behavior**
	Management- and handling-induced behavioral aberration (phobia)
Description	Violent avoidance behavior in the form of uncontrolled rearing up on the hind legs
Causes*	1: Organic disease, pain
	2: Fear
	3: Unclear rank order
	4: Lack of exercise
Therapy	1:
	• Medical treatment
	• Appropriate equipment
	2:
	• Counter-conditioning (classical, operant)
	• Trust-building measures
	3:
	• Counter-conditioning (punishment)
	• Exhaustion
	• Rank order exercises
	1– 4:
	• Appropriate management and feeding according to species-specific requirements
	• Good riding skills
Prevention	• Consistent and determined handling from the beginning of training
	• Appropriate basic training (groundwork)
	• Good riding skills
	• Regular health checks
	• Appropriate management and feeding according to behavioral needs

*Numbers used for causes correspond to numbers used in the therapy section

Bucking

Description. Occasional bucking represents normal horse behavior (**149**). It is shown during play or in high spirits, for example when being turned out onto pasture, and it is infectious. This type of bucking loosens the back musculature and helps to get rid of built-up excitement. Seeing a horse buck like that should be viewed positively because is part of the natural expression of any healthy horse.

When bucking under saddle, the horse jumps up and down violently without any regard for the rider's influence, and can catapult the rider from the saddle. Bucking like this is an unwanted behavior. In exceptional cases, such as when a phobia is present, it can also represent a handling-induced behavioral aberration.

Predisposition. A short and tight but strong back predisposes to bucking. These horses will show a strong tendency towards violent bucking

as foals and also later, as soon as they are turned out into a pasture or paddock. "Highly bred" horses and very excitable horses are also predisposed. Bucking is therefore often observed in refined pony and draft horse breeds, which are stocky and built almost squarely and are easily excitable.

By nature, some horses are particularly ticklish underneath the belly. They tend to buck as soon as something splashes (e.g. water) or hits (e.g. pieces of dirt, gravel) against the underside of their abdomen. Increased ticklishness can also be observed in mares in heat and those with ovarian dysfunction (constant heat). They therefore also tend to buck frequently.

Causes. Pain, fear, and rank order problems are the primary causes of bucking. If successful, that is, if the rider falls off or gives up, and pain and fear subside or the horse is allowed to do as it pleases, a rapid learning effect sets in.

If a horse bucks, one should first of all con-

149 Bucking is normal behavior of healthy horses.

sider pain. If the horse, for example, bends its back to avoid the brush during grooming, this may indicate a painful process in the spinal region. Horses with back or skin problems affecting the saddle region generally tend to buck more often. In many cases, pain is caused by equipment deficits and riding mistakes. Among others, these causes include pressure-exerting, ill-fitting saddles, rubbing saddle blankets which have become stiff from sweat, too rapid tightening of the girth, riding with a high degree of collection without the necessary looseness, a stiff seat, and an un-giving, hard hand. The horse can draw attention to these painful influences only by means of its movements and reactions. It does not have another language. Next to rearing and bolting, bucking is the horse's way of expressing pain.

A similar behavioral pattern arises if fear is the cause. Excessive demands during work, for example, can lead to fear-induced bucking. In most cases, however, fear is the consequence of pain. The original cause often lies in mistakes that are made when first getting the horse used to the saddle and rider. In many cases, training steps occur too rapidly and the horse does not learn to associate the rider on its back with a trusted person. In addition, it cannot see the rider for the most part without turning its head because the rider is in the blind spot. An

unidentified being on its back, however, represents danger for the former flight animal, while the weight further signals an attack. Under these circumstances, therefore, it is only natural if the horse tries to get rid of the "predator". In isolated cases, the negative experience associated with riding can be so extreme that it develops into a phobia. This can occur if horses are "broken in" as is still customary in some countries today. The goal of this method is to break an inexperienced horse to ride by letting it buck until it stops from exhaustion (p.130). Very sensitive and fearful animals can acquire a behavioral aberration in the narrower sense in this manner.

Rank order problems are most often associated with fear or pain. They can, on the other hand, also elicit bucking *per se* as a trial of strength. In many cases, however, such an animal also suffers from a lack of exercise and tries to "vent" and satisfy its need for exercise and running in this manner. Lack of basic training or a weak rider is often responsible for this type of behavior. In many cases, it also occurs in horses that have not learned that bucking is only acceptable "in private", for example on a pasture, but not under saddle.

Some animals buck with the intention of getting rid of the rider. Independent of the original cause, they have learned to evade the uncomfortable sensation of being ridden in this manner. If this is the case, bucking can turn into a reflex-like behavior. These animals will show the unwanted behavior in any situation, even if the original causes such as equipment deficits and riding skills have been corrected.

Therapy. First of all, and independent of the etiology of bucking, the horse should be kept under appropriate management conditions, because in many cases, overexcitement and a built-up need for exercise contribute to the unwanted behavior. In addition, feeding should be adjusted by reducing the concentrate portion in exchange for an increased roughage portion or more frequent pasture access. Horses with a tendency to buck need a considerable amount of exercise. Exercise, however, should occur in a calm, relaxed, and disciplined manner under human control. Aside from riding, therefore, walking on a lunge line or a hot-walker, as well as pasture turn-out during the day, are appropriate. Letting the horse "vent" by bucking prior to riding is not an appropriate way to make up for a lack of exercise. On the contrary, it allows the horse to maintain its habit and, without a warm-up period, is also dangerous for tendons, ligaments, and joints.

If pain is the cause of bucking, appropriate medical treatment is required. Additional palpation of the body, for example by using the Tellington-Touch, can help to detect and treat muscle tension. Different massage techniques, some of which were designed specifically for horses, can be helpful in the same manner. Furthermore, pinching or pressure-exerting parts of the saddle and bridle must be removed and exchanged for appropriate equipment. Special emphasis should be placed on a saddle with enough room under the pommel and a large contact surface (large panels). It should go without saying that the rider needs to care for the equipment in a manner that prevents it from pinching or exerting undue pressure. In addition, it should be ensured before each mounting that the saddle pad is placed smoothly and with the direction of the hair, and that the withers are protected but not constricted by the saddle pad.

Bucking caused by riding mistakes can only be corrected by an appropriate improvement of the rider's skills (**146**). Generally, but especially in bucking horses, the girth should not be tightened completely until after mounting and warming up of the horse. The rider must sit very elastically and must have a giving hand. In many cases, a more careful influence on the horse is sufficient to control the problem

behavior. With horses that buck only in the arena but not on the trail, frequent relaxation periods at a loose rein during the dressage lesson can work wonders (pain diagnosis!). If the opposite is the case and the horse bucks as soon as it gets to go out on the trail, the built-up need for exercise needs to be decreased. Aside from the previously mentioned general measures for improved management, one should therefore change one's trail riding habits. Foremost, relaxation has to be ensured. Inviting cantering stretches should be avoided and instead, the horse should be trotted for extended periods of time. Once the rides have become controllable at a trot, one can go back to cantering exercises. It is best to let the horse go uphill at first. To prevent bucking, the horse is bent around the rider's leg and collected prior to cantering. If it still wants to buck, which it indicates by lowering its head, the reins are shortened on one side and the horse's head is lifted up energetically. In this manner, bucking can be prevented in advance.

> Tip: in order to buck, the horse has to lower its head and neck. It cannot buck with a raised head. If the horse pulls its head down, the head should be energetically raised up and to the side while at the same time driving the horse forward.

If a horse bucks exclusively to throw the rider, and if fear and pain can be excluded, counter-conditioning and punishment of the unwanted behavior are indicated (p.128). Punishment must take place during or immediately after bucking. Because lashes with the whip would provoke further bucking in this case, it is less dangerous to force the horse into an obedience exercise such as the "windmill" immediately following the last bucking jump (**150**). For this exercise, the horse is turned in a tight circle several times, which represents a very effective subordination exercise (p.129). Another variant is the use of exhaustion therapy, letting the horse canter uphill even if it begins to breathe heavily. The problems associated with this method were discussed earlier (p.130). Exercises that serve to clarify rank order are definitely of use with this type of bucking.

A completely different method of correction, desensitization, is indicated if the horse bucks out of fear. This type of therapy should also be employed in the case of learned behavior, which is originally attributable to fear. It is also the

150 "Windmill walking" is a rank order exercise that has the effect of punishment. It can be performed exclusively by shifting the rider's weight without use of the reins.

method of choice if phobia-like fear is present. With the latter, it might be necessary to get the horse used to carrying a weight in a stepwise manner. This approach is comparable to that used for the treatment of girthiness (p.209). Instead of mounting the horse, it is less dangerous to apply two sandbags, whose weight is successively increased to about 80–100 kg (176–220 lb). They must be fastened very well and must under no circumstances come loose if the horse begins to buck. If this reaction occurs, the weight of the sand bags must again be decreased until no adverse reaction is elicited. This stepwise adaptation to the weight or, respectively, the rider, is supported by operant or classical counter-conditioning. In parallel, trust-building measures and rank order exercises should be employed.

Prevention. Appropriate management and feeding without excessive amounts of concentrate are essential prerequisites for the prevention of bucking. Special emphasis should be placed on sufficient opportunity for exercise by means of pasture access or exercise in a group. For horses with a great need for exercise and for easily excitable horses, additional opportunities for exercise such as daily exercise on a hot-walker or frequent ponying can have a relaxing and calming effect.

The most important measure to prevent bucking is to allow the horse to get used to the saddle and the weight of the rider in a fear-free and thorough manner at the beginning of training. Young horses must slowly be adapted to carrying a saddle. For the initial stages, especially light saddles (plastic saddles, various

custom-made Western saddles) and saddles with a large contact surface (large panels, Western saddles) are particularly useful. The saddle pad should be soft and as thick as possible, so that the young horse's back is well cushioned. A particularly careful method to get a horse used to the saddle is stepwise adaptation combined with rewarding (classical and operant conditioning). Initially, the horse is adapted to having a blanket and girth placed on its back. In the next step, it learns to carry a saddle while being led. Walks and hikes and walking across ground poles and obstacles help the horse to get used to the saddle under different circumstances. Only when this preparation period has been completed, should the horse be lunged with a saddle for the first time. The goal is to not provoke bucking during any of these exercises. If one proceeds in this manner from the beginning, the horse will not associate carrying of the saddle with bucking in any situation. Aside from good riding skills and horse-friendly equipment, this is the best method to prevent bucking from starting in the first place.

> Tip: the horse has to learn that bucking is allowed in its free time but is not tolerated under saddle. Work should therefore be designed in a manner that bucking is not elicited by any exercise. "Letting the horse buck it off" on a lunge line, which is commonly practiced, should be avoided from the start.

	Bucking
Classification	**Unwanted behavior**
	Management- and handling-induced behavioral aberration (phobia)
Description	Violent avoidance behavior in the form of uncontrolled jumping
Causes*	1: Organic disease, pain
	2: Fear
	3: Unclear rank order
	4: Lack of exercise
Predisposition	• Exterior (short, tight, and strong back)
	• Easily excitable horses
Therapy	1:
	• Medical treatment
	• Appropriate equipment
	2:
	• Counter-conditioning (operant, classical)
	• Trust-building measures
	3:
	• Counter-conditioning (punishment)
	• Exhaustion therapy
	• Rank order exercises
	1–4:
	• Appropriate management and feeding according to species-specific behavioral needs
	• Good riding skills
Prevention	• Appropriate basic training from the beginning
	• Appropriate equipment
	• Regular health checks
	• Appropriate management and feeding according to behavioral needs

*Numbers used for causes correspond to numbers used in the therapy section

Differential diagnosis. Crow-hopping out of mere pleasure to move, which can also occur under saddle, needs to be differentiated from true bucking. It arises from an urge to play and from high spirits, and is dependent on the individual horse's temperament and age, as well as management factors, feeding, and the opportunity for exercise. Well balanced horses, which have constant access to pasture and are not overfed with concentrate, will only buck at "playing time". This can also take place during riding when the ground is soft and a fresh wind blows such as in the spring and fall. Even the best behaved horse will not be able to suppress a crow-hop or two under these circumstances, especially if it sees a stubble field. In contrast to true bucking, however, this can easily be sat out because the hop is incorporated into the canter. In addition, the horse will remain controllable by appropriate aids. A horse should not be punished for this type of behavior. Should the crow-hopping take on unwanted dimensions, however, it suffices to terminate it by the rider's

influence and a loud "no". This correction is indicated because serious bucking can often develop from uncontrolled crow-hopping.

Girthiness

Description. If a horse suffers from girthiness, it shows a more or less strongly developed avoidance behavior whenever it is saddled and the girth is tightened (**151**). If less severe or moderately severe girthiness is present, the horse communicates its dislike of the saddle by reactions such as stepping off to the side, head tossing, or arching of the back, or it may bite or kick at the girth or the person placing the saddle. With severe girthiness, the horse bucks, rears or throws itself to the ground as soon as the girth is tightened, the rider begins to mount, or the saddle is merely placed on its back. Some horses will even refuse to be led with a saddle. While horses accept the saddle after a certain time with the former two variants and can be

151 Turned back ears and evasion during saddling are some of the signs of girthiness.

ridden, this is no longer possible with the severe form. These animals will at times resist the rider so violently that he runs the risk of being thrown off or being buried underneath the horse.

Predisposition. Certain deficiencies in a horse's conformation can predispose it to girthiness. Horses with a higher croup than withers, for example, often have a back that makes it difficult to place the saddle correctly, which can easily lead to pressure sores and therefore pain. Horses with a short and strong back, which tend increasingly towards bucking, are also more frequently affected by girthiness. In addition, a certain breed disposition exists based on personal observations in practice. Easily excitable horses such as thoroughbreds, refined warmbloods, and Arabians suffer particularly often from girthiness. This may be associated with their thin hair coat and sensitive skin.

Causes. Fear and pain have to be considered as the primary causes. They are generally attributable to negative experiences which occurred during saddling and riding. In most cases, mistakes were made when getting the horse used to the saddle and when riding it for the first time. For example, horses with girthiness have often been ridden too early, and preparatory exercises were insufficient or did not take place at all. Riding mistakes, which lead to

tensing of the back musculature, can also result in girthiness. This includes, for example, training aids that force the horse into a dressage-type position or the immediate "collection" without previous relaxation (**148**). Getting a horse used to the saddle with the help of the exhaustion method should also be viewed critically because it lies within the nature of the method that the horse will associate it with fear and a negative general mood. This method, which involves saddling the horse, tightening the girth and letting it buck until it "understands that the behavior does not lead to anything" and "gives up", can result in permanent trauma to sensitive horses. The potential result is a saddle phobia with fear reactions that drastically digress from normal, such that they have to be considered a definite behavioral aberration. In general, however, fear will not be developed to this extreme and a mere unwanted behavior is present. This is easier to treat than a truly aberrant behavior.

Therapy. It is certainly the wrong approach to punish girthy horses. On the contrary: the trusting relationship between animal and human has to be re-established and with the help of systematic desensitization, the horse has to slowly be re-adapted to the saddle. This method is supported by counter-conditioning and positive reinforcement (p.128). Before beginning any behavioral therapy, however, the horse must be examined and, if necessary, treated for any painful conditions. Furthermore, poor equipment (especially saddle, girth, and saddle pad), which may exert pressure, impair the horse's movement or in any other way cause pain, has to be changed. As was described for bucking, light Western saddles and saddles with large panels are recommended: because of their larger contact surface, they provide more comfort for the horse than the customary multi-purpose saddle. The contact surface of the multi-purpose saddle is comparatively small and exerts more localized pressure on the horse's back. If this type of saddle is not fitted correctly, back problems are imminent. Newer developments in this field offer the advantages of a large contact surface that conforms to the horse's back while being optically indistinguishable from the multi-purpose saddle.

At the beginning of the desensitization program, the horse is first adapted to having its back and abdomen touched. Massage techniques such as the Tellington-Touch are particularly useful. In this manner, tension is released and the horse's aversion against having a human approach its back is reduced. Once the horse does not try to evade the massage anymore, the next step can follow. It depends on the severity of the girthiness. In less severe cases, one can begin at this point to place the saddle carefully. Each practice sequence is rewarded so that the horse associates the originally frightening process with a positive event. For several days, the horse is then allowed to get used to carrying the saddle. For example, one can work it on a lunge line, do groundwork exercises, or pony it with the saddle in place. One can also feed the horse with the saddle in place or leave it tied up for a period of time. During the first exercise sequences, the girth must not be tightened all the way. A certain habituation period should be allowed before it is properly tightened slowly and in intervals.

As soon as the horse accepts the saddle as an everyday occurrence and something entirely normal, it can be mounted for the first time. Prior to mounting, one should make the horse complete several familiar exercises for about 15–20 minutes. It is then taken to a familiar place and held by a helper, who is positioned at its head and distracts it by talking, praising, or feeding. If the horse remains calm and relaxed, the rider is given a leg up and mounts without the girth being tightened completely. Tightening of the girth takes place later on at a quiet walk after having made a few turns. In doing so, it is important that the horse is allowed to go forward freely with only light influence of the reins and without any leg aids. It can at times be helpful to have someone lead the horse for the first few minutes.

In cases of severe girthiness, the horse is initially adapted to carrying a saddle blanket and surcingle. As was described for saddling, the exercise is split up into several small steps that take place under positive reinforcement. At first, the horse is adapted to the girth pressure by running the girth along the abdomen; thereafter, the horse is led with the surcingle fastened loosely; and finally, the horse is equipped with a blanket and surcingle and completes exercises such as walking over ground poles. This is practiced and positively reinforced until the horse no longer shows adverse reactions. Once this is achieved, placement of the saddle can be begun as described earlier.

If a phobia-like fear is present, it is recommended first to reduce the avoidance behavior by extinction (p.131). For this purpose, the horse is initially not confronted with the saddle at all for an extended period of time. It can, for example, be sent on a "pasture holiday" for the duration of the summer. Following this break, the trusting relationship and the rank order have to first be re-established. Groundwork is the most useful means of doing so. Following this period, systematic desensitization as was described for severe girthiness, is undertaken. The combination with classical conditioning (rewarding sound and feed) has proven especially successful.

Based on practice experience, the success of correction by desensitization can be enhanced, provided that all factors such as equipment have been optimized, if the horse is taken on long trail rides, which preferably last for several days, immediately following the termination of therapy.

Prevention. Girthiness can be avoided if the horse is trained to tolerate the saddle calmly and in a stepwise manner under positive reinforcement. If one proceeds similarly to the described desensitization method, the horse will make positive associations with the unfamiliar situation from the beginning.

During further use, girthiness often occurs insidiously; for example, the horse does not stand still when mounting or steps to the side when being approached with the saddle. One should react to these slight signs and take the appropriate diagnostic and therapeutic measures. Girthiness during further use of the horse can be avoided if a well fitting and well cared for saddle and other equipment is used, if the girth is tightened in a stepwise fashion, and if the horse is ridden in a manner that does not lead to painful tension of the back musculature. The horse therefore has to be warmed up thoroughly prior to work, forced collection with the help of training aids should be avoided, and the rider should work hard in order to achieve a correct seat and use of the reins.

Conclusion. Girthiness is preventable if the horse gets used to the saddle slowly. The saddle must fit well, have enough room under the pommel and a large contact surface, and be sufficiently stiff. Furthermore, the rider should sit lithely in the saddle in order to activate the horse's back musculature.

Girthiness

Classification	**Unwanted behavior**
	Handling-induced behavioral aberration (phobia)
Description	More or less violent avoidance behavior during saddling and mounting
Causes*	1: Organic disease, pain
	2: Fear
Predisposition	• Conformation (difficult saddle placement, short, strong back)
	• Easily excitable horses
Therapy	1:
	• Medical treatment
	• Appropriate equipment
	2:
	• Desensitization with counter-conditioning (positive reinforcement)
	• Trust-building measures
	1 and 2: Good riding skills
Prevention	• Stepwise adaptation to saddle and rider with positive reinforcement
	• Appropriate equipment
	• Good riding skills
	• Regular health checks

*Numbers used for causes correspond to numbers used in the therapy section

Glossary

Adaptation: Adjustment; development of characteristics which make a living being more suitable for its respective environment, i.e. increase its life expectancy and reproductive success as well as that of its offspring.

Aggression: Collective name for all elements of attacking, defensive, and threatening behavior (synonym: aggressive behavior, aggression behavior).

Aggressiveness: Extent of the readiness to attack of an individual or species.

Agonistic behavior: Generic term for the entirety of all behaviors related to combative conflict between individuals. The term comprises aggression (see above) and flight.

Activity area: Living quarters.

Ambivalent behavior: Term denoting the simultaneous or rapidly alternating occurrence of movements and body postures belonging to different, often opposed, areas of behavior. It occurs if two behavioral tendencies are activated simultaneously.

Anamnesis: Patient history; type, beginning, and progression of current complaints or behavioral aberrations, which are retrieved during a conversation.

Anthropomorphic: Humanizing, suggesting human characteristics for animals or inanimate things.

Appetency behavior: Searching behavior; Active seeking out of a triggering stimulus situation.

Circadian rhythm: Night-day rhythm.

Circannual periodicity: Yearly periodicity.

Classical conditioning: During classical conditioning, a natural stimulus (e.g. the sight of feed, original or unconditioned stimulus) for a response is combined with an artificial, initially indifferent signal (signal or conditioned stimulus). After a number of concurrent presentations, the signal stimulus alone is capable of eliciting the accompanying response: a conditioned reflex has been created.

Conditioning: A collective term for experimental processes, which result in a behavioral pattern or other response becoming dependent on certain conditions.

Conflict behavior: Behavioral patterns, which occur in a conflict situation, i.e. at a time when two incompatible behavioral tendencies (e.g. attack and flight) are activated simultaneously and neither one is clearly dominant.

Coping: Adaptation strategy; attempt of the organism to adapt to inadequate living conditions.

Critical phase: The stage of life in which a creature is particularly receptive for certain experiences.

Damaging fight: In contrast to the ritualized fight, where the opponent is only forced aside, a fight in which animals can hurt or even kill each other.

Deprivation: Deficit, withdrawal of experience.

Desensitization: In ethology, a learning behavior that is based on stepwise adaptation and counter-conditioning.

Displacement activity: An unexpected movement or action, which occurs outside the behavioral context for which it was originally developed. It appears in conflict situations and is generally "unsuccessful" in the sense that it does not serve the biological purpose to which it was originally adapted.

Domestication: The process of creating domestic animals.

Dominance: In ethology, the term is used to denote an individual's position within the social rank order. The superior animal is denoted as dominant, the inferior individual as subordinate.

Drive: A strong motivating tendency or instinct related to self-preservation, reproduction, or aggression that prompts activity toward a particular end.

Emotional build-up: Increased readiness to exhibit a behavioral pattern after having been prevented from exhibiting it for an extended period of time.

Essential behavioral pattern: Inborn coordinated movement, the completion of which is essential for an animal's well-being. Prevention results in behavioral aberrations.

Estrus: Heat; collective term for the entirety of changes that occur in female mammals in connection with the periodic recurrence of sexual activity.

Ethogram: Behavioral inventory; a list of all behavioral patterns of a species.

Ethology: Study of animal and human behavior.

Evolution: Phylogenetic development of animals and plants (biological or genetic evolution).

Flehmen: A facial expression exhibited by many mammals, especially hoofed animals and cat-like predators. Equids roll their upper lip upwards while leaving the teeth closed, such that the inside of the upper lip, the upper incisors and the gums are visible. Flehmen enables intensive olfactory examination of substances with the help of the vomeronasal organ.

Following behavior: Collective term for spatial following, which is exhibited by young animals of many species towards their parents or dam.

Food imprinting: Rapid and lasting determination of certain food preferences similar to imprinting.

Frustration: Emotional tension, elicited by the absence of an expected, emotion-releasing action. The object, which the behavior is usually directed against, is present but completion of the behavioral pattern is prevented by external influences.

Functional area: Generic term (in ethological language) for behavioral patterns with identical or similar function and effect, e.g. locomotion, feed intake or resting.

Habituation: An animal's ability to get used to and no longer react to repeatedly occurring stimuli, which are connected neither with positive nor negative effects (synonym: adaptation, stimulus adaptation, stimulus-specific fatigue, stimulus-specific weakening of response, "central nervous" adaptation).

Hypertrophy: Enlargement of a tissue or organ. In ethology: excessive occurrence of a behavioral pattern.

Imitation: Copying; learning by observation.

Imprinting: In ethology, imprinting is understood as a relatively rapid learning process occurring early in life, which differs from other learning processes in two characteristics: (a) the existence of a defined critical period; (b) a very stable, potentially irreversible result.

Individual distance: The distance to which members of the same species maximally approach each other. Crossing of this distance results in aggression or evasion by one of the animals.

Inner clock: Sense of time, biological clock. The ability to (endogenously) determine time independent of external stimuli (e.g. position of the sun).

Instinct: Inborn readiness to act.

Macrosmatics: Individuals with a strongly developed sense of smell.

Maturation: Perfection of a behavioral pattern without practice.

Microsmatics: Individuals with a weakly developed sense of smell.

Misdirected imprinting: Bonding to an object other than the natural one caused by a "wrong" experience during the critical period (synonym: imprinting on a foreign object).

Morphology: The branch of biology that deals with structure or form.

Motivation: An animal's readiness to carry out a certain action. It is determined by a number of exogenous (external) and endogenous (internal) factors (synonym: mood, specific readiness to act, driving force, urge, drive).

Mutation: Alterations within the genetic make-up of a cell.

Ontogeny or ontogenesis: The origin and development of an individual from the fertilized egg until death.

Operant conditioning: During operant (instrumental) conditioning, a new movement (action) is brought into context with the reduction of a need. This movement initially occurs spontaneously. If it is rewarded repeatedly, the animal establishes a connection and the movement in question will be exhibited in similar situations with increased frequency.

Paleontology: The study of the forms of life existing in prehistoric or geologic times.

Pheromone: Hormone-like substance, which is produced in certain glands and emitted to the outside. Functions of pheromones include social communication (sexually attractive substances, scents to mark territory, and so on); (synonyms: exohormone, ethohormone, sociohormone or social hormone).

Phobia: Excessive, inappropriate fear reaction, which is elicited by certain objects or situations.

Phylogeny or phylogenesis: The history and evolutionary development of a species. Phylogeny of behavior: the evolutionary development of behavioral patterns.

Population: "Unit of inhabitants". The total number of individuals belonging to a species that inhabit a certain area.

Rank order: Social hierarchy, "pecking order". The regulated distribution of "rights and duties" within a group of animals.

Reflex: The invariably and immediately occurring response of a target organ (executive organ) to a sensory stimulus. If the stimulus–response–relationship has a hereditary basis, an unconditional reflex exists (e.g. pupillary light reflex). If the relationship between stimulus and response is created by conditioning, the reflex is denoted as conditioned ("based on experience").

Reinforcement: In ethology, a collective term for all events denoted as "reinforcement", which occur after a behavioral pattern is exhibited by the animal, and result in a subsequent increase of the frequency and/or intensity of this action.

Residual-reactive behavior: A behavior diverging from the norm, which persists despite correction of the original deficits.

Ritualization: Symbolic continuation of an originally functionally important behavioral pattern in another functional area.

Ritualized fighting: Inborn, strictly regulated fighting behavior directed against members of the animal's own species, which is ritualized enough to avoid serious injury in general.

Self-mutilation: Aggressive behavior such as biting directed against the individual's own body.

Social facilitation: "Contagion". The widespread tendency of members of social species simultaneously to do the same thing.

Species: In biology, a species represents a "reproductive unit", i.e. a group of individuals, who under natural conditions are able to reproduce unrestrictedly and produce fertile offspring.

Stereotypy:
(a) In general: constant, uniform repetition of behavioral patterns or articulations.
(b) In the sense of aberrant behavior: behavioral patterns, which are repeated nearly identically and are exhibited without an apparent functionality.

Trigger mechanism: Stimulus filter which, out of the abundance of stimuli acting on the individual, selects the one for which a readiness to act exists.

References

Ahlswede, L. (2000): Gesundheitliche Aspekte und Sorgfaltspflichten bei der Jungpferdeaufzucht. *Dtsch. tierärztl. Wschr.*, **107**, 104–106.

ALB (1998): *Offenlaufställe.* Arbeitsblatt Landwirtschaftliches Bauwesen (ALB), ALB Bayern, 85586 Poing/Grub.

Berger, J. (1986): *Wild horses of the Great Basin. Social Competition and Population Size.* The University of Chicago Press, Chicago and London.

Bey, O. (1993): *Nutzung des Pferdes aus der Sicht des Tierschutzes.* Diss. med. vet., Gießen.

Beyer, S. (1998): *Konstruktion und Überprüfung eines Bewertungskonzeptes für pferdehaltende Betriebe unter dem Aspekt der Tiergerechtheit.* Diss. agr., Gießen.

BMELF (1992): Leitlinien Tierschutz im Pferdesport. Hrsg.: Bundesministerium für Ernährung, Landwirtschaft und Forsten (BMELF), Referat Tierschutz, Bonn.

BMELF (1995): Leitlinien zur Beurteilung von Pferdehaltungen unter Tierschutzgesichtspunkten. Hrsg.: Bundesministerium für Ernährung, Landwirtschaft und Forsten (BMELF), Referat Tierschutz, Bonn.

Boyd, L.E., Carbonaro A.D. and Houpt K.A. (1988): The 24-hour time budget of Przewalski horses. *Appl. Anim. Behav. Sci.*, **21**, 5–17.

Brückner, R. (1995): *Dein Pferd – sein Auge seine Sehweise.* Selbstverlag Basel.

Brummer, H. (1978): Verhaltensstörungen. In: *Nutztierethologie.* Hrsg., Sambraus, H.H., Paul Parey Verlag, Berlin, 281–292.

Caanitz, Heidrun (1996): *Ausdrucksverhalten von Pferden und Interaktionen zwischen Pferd und Reiter zu Beginn der Ausbildung.* Diss. med. vet., Hannover.

Dallaire, A. and Ruckebusch, Y. (1973): Sleep patterns in the pony with observations in partial perceptual deprivation. *Physiol. Behav.*, **12**, 789–796.

Denoix, J.-M. und Pailloux, J.-P. (2000): *Physiotherapie und Massage bei Pferden.*
Eugen Ulmer Verlag, Stuttgart.

Deutsche Reiterliche Vereinigung (FN) (1993): Orientierungshilfen Reitanlagen- und Stallbau. FN-Verlag, Warendorf.

Deutsche Reiterliche Vereinigung (FN) (1994): Richtlinien für Reiten und Fahren. Bd. 1, Grundausbildung für Reiter und Pferd. FN-Verlag, Warendorf.

Dillenburger, E. (1982): *Entwicklung der Verhaltensweisen von Fohlen von der Geburt bis zum Absetzen.* Diss. agr., Stuttgart-Hohenheim.

Dodman, N.H., Shuster, L., Court, M.H., Dixon, R. (1987): Investigation into the use of narcotic antagonists in the treatment of a stereotypic behaviour pattern (crib-biting) in the horse. *Am. J. Vet. Res.*, **48**, 311–319.

Duncan, P. (1980): Time-budgets of camargue horses. *Behaviour, 72*, 26–49.

Ebhardt, H. (1958): *Verhaltensweisen verschiedener Pferdeformen.* Säugetierkundliche Mitteilungen Bd IV (1), 1–9, Stuttgart.

Engelhardt, B. (1990): *Zur Geschichte der Untugenden des Pferdes – Symptome, Ursachen, Behandlung und Forensik.* Diss. med. vet., Gießen.

Erasimus, L. (1988): *Untersuchungen über die Beziehung zwischen sozialer Rangordnung und Reiteignung bei österreichischen Lipizzanerhengsten.* Diss. agr., Wien.

Feige, K. und Wehrli, M. (1998): Lichtinduziertes Headshaking und dessen Therapie mit Cyproheptadin. In: *15. Arbeitstagung der Fachgruppe "Pferdekrankheiten"*, Deutsche Veterinärmedizinische Gesellschaft (DVG), Wiesbaden, 238–246.

Fraser, A. (1992): *The behaviour of the horse.* CAB International, Wallingford.

Frentzen, F. (1994): *Bewegungsaktivitäten und -verhalten in Abhängigkeit von Aufstallungsform und Fütterungsrhythmus unter besonderer Berücksichtigung unterschiedlich gestalteter Auslaufsysteme.* Diss. med. vet., Hannover.

Frey, W. (1995): *Verschollen – Chinas Wildpferde*. BBC Wildlife.

Gerken, M., Kiene, M., Kreimeier, P. und Bockisch, F. (1996): Verhalten von Trabrennpferden in Gruppenauslauf-haltung und in Einzelhaltung. In: *Aktuelle Arbeiten zur artgemäßen Tierhaltung*. Kuratorium für Technik und Bauwesen in der Landwirtschaft (KTBL), Darmstadt, Deutsche Veterinärmedizinische Gesellschaft (DVG), Gießen, 132–142.

Goldschmidt-Rothschild, B. und Tschanz, B. (1978): Soziale Organisation und Verhalten einer Jungtierherde beim Camargue-Pferd. *Z. Tierpsychol.*, **46**, 372–400.

Grabner, A. (2000): Infektionsbedingte Verhaltensstörungen beim Pferd – dran denken ist notwendig. In: *Verhaltensstörungen*. Hrsg., Lindner, A., Arbeitsgruppe Pferd, Laurahöhe 14, Essen.

Grauvogl, A. (1997): *Artgemäße und rentable Nutztierhaltung*. VerlagsUnionAgrar, BLV-Verlag, München, Frankfurt, Wien.

Grizmek, B. (1987): *Säugetiere*. Band 4, Kindler-Verlag, München, 557–596.

Hackbarth, A. (1998): *Liege- und Spielverhalten von Pferden in Offenlaufställen mit getrennten Funktionsbereichen*. Di-plomarbeit, Fachhochschule Weihenstephan, Freising.

Hart, B.L. and Hart, L.A. (1991): *Verhaltenstherapie bei Hund und Katze*. Enke Verlag, Stuttgart.

Heffner, H.E. und Heffner, R.S. (1983): The hearing ability of horses. *Equine Pract.*, **5**, 27–32.

Heidemann, S. (1985): *Untersuchungen über das Verhalten von Pferden beim Autotransport*. Diss. med. vet., Gießen.

Henderson, J., Waran, N. and Young, R. (1997): Behavioural enrichment for horses: The effect of foraging device (the "Equiball") on the performance of stereotypic behaviour in stabled horses. In: Mills, D., Heath, S., and Harrington, L. (Eds), *Proceed. of the 1st Internat. Conf. Vet. Behav. Med.*, University of Guelph, Ontario, Canada, 1–7.

Herre, J. und Röhrs, M. (1990): *Haustiere – zoologisch gesehen*. Gustav Fischer Verlag.

Houpt, K. (1986): Stable Vices and Trailer Problems. *Veterinary Clinics of North America, Equine Practice*, **2/3**, 623–633.

Houpt, K. (1995): Influences on Equine Behaviour. In: *The Thinking Horse*. Equine Research Centre, University of Guelph, Ontario, Canada, 1–7.

Houpt, K.A. and Houpt, T.R. (1989): Social and illumination preferences of mares. *J. Anim. Sci.*, **66**, 2159–2164.

Houpt, K.A. (1998): *Domestic Animal Behavior for Veterinarians and Animal Scientists*, 3rd edn. Iowa State Press and Manson Publishing/The Veterinary Press.

Immelmann, K. (1982): *Wörterbuch der Verhaltensforschung*. Verlag Paul Parey, Berlin, Hamburg.

Keiper, R.R. and Sambraus, H.H. (1986): The stability of equine dominance hierachies and the effects of kinship, proximity and foaling status on the hierachy rank. *Appl. Anim. Behav. Sci.*, **16**, 121–130.

Kiley-Worthington, M. (1976): Tail movements of ungulates. *Behav.*, **56**, 69–115.

Kiley-Worthington, M. (1983): Stereotypes on Horses. *Equine Practice*, **5**, 34–40.

Kiley-Worthington, M. (1989): *Pferdepsyche – Pferdeverhalten*. Albert Müller-Verlag, Rüschlikon, Zürich, Stuttgart, Wien.

Klingel, H. (1972): Das Verhalten der Pferde (Equidae). In: *Handbuch der Zoologie*. Hrsg., Helmcke, J.-G, Starck, D., Wermuth, H., **10**(24). Verlag Walter de Gruyter, Berlin. 1–68.

Kolter, L. (1987): Bau und Handhabung von Gruppenställen mit Auslauf für Pferde. – Modellvorhaben Rexhof. Hrsg.: Bundesministerium für Ernährung, Landwirtschaft und Forsten, Bonn.

Krull, H.D. (1984): *Untersuchungen über Aufnahme und Verdaulichkeit von Grünfutter beim Pferd*. Diss. agr., Stuttgart-Hohenheim/Hannover.

Kusunose, R., Hatakeyama, H., Kubo, K., Kiguchi, A., Asai, Y., Fujii, Y. and Ito, K. (1985): Behavioural studies on yearling horses in field environments. 1. Effects of field size on the behaviour of horses. *Bulletin of Equine Research Institute*, **23**, 1–6.

Lane, J.G. and Mair, T.S. (1987): Oberservations on headshaking in the horse. *Equine Vet. J.*, **19**, 331–336.

Lebelt, D. (1996): *Verhaltensphysiologische Untersuchungen zum Koppen des Pferdes*. Diss. med. vet., München.

Lebelt, D. (1998): *Problemverhalten beim Pferd*. Enke Verlag, Stuttgart.

Loeffler, K. (1990): Schmerzen und Leiden beim Tier. Berl. Münch. *Tierärztl. Wschr.*, **103**, 257–261.

Lorenz, K. (1949): Durch Domistikation verursachte Störungen arteigenen Verhaltens. *Z. Angew. Psychol. Charakterk.*, **59**, 2–81.

Luescher, A., McKeown, D. and Dean, H. (1996): A cross-sectional study on compulsive behaviour (stable vices) in horses. In: *Proceed. of the Internat. Conf. Equine Clinic. Behav.*, Schweizerische Vereinigung für Pferdemedizin, 6–7.08.96, Basel.

Luescher, A., McKeown, D. and Halip, J. (1991): Reviewing the causes of obsessive-compulsive disorders in horses. *Vet. Med.*, **86**, 527–530.

Madigan, J.E., (1996): Evalution of treatment of headshaking syndrome. In: *Proceed. of the Internat. Conf. Equine Clinic. Behav.*, Schweizerische Vereinigung für Pferdemedizin, 6–7.08.96, Basel.

Madigan, J.E., Kortz, G. Murphy, C. and Rodger, L. (1995): Photic headshaking on the horse: 7 cases. *Equine Vet. J.*, **27**, 306–311.

Mair, T.S. and Lane, J.G. (1990): Headshaking in horses. *Practice*, **12**, 183–186.

Marsden, D. (1995): An investigation of the heredity of susceptibility of stereotypic behavior patterns – stable vices – in the horse. *Equine Vet. J.*, **27**, 415.

Mason, G. (1991): Stereotypies – a critical review. *Anim. Behav.*, **41**, 1015–1037.

McDonnell, S. (1998): Pharmacological aids to behaviour modifications in horses. *Equine Vet. J.*, Suppl. **27**, 50–51.

McFarland, D. (1999): *Biologie des Verhaltens. Evolution, Physiologie, Psychobiologie.* Spektrum Akademischer Verlag. Heidelberg, Berlin.

McGreevy, P.D., Richardson, J.D., Nicol, C.J. and Lane, J.G. (1995a): Radiographic and endoscopic study of horses performing an oral based stereotypie. *Equine Vet. J.*, **27**, 92–95.

McGreevy, P.D., Cripps, P., French, N., Green, L. and Nicol, C.J. (1995b): Management factors associated with stereotypic and redirected behaviour in the thoroughbred horse. *Equine Vet. J.*, **27**, 86–95.

McGreevy, P.D., French, N. and Nicol, C.J. (1995c): The prevelance of abnormal behaviour in dressage, eventing and endurance horses in relation to stabling. *Vet. Rec.*, **137**, 36–37.

McGreevy, P.D. and Nicol, C.J. (1995): Behavioural and physiological consequences associated with prevention of crib-biting. In: *Proc. 29th Internat. Congr. Internat. Soc. Appl. Ethology.* UFAW, London, 135–136.

Meyer, H. (1995): *Pferdefütterung.* Blackwell-Wissenschaftsverlag, Berlin, Wien, Oxford, melbourne, Paris.

Meyer, H. (2000): Zum Leiden und zu seiner Feststellung. *Pferdeheilkunde*, **16**, 45–65.

Mill, J., Lewin, W. and Preis, H. (1996): Possibilities for the use of electroencephalography in equine veterinary medicine. *Pferdeheilkunde*, **12**, 710–711.

Miller, R. (1995): *Prägungstraining.* Kierdorf Verlag, Wipperfürth.

Nobis, G. (1997): Die Geschichte des Pferdes – seine Evolution und Domestikation. In: *Handbuch Pferd.* Hrsg., Thein, P. BLV-Verlag München, Wien, Zürich, 8–24.

Pfeil-Rotermund, S. und Zeeb, K. (1994): Zum Ausdrucksverhalten von Springpferden. In: *Aktuelle Arbeiten zur artgemäßen Tierhaltung.* Kuratorium für Technik und Bauwesen in der Landwirtschaft (KTBL), Darmstadt, Deutsche Veterinärmedizinische Gesellschaft (DVG), Gießen, 20–30.

Pirkelmann, H. (1991): Baulich-technische Einrichtungen und Arbeitswirtschaft in der Pferdehaltung. In: *Pferdehaltung.* Hrsg., Pirkelmann, H., Verlag Eugen Ulmer, 74–160.

Pirkelmann, H., Zeitler-Feicht, M.H., Fader, C. und Wagner, M. (1993): *Rechnergesteuerte Versorgungseinrichtungen für Pferde im Offenlaufstall.* Forschungsbericht, W. Schaumann-Stiftung.

Pirkelmann, H. (1999): Offenlaufställe für die Pferdehaltung. *Pferde Zucht und Haltung*, 7, 48–53.

Preuschoft, H. (1993): Zügelführung sensibler machen. *Pferdespiegel*, **9**, 41–44.

Preuschoft, H. (1999): Über die Wirkung von Gebissen und Hilfszügeln. Seminar "Interaktion Reiter und Pferd – auch ein Tierschutzthema – ein Denkanstoß für die Verständigung zwischen Reiter und Pferd". *Haupt- und Landgestüt Schwaiganger.* 4 Juli 1999.

Radtke, K. (1985): *Über die Bewegungsstereotypie Weben beim Pferd.* Diss. med. vet., München.

Rai, F. (1996): *Natürliches Reiten.* Weltbild Verlag GmbH, Augsburg.

Rees, L. (1986): *Das Wesen des Pferdes*. Albert Müller Verlag, Rüschlikon-Zürich, Stuttgart, Wien.

Rehm, G. (1981): Auswirkungen verschiedener Haltungsverfahren auf die Bewegungsaktivität und auf die soziale Aktivität bei Hauspferden. In: *Aktuelle Aspekte der Ethologie in der Pferdehaltung*. FN Verlag, Warendorf, 81–101.

Rodewald, A. (1989): *Fehler bei der Haltung und Nutzung als Schadensursache bei Pferden in Reitbetrieben*. Diss. med. vet., München.

Ruckebusch, Y. (1972): The relevance of drowsiness in the circadian cycle of farm animals. *Anim. Behav.*, **20**, 637–643.

Sambraus, H.H. (1975): Ethologie der landwirtschaftlichen Nutztiere. *Schweiz. Arch. Tierheilk.*, **117**, 193–218.

Sambraus, H.H. (1978): *Nutztierethologie*. Verlag Paul Parey, Berlin, Hamburg.

Sambraus, H.H. und Rappold. D. (1991): Das "Koppen" bei Pferden. *Pferdeheilkunde*, 7, 211–216.

Sambraus, H.H. (1994): *Atlas der Nutztierrassen*. Verlag Eugen Ulmer, Stuttgart.

Sambraus, H.H. (1997a): Normalverhalten und Verhaltensstörungen. In: *Das Buch vom Tierschutz*. Hrsg., Sambraus, H.H., Steiger, A., Enke-Verlag, 57–69.

Sambraus, H.H. (1997b): Grundbegriffe im Tierschutz. In: *Das Buch vom Tierschutz*. Hrsg., Sambraus, H.H., Steiger, A., Enke-Verlag, 30–38.

Schäfer, M. (1991): Ansprüche des Pferdes an seine Umwelt. In: *Pferdehaltung*. Hrsg., Pirkelmann, H., Verlag Eugen Ulmer, 15–73.

Schäfer, M. (1993): *Die Sprache des Pferdes*. Franckh-Kosmos-Verlag, Stuttgart.

Schäfer, M. (2000): *Handbuch der Pferdebeurteilung*. Franckh-Kosmos-Verlag, Stuttgart.

Schmid, E. (1994): *Haltung und Pflege von Pferden in Süddeutschland unter Berücksichtigung der Hufgesundheit*. Diss. med. vet., München.

Schnitzer, U. (1996): Grundsätze der Gymnastizierung des Reitpferdes. *Pferdespiegel*, **3**, **4**, **5** and 7, jeweils 41–44.

Schnitzer, U. (1999): Einige Auswirkungen des Sozialverhaltens der Pferde beim Reiten. *Pferdespiegel*. Rudolf-Diesel-Strasse 5, 8411 Winterthur.

Smith, B.L., Jones, J.H., Carlson, G.R. and Pascoe, J.R. (1994): Body position and direction preferences in horses during road transport. *Equine Vet. J.*, **26**, 374–377.

Stamp Dawkins, M. (1980): *Leiden und Wohlbefinden bei Tieren*. Verlag Eugen Ulmer, Stuttgart.

Stevens, E.F. (1990) Instability of harems of feral horses in relation to season and presence of subordinate stallions. *Behaviour*, **112**, 149–161.

Stohler, T. (1996): Das "Kopfschlagen" (head shaking) beim Pferd. In: *Proceed. of the Internat. Conf. Equine Clinic. Behav.*, Schweizerische Vereinigung für Pferdemedizin, 6–7.08.96, Basel.

Stupperich, A. (1998): Handbuch Pferdeweide. Franckh Kosmos-Verlag, Stuttgart.

Sweeting, M.P., Houpt C. und Houpt T.A. (1985): Social facilation of feeding and time budgets in stabled ponies. *J. Anim. Sci.*, **60**, 369–371.

Tellington-Jones, L. und Taylor, S. (1995): *Die Persönlichkeit ihres Pferdes*. Franckh-Kosmos Verlag, Stuttgart.

Tembrock, G. (1964): *Verhaltensforschung*. VEB Gustav Fischer Verlag, Jena.

Tschanz, B. (1979): *Sozialverhalten beim Camarguepferd – Dokumentierverhalten bei Hengsten*. Publikation zu wissenschaftlichen Filmen, Göttingen, Biol. **12**/12 – D 1284.

Tschanz, B. (1993): Erkennen und Beurteilen von Verhaltensstörungen mit Bezugnahme auf das Bedarfskonzept. In: Buchholtz, C. et al., *Leiden und Verhaltensstörungen bei Tieren*. Tierhaltung 23, Birkhäuser Verlag, Basel, Boston, Stuttgart, 65–76.

Tyler, S.J. (1972): The behaviour and social organization of the new forest ponies. *Anim. Behav.*, 5, 87–193.

Ubbenjans, M. (1981): Untersuchungen zur Haltung von Reitpferden auf künstlichen Bodenbelägen. In: *Aktuelle Aspekte der Ethologie in der Pferdehaltung*. Hrsg., Deutsche Reiterliche Vereinigung (FN) und Zeeb, K., FN-Verlag, Warendorf, 105–115.

Ulbricht, M. (1994): *Ausbildung, Berufsbild und Arbeitspraxis der Hufbeschlagschmiede und ihre Beurteilung unter Tierschutzgesichtspunkten*. Diss. med. vet., München.

Ullstein, H. (1996): *Natürliche Pferdehaltung*. Müller Rüschlikon Verlags AG, CH-Cham.

Vecchiotti, G. and Galanti, R. (1986):
Evidence of heredity of cribbing, weaving
and stall-walking in thoroughbred horses.
Livest. Prod. Sci., **14**, 91–95.

Veltjens, C. (1987): *Der Einfluss endogener
und exogener Faktoren auf Erkrankungen
des Bewegungs- und Atmungsapparates bei
Pferden verschiedener deutscher
Zuchtgebiete*. Diss. agr., Bonn.

Wackenhut, K.S. (1994): *Untersuchungen zur
Haltung von Hochleistungspferden unter
Berücksichtigung der Richtlinien zur
Beurteilung von Pferdehaltungen unter
Tierschutzgesichtspunkten*. Diss. med. vet.,
München.

Waring, G.H. (1983): *Horse behaviour*. Noyes
Publications, Park Ridge, New Jersey.

Winskill, L. C., Waran, N.K. and Young R.J.
(1996): The effect of a foraging device (a
modified "Edinburgh Foodball") on the
behaviour of the stabled horse. *Appl.
Anim. Behav. Science*, **48**, 25–35.

Wintzer, H.-J. (1999): *Krankheiten des
Pferdes*. Paul Parey Verlag, Berlin.

Wolff, A. and Hausberger M. (1994):
Behaviour of foals before weaning may
have some genetic basic. *Ethology*, **96**,
1–10.

Wolff, A. and Hausberger M. (1996):
Learning and memorisation of two
different tasks in horses: the effects of age,
sex and sire. *Appl. Anim. Behav. Sci.*, **46**,
137–143.

Zeeb, K. (1997): Artgerechte Pferdehaltung
und verhaltensgerechter Umgang mit
Pferden. In: *Handbuch Pferd*. Hrsg.,
Thein, P., BLV-Verlag, München, Wien,
Zürich, 128–153.

Zeitler-Feicht, M. H. und Grauvogl, A.
(1992): Mindestanforderungen an die
Sport- und Freizeitpferdehaltung unter
Tierschutzgesichtspunkten. *Der praktische
Tierarzt*, **73**, 781–796.

Zeitler-Feicht, M. H. (1993):
Mindestanforderungen an die Beleuchtung
und Stalluft in der Pferdehaltung unter
Tierschutzgesichtspunkten. *Tierärztl.
Umschau*, **48**, 311–317.

Zeitler-Feicht, M.H. (1994): *Das Verhalten
von Hauspferden*. Fortbildungsskript,
Akademie für Tiernaturheilverfahren
(ATM), Bad Bramstedt.

Zeitler-Feicht, Margit H. (1996):
Mindestanforderungen an die
Gruppenhaltung von Pferden unter
Tierschutzgesichtspunkten. *Tierärztl.
Umschau*, **51**, 611–614.

Zeitler-Feicht, M.H., Prantner, V., Thaller,
G.,und Fader, C. (1999): Zum
Liegeverhalten von Pferden in
Offenlaufställen. In: *Aktuelle Arbeiten zur
artgemäßen Tierhaltung*. Kuratorium für
Technik und Bauwesen in der
Landwirtschaft (KTBL), Darmstadt,
Deutsche Veterinärmedizinische
Gesellschaft (DVG), Gießen, 81–89.

Zeitler-Feicht, M.H. (1999):
Verhaltensstörungen des Pferdes. In:
*Tagungsbericht der Deutschen
Veterinärmedizinischen Gesellschaft e.V.
(DVG)*, Fachgruppe "Tierschutzrecht",
DVG-Verlag, Gießen, 132–143.

Zeitler-Feicht, M.H., (2000): Prophylaxe von
Verhaltensproblemen beim Pferd. In:
*Tagungsbericht der Deutschen
Veterinärmedizinischen Gesellschaft e.V.
(DVG)*, Fachgruppe "Angewandte
Ethologie", DVG-Verlag, Gießen,
136–144.

Zierz, J. (1993): *Die Quantifizierung akuter
Schmerzen beim Pferd mittels physiologischer
und ethologischer (klinischer und
verhaltenstypischer) Parameter sowie deren
Korrelation zur aktuellen
Plasmakonzentration von Adrenalin und
Noradrenalin. Ein Beitrag zur
Schmerzmessung beim Pferd*. Diss. med.
vet., Berlin.

Index